GrassRo

MW01264494

Portland

**GrassRoutes**

Portland

An Urban Eco Guide

Serena Bartlett

with Daniel Laing

SASQUATCH BOOKS
SEATTLE

*To chocolate ganache, poodles, lakes in summer, gardening,
the rosy city of Portland, and anything that brings people
as much joy as these things bring me*

In memory of dear, sweet Bonnie

*Certainly, travel is more than the seeing of sights; it is a change
that goes on, deep and permanent, in the ideas of living.*

—Miriam Beard

Printed in the United States of America
Published by Sasquatch Books
Distributed by PGW/Perseus
15 14 13 12 11 10   9 8 7 6 5 4 3 2 1

Cover design: Rosebud Eustace
Cover and interior illustrations: Daniel Laing
Interior design: Rosebud Eustace
Interior composition: Sarah Plein
Interior maps: Lisa Brower/GreenEye Design

Library of Congress Cataloging-in-Publication Data is available

ISBN-10: 1-57061-610-8
ISBN-13: 978-1-57061-610-5

Sasquatch Books
119 South Main Street, Suite 400
Seattle, WA 98104
(206) 467-4300
www.sasquatchbooks.com
custserv@sasquatchbooks.com

CONTENTS

Acknowledgments

I would like to thank the writers and travelers before me, and the people who have listened to their inner voice to speak up in a world of beauty and contradictions. Thanks to my talented contributors, my friends, and my family for their encouragement and support (and for spending time with me across this globe, laughing with me, and always inspiring me to live out my dreams). Thanks, Bear and Khempo.

Contact Us

The places and events listed in this guide are ones we thought were outstanding. Cities are constantly changing, so please contact us if you feel there is something we missed or if you find out-of-date information. Updates, new venues, and corrections will be posted on our web site. We would love to hear from you! E-mail us at *info@grassroutestravel.com*.

The GrassRoutes Story

Like cracking open a dusty geode, travel has revealed to me the many facets of the world, allowing me to compare my known surroundings with the previously unexplored. No other activity has had quite the same impact, offering a unique experience of both commonalities and differences in the quilt of humanity. After each journey, my reality was challenged with new ways of thinking and acting, and I found I had new interests and an altogether different perspective. The most important souvenir I brought home wasn't tangible—it was a more open mind.

I became a detective of sorts, unearthing cultures and becoming familiar with local customs by seeking out nontraditional attractions and cities off the beaten path. Wherever I was, the locals gave me the chance to have unique experiences rather than manufactured ones. When I returned home, I kept up the habit, discovering a wealth of intrigue in my own country. Whether trekking across another continent or walking a few blocks to a nearby neighborhood, no matter what my pocketbook dictated, I always managed to find new cultural gems.

GrassRoutes was born out of my growing collection of ideas and inspirations drawn from my journeys. I made up my mind to promote world citizenship, but search as I might, I found no vehicle that expressed my ideas about travel, so I decided to create one.

The concept evolved from a bundle of notes collected on the road. Since I have always viewed cities as whole entities, I didn't want my guides to be divided into chapters covering specific neighborhoods. Also, chowing down on some messy barbecue doesn't equate with dining on braised rabbit, so I chose not to organize the guides simply by activity. GrassRoutes guides had to be designed around the mood of the traveler and the timing.

But organization wasn't the only thing I wanted to do differently. GrassRoutes, true to its name, champions local businesses and their corresponding contributions to the greater good of the community. Restaurants that serve sustainably grown produce share these pages with shops that showcase works by local artists. Wildlife preserves are in the mix with amusements that use energy-saving techniques. Volunteer listings give visitors the opportunity to interact with residents while giving back. Being conscientious about society and environment is a recipe for peace: This is one message I hope to convey.

Another is that travel can fit a limited budget. GrassRoutes is more than a guide to a city's attractions—it is a reaffirmation that authentic cultural experiences are not out of reach for anyone.

As you enjoy your travels, you can be satisfied knowing that you are a conscientious consumer. With such a bounty of local businesses dedicated to the spirit of positive change, it is becoming easier to support such a philosophy. Each listing in every GrassRoutes guide meets this standard in one aspect or another. So while you are venturing out into the world and meeting real people in new places, your dollars are staying in the community.

In this spirit, I bring you GrassRoutes guides, created to benefit readers and communities. I hope you will try something new, even if you thought it was not possible. All you need to have a genuine cultural escapade is an inquiring mind, a detective's spirit, and the desire to get acquainted with the world around you.

Read more about the GrassRoutes philosophy:
www.grassroutestravel.com/story

Urban Eco-Travel Tips

To help you prepare for your adventure, here are some tips that I have compiled over my years of world travel.

Trip Planning

Don't overplan. Pick dates that make sense, and make the fewest reservations you can get away with to take into consideration factors of time, exhaustion, and exploration.

Before embarking on a trip, tell as many people as will listen where you are going, and get their feedback and tips. Have the same talkative approach when you get to your destination so you can meet locals and learn their favorite spots.

Look at books and magazines featuring the culture and history of the area before embarking on your trip, and keep a well-organized travel guide and a clear map with you while you are exploring.

Time Allotment

When picking dates, consider what kind of trip you want to have. One game plan is to spread out your time between different sights as a good introduction to an area. Another is spending prolonged time in one or two cities to truly get to know them. Either way, in my experience it is good to slow down the tempo of travel enough to smell the proverbial roses.

Reservations

Be sure to reserve a hotel for at least the first night so you have somewhere to go when you get off the plane. Even if you prefer to travel on a whim, I recommend starting on day two—after you get your bearings.

Before you book a room, try to get an idea of your destination first, so you can place yourself in the area that most interests you. If your entire vacation will be spent in the same area, I suggest staying in the same centrally located hotel the whole time so you avoid having to carry your stuff around. After all, you probably didn't travel to see different hotels, but to see the city itself!

Whenever you do book a hotel, make sure you know its cancellation policy.

In general, don't reserve many transit engagements. That way, if you want to extend your stay in a given spot, you can do that without too many trials and tribulations. Local transit arrangements are usually easy to book without much advance notice.

Restaurants tend to have widely varying policies on reservations, so check ahead to see whether your dream meal requires one. Or forgo the reservations: When you get to your destination, look around and act on a whim, or best of all, get the locals' advice. It is hard to get a good sense of a restaurant from its web site.

Be sure to reserve tickets for any special events you'd like to attend.

Packing

Pack light, but anticipate a variety of activities. I like to have a good pair of pants that can match with different shirts. I also bring one dressier outfit and a bathing suit.

Bring more than enough underwear, but wear clothes that can keep their shape for two or three days of use, especially pants or skirts. You'll be meeting and interacting with new people every day, so no one will know you wore the same outfit two days in a row.

Buy sundry items like sunscreen after you arrive. Remember, you will have to carry what you bring, so don't weigh yourself down.

Check the climate and current weather conditions of your planned locations and pack accordingly.

Try taking your luggage for a stroll in your own neighborhood before hitting the road. Then you'll know right away if you've overpacked, with enough time to do something about it.

Read GrassRoutes' latest packing tips and gadgets: *www.grassroutestravel.com/packing_tips*

Toiletries

It is amazing the time, energy, and stress saved by bringing along a few extra items in your toiletry kit. These things boost my self-sufficiency when I am on the road, and I always like that. I'm not talking about remembering to bring your toothbrush and toothpaste—I'm talking about finessing your toiletry kit, because let's face it, what you put in there is personal. The following is a list of some handy items for both sexes, followed by a list of girls-only things.

General

Aspirin/ibuprofen/acetaminophen—Whatever your choice for general pain relief, these products can be surprisingly hard to come by at times, and sold by the pair they are way overpriced.

Gauze and tape—I find this combo to be more flexible than adhesive bandages for various cuts and helpful for off-the-cuff art projects, too. For an instant spa treatment, use the gauze as cheesecloth, wrap an extra tea bag from the hostel/hotel inside, wet the package with warm water, and place it over your eyes after you get back from a long day.

Clove oil—This fast-acting tooth pain remedy numbs lightly. You won't catch me traveling without it.

Hand sanitizer and tissues—Because you never know.

Arnica and calendula creams (avoid the gel versions if possible): Arnica goes on bruises and sore muscles; calendula goes on open wounds and scrapes. If you want simple and effective natural remedies for such ouchies, I recommend packing tubes of these two creams.

Leatherman multitool—Even for city travel, I don't think I've gone on a trip and *not* used mine, if only to get a wine bottle open.

Tabacum and a handkerchief—If you have a tendency for motion sickness, there's no better trick than the one a fellow travel writer taught me: Tie a handkerchief around your eyes (not too tight!) and take the recommended dose of this natural remedy. Try to get near a vent or moving air, face forward, and you'll be much more likely to turn around that sick feeling.

First aid antibiotic ointment—From paper cuts to all-out scrapes, healing ointment protects against infection on the road. And it doubles beautifully for shaving cream, never leaving red bumps, in case the airport security folks made you dump your canister.

For Girls Only

Mannose—If you have a tendency for compromised urinary tract health on the road, I recommend this age-old remedy for eliminating the issue. Mannose-D is in cranberries, and taking one teaspoon of mannose is like drinking five bottles of undiluted, unsweetened cranberry juice. This remedy is available at health food stores and natural medicine outlets.

Lavender oil—This essential oil emits a calming scent and masks body odors. I mix mine with a little lotion to avoid putting oil directly on my skin, because it can be too concentrated, especially for sensitive skin.

GladRags pads—Try these reusable pads and Keeper Cups if you are willing—they save tons of trash and have traveling bags to make their use doable on the road. Admittedly, these products are not for everyone.

Instant ice pack and instant heat pad—I don't know about you, but cold cures my headache pretty fast, and heat calms my sore back or upset tummy quickly. Learning about cold and heat's ability to relieve pain and relax tenseness in my body has changed my travels for the better. Just make sure you don't buy Icy Hot patches—those are completely different than plain heat pads. For "that time of the month," it's great having these temperature options on hand.

Safety

All major cities around the world have some amount of crime. Please use your wits and stay safe. Try to avoid traveling alone to new places at night.

En Route

Travel with equipment that helps make the journey to your destination peaceful. When I travel, I bring earplugs, headphones, and a sleep mask so my voyage will be blissfully quiet. I find this is easier than asking others to tone it down.

Get enough sleep before you fly. I recommend drinking lots of water the day before traveling and the day of—more if you tend to get dehydrated easily or are prone to headaches from dry plane air. Boosting your dose of vitamin C won't hurt either. To prevent your ears from popping on takeoff and landing, purchase a natural gum, like rainforest-friendly, chicle-based chewing gum.

When You Get There

Don't plan two activity-heavy days back to back. In general, it is good to have a combination of restful, educational, and physical experiences. Balance your time rather than trying to jam in too much activity. Ask yourself what you really want to see, and cut out the rest. Keep in mind that you can always come back, and be realistic about what you and your friends and family have the energy for.

Consider breaking into smaller groups when people in your party have different ideas of what they want to see and do.

Carbon Offsets

Despite the debate about the effectiveness of carbon offsets, they represent an important stopgap measure that can really do a lot of good. Carbon offset providers use a calculator programmed to estimate what a given trip will rack up in carbon dioxide emission. This mechanism considers factors like trip distance and the number of passengers in a vehicle so you'll only be responsible for your share. To offset the estimated carbon dioxide emission, you then pay one of these providers to plant trees or otherwise reduce carbon elsewhere.

You aren't throwing your money away if you know where to get certified offsets. For instance, some of the best carbon offset products are certified by Green-e, a consumer protection program run by Center for Resource

Solutions. Other carbon offset providers doing a stellar job, and thus endorsed by Environmental Defense Fund (*www.fightglobalwarming.com*), are Carbon fund.org and AtmosClear (*www.atmosclear.org*).

Major travel web sites are helping out by making carbon offsetting a click option when you purchase your ticket.

Green Travel

Air travel is not great in terms of being carbon neutral, but many airlines are starting to invest in energy efficiency to make up for their jet fuel emissions. When you book a flight, pressure them to do so, or buy your own credits when you fly from one of the certified carbon offset providers. Travel often necessitates flying, so try to use airlines that are more conscientious when you can, and you are sure to make a more positive contribution to the greater good. Weigh your options and do the best you can.

Public transit and biking are the greenest solutions there are, but other great ways to get around exist, like using vehicles that run on compressed natural gas, electricity, fuel cells, or biofuels. In these pages, I point you to the latest and greatest green transit solutions in the area you'll be visiting.

Read more about green travel: *www.grassroutestravel.com/green_travel*

Eating

These days eating green is a tricky undertaking. Here are some tips to stay conscientious and also get your grub on whether you're away or at home.

- Lots of smaller farms operate organically but just don't have the bucks to maintain an organic certification stamp. Search these out on your next farmers market excursion.

- Organic produce that's out of season, shipped from far away, can be more taxing on the environment than buying conventional, local produce in season.

- Biodynamic farming is a wonderful philosophy of growing that takes into consideration many factors beneficial to the earth. It isn't always easy finding biodynamic produce; try farmers markets or search online for a biodynamic CSA (a group of farmers or consumers promoting community-supported agriculture). Otherwise, buy local, in season, and organic.

- For more affordable and accessible organics, buy from a local farm, join a CSA, or subscribe to an organic food box service.

- Find out which conventional produce you should avoid because it's grown unsustainably or requires soil sterility and high levels of chemicals that stay on board when you take a bite. Stone fruits and leafy veggies are two examples of things to buy organic, always.

- Conventional produce that doesn't require a large amount of pesticides or to which pesticides aren't as apt to stick, such as fruits and vegetables with thick peels, are safe to eat.

- When you are ordering at one of the restaurants in this book, you may find some ingredients that aren't sustainable on the menu. Just go for the dishes you know have ingredients that can be sustained.

- Kosher, halal, and organic, hormone-free meats are always better choices in terms of taste, quality, humaneness, and sustainability.

- When buying packaged products or frozen goods, be extra careful to check the country of origin. My rule of thumb is the closer, the better. Some countries have unreliable quality control practices that degrade the soil, pollute the environment, and strain working and living conditions. Michael Pollan has a particularly interesting and well-informed explanation of this in his book *In Defense of Food: An Eater's Manifesto* (*www.michaelpollan.com/indefense.php*).

- Be especially careful when it comes to seafood. Shrimp, tuna, big fin fish—all no-nos. Squid, catfish, tilapia, anchovies, and mackerel, on the other hand, are all totally tasty and easy to sustain. The Monterey Bay Aquarium has an up-to-date explanation of the best seafood choices: *www.montereybayaquarium.org/cr/seafoodwatch.aspx*

Read more about eco-friendly dining: *www.grassroutestravel.com/eating*

Banking

Did you know that the most important factor in true sustainability is economic? Think local jobs, banks that give loans to new small businesses, and more. Business owners who live where they work care about the longevity of their community and local environment, and when you spend your money at locally owned businesses, you support that sincere effort.

Most of the businesses in these pages have direct links to the local economy, injecting most of their revenue right back into the community. Don't consider the sustainability movement without looking into the economics of it—indeed the solution to many challenges in society today lies in the communion between green industry and economics. For more info, check out Van Jones's Green For All (*www.greenforall.org*) or the Business Alliance for Local Living Economies (*www.livingeconomies.org*).

For specific establishments and more about keeping money circulating locally, see "Community-Supporting Banks" on page 228, and refer to *www.grassroutestravel.com/buy_local*.

Using GrassRoutes Guides

Organization by type of venue runs the risk of muddling, say, an upscale restaurant with a drive-thru, just because both are technically restaurants. Instead, shouldn't guides be organized by what kind of experience you are looking for?

GrassRoutes guides employ a new system of organization that makes searching for activities, restaurants, and venues easy. This guide is organized by situation, with chapters such as "Stay Up Late," "Do Lunch," and "Hang Out" that pay attention to your state of being.

All phone numbers are in the (503) area code unless otherwise stated.

As authors, we want to tell our experiences from our own perspectives. The initials after each review denote the author:

SB: Serena Bartlett
DL: Daniel Laing
MM: Marisa McClellen
NK: Nicky Kriara
RM: Raina Rose McClellen
JF: Jamie Freedman

Our Criteria

Urban Eco-Travel is defined by businesses and activities that give back to their local communities through environmental, social, or economic means. To appear in a GrassRoutes guide, a business and/or activity *must* have a local presence or be locally owned. In addition, if we can answer *yes* to at least one of the following questions, the destination passes our test:

- Does it bank locally?
- Does it hire locals?
- Does it use energy-efficient appliances?
- Does it sell fair-trade merchandise?
- Does it have a positive community benefit (for example, bringing people together or providing community outreach)?
- Does it use fair-trade, organic, or locally grown products?
- Is its location environmentally sound (for example, the building is not on a landfill, or the building is made with green materials)?
- Does it participate in reuse/garbage reduction?
- Does it care about the environment, community, and economy around it?
- And last, but certainly not least, do we love the place? Does something make it special? Does it blow our minds?

With these considerations in mind, we've created a series of icons to accompany our reviews. These icons (see key on the following page) indicate which of the criteria above are particularly noteworthy at a specific business or organization.

art/cultural/historic preservation			free
banks locally			green cleaning
bikeable			green energy use
cash only			hires locals
community pillar			inspirational
composts			local organic produce/ ingredients
cost: cheap			locally owned
cost: moderate			on public transit route
cost: pricey			recycled material use
dog friendly			recycles
educational			reservations recommended
electric vehicle use			romantic
employee health care			vegetarian
employees reentering workforce			WiFi available
fair trade			

The GrassRoutes Team

Serena Bartlett

A natural born contrarian, Serena has lived and traveled in more than 25 countries. She is an award-winning author and an active spokesperson for inspiring ways to tread more lightly on the planet. With degrees from Friends World College (now Global College) and Long Island University, she had the world as her classroom. Serena is a regular contributor to a number of national and Bay Area publications, and has written stories on everything from shampoo-making with garden ingredients to green business tips to an interview with one of her role models, Riane Eisler. She has appeared on ABC's *View from the Bay*, KRON4's *Bay Area Backroads*, and other programs as a green travel expert, and has been a featured guest on KPFA and KGO radio. Serena revels in creative solutions for becoming more self-reliant, like sewing her own sheets and quilts, designing jewelry, making wild forays in the kitchen, and growing her own edible garden. She is a ski bum at heart and a swimming junkie, equally comfortable on a pack trip with her poodle or as a city slicker. Discover more about Serena at *www.serenabartlett.com* and at *www.grassroutestravel.com*, and read her regular blog updates at *www.grassroutestravel.com/blog* and *www.grassroutestravel.com/blogeats*.

Daniel Laing

Born and raised in Oakland, Daniel's style of freehand line drawing continues to evolve with each new GrassRoutes guide. His art has been shown at several galleries, design studios, and cafes. Daniel studied anthropology at UC Berkeley, where he learned to see beyond the superficial by putting aside preconceived notions. He can be found zipping around the streets of Oakland and San Francisco on his speedy bike, scaling the bouldering walls at the local climbing gym, in the front row of a Sonic Youth concert, or buried in a book. See more of Daniel's designs and artwork at *www.grassroutestravel.com/illustrations* and *www.daniellaing.com*.

Marisa McClellan

Despite living in Philadelphia for the last eight years, Marisa will always be a Portlander at heart (and she continues to drive her 1992 Subaru station wagon in order to prove it). Her family moved to the City of Roses when she was eight years old, and she grew up among the bridges, coffeehouses, and thrift stores of PDX.

When not lovingly expounding on all the wonderful things her hometown has to offer, Marisa can be found filming an independently produced online cooking show called *Fork You* (*www.forkyou.tv*); writing about jam making, canning, pickling, and preserving at Food in Jars (*www.foodinjars.com*); and working as a web producer for the official tourism marketing organization in Philadelphia. She lives in Center City with her Fork You co-host and husband, Scott McNulty.

Nicky Kriara

Nicky is a multimedia visual artist and Portland native. Her enthusiasm for travel tends to lead her away from Oregon, but her affection toward the Pacific Northwest always brings her back. She has a Bachelor of Fine Arts from the University of Oregon, where she studied ceramics and installation art. Kriara owned Epitome Gallery (2004–2006) in Portland's Old Town and continues to show her work in galleries throughout the United States. *www.nickykriara.com*

Raina Rose McClellan

With an ever-growing patchwork of fans across America, Raina Rose's song stylings are becoming one of the new sounds of folk. Her newest album, *When May Came*, was released in early 2010 to much acclaim, and many of her songs from her four albums were inspired by her upbringing in Portland. She is still intimate with the Rose City scene, especially when it comes to music, but she regularly tours, so find out where to catch her live at *www.rainarose.com*.

Jamie Freedman

Diving into each music scene she finds herself in, Jamie is an ethnomusicologist who has lived and traveled all over the world. She is a musician herself, writes for Examiner.com, and helps organize Girls Rock Camps. Check out her play lists in other GrassRoutes guides, and visit her regularly updated blog for new tunes and shows: *www.alwaysmoretohear.com*

Dutsi Bap

Our cheerleader, research assistant, and referee, Dutsi boosts morale and provides support crucial to the GrassRoutes team. When he's not on the road testing out new locations, he visits local nursing homes to spread joy and fluffiness. He completed therapy dog certification and believes that the meaning of life is to eat roast chicken, run in the park, and take long naps at the feet of our writers. Dutsi also loves our freecycled leather couch!

Portland and Environs

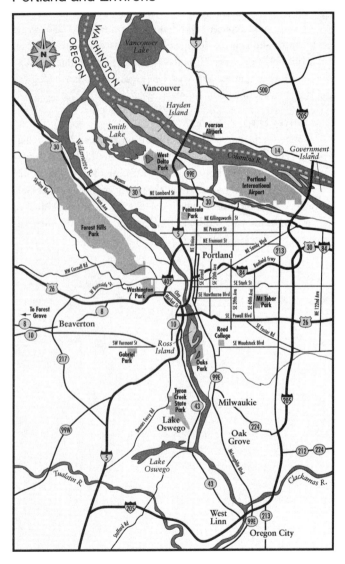

Northwest Portland

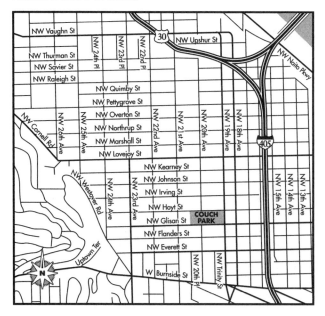

Hawthorne District

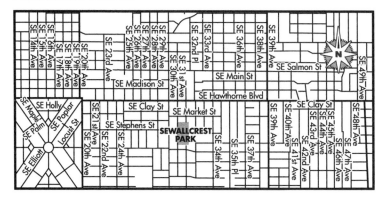

North Mississippi

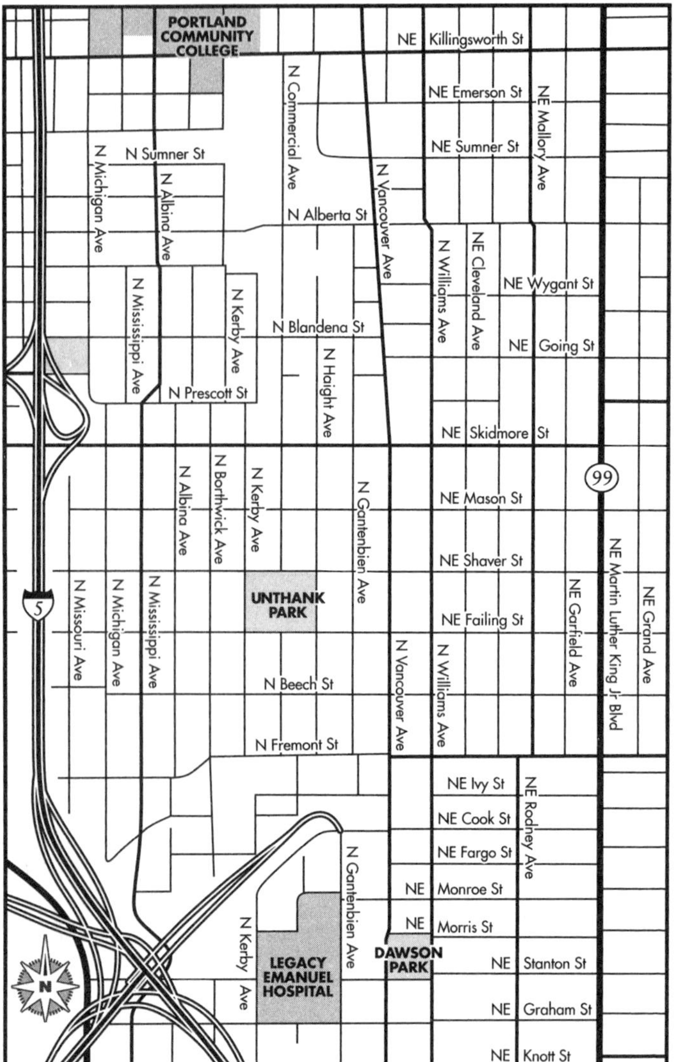

Sellwood/Westmoreland

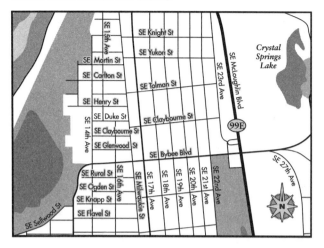

Irvington

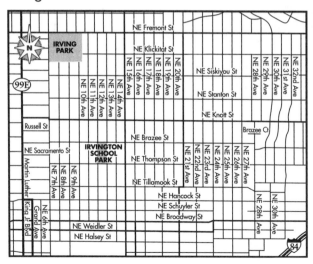

Southern Oregon Coast (for "Detour" chapter)

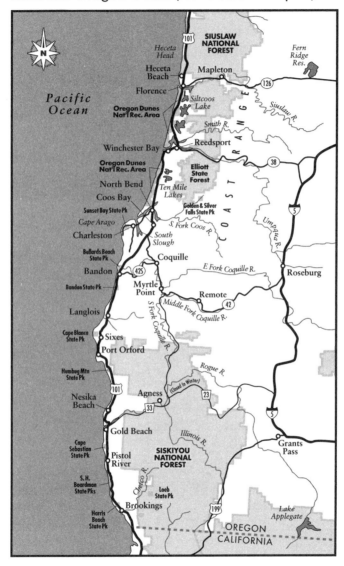

PORTLAND
About Portland

"Keep Portland Weird" is a slogan you'll often see staring at you from the rear bumper of a car driving down Portland's boulevards. This phrase sums up the spirit of preservation in Oregon's largest city, which was designed to retain a small-town feel. It's strange to think that Portland was once a 640-acre plot purchased for a quarter, and even stranger that it was almost called Boston.

The story of how the City of Roses came to be begins in 1843 when drifter William Overton attempted to file a claim for the 640-acre site known as "the clearing," but lacked the 25 cents to do so. Enthralled by the beautiful landscape, Overton made a deal with Massachusetts lawyer Asa Lovejoy, who gave him the 25 cents in exchange for an equal share of the land. Overton eventually continued his drifter lifestyle, selling his share to Francis Pettygrove. The new partners concurred that their budding township deserved a name, but they could not come to an agreement. Lovejoy was determined to name it after his hometown of Boston, while Pettygrove wanted the honor to go to his native Portland, Maine. Neither was willing to yield, and so the coin toss of the century was held to settle the matter. Consequently, the coin they used became known as the Portland Penny. In 1851, less than a decade after that fateful coin toss, Portland was incorporated as a city.

Lovejoy and Pettygrove, who have been memorialized with street names, predicted that Portland would evolve into a prosperous and popular destination, owing to its prime location on the Willamette River and its abundant natural resources. Indeed, it became a major transportation center during the Civil War, with docks built for shipping lumber, fish, and wheat to the rest of the nation and the world. Portland's popularity as a port city, coupled with government corruption, resulted in increased abductions of men to work as slave labor on sailing ships. Notorious in this "shanghaiing trade" was hotelier Joseph "Bunco" Kelly, whose deceitful tricks earned him his nickname. Bunco once delivered an Indian statue wrapped in blankets as another would-be slave to a ship captain, who threw it overboard in a fit of rage upon discovering the ruse. The statue was discovered nearly 60 years later by a pair of dredge operators.

Portland's seamy underground took a turn for the better with the flourishing of the lumber industry and the wealth earned from providing goods for the California gold rush. City officials regulated the waterfront's questionable activities. The subterranean tunnels beneath the city streets that were once used to cart hapless drunks to an unwanted life at sea soon became a historical curiosity. Business owners shifted their concern from making a profit on trickery to improving worker conditions. For example, lumber baron Simon Benson commissioned 20 drinking fountains when he learned that his employees were substituting alcohol for water in the downtown areas, because fresh water was not readily available. Beer consumption reportedly decreased 25 percent following the installation of the Benson Bubblers. The elegant fountains are now surrounded by public parks, outdoor art, coffee carts, bookstores, and of all things, microbreweries.

Just 20 years prior, the city gained a nickname, which really helped put Portland on the map. The *City of Roses* derives from the warm summers and rainy but temperate winters, which make it an ideal location for growing roses, proven in the explosion of spring blossoms. The earliest known reference to Portland as the City of Roses dates back to an 1888 Episcopal Church convention. At the Lewis and Clark Centennial Exposition of 1905, Mayor Harry Lane suggested a festival of roses for the city, and the nickname's appeal began to spread. Two years later, the first Portland Rose Festival was held, and it remains an annual tradition.

Over the years and throughout its many stages of growth during the 20th century, new festivals and traditions have sprung up in the City of Roses. This bridged, criss-crossed place is now big on books and book festivals, microbreweries and beer fests, and a vivid arts community with a slew of monthly—even weekly—events. Spiffy cocktails are spreading from Portland to cities all over the country, and the hipster scene, indie music, and DIY movement are making the same migration. Portland is a place for doers, a place for people with relaxed and friendly attitudes but refined senses when it comes to eating, drinking, listening, smelling . . .

Today, the city is known far and wide for its exports of hipster culture, indie music, cycling innovations, cult writing, but perhaps most for its dedication to green transportation. Even in European circles, Portland is widely known for its commitment to alternative modes of transportation, land conservation policies, and overall attention to green practices. The city ranked number one in overall sustainability ratings in 2006 and is proud to hold the title of "role model for the nation" by SustainLane. Portland has been rated as one of the cleanest U.S. cities and is third among the top 10 cities making the best use of renewable energy in city operations (the crown goes to GrassRoutes' hometown of Oakland, California). Portland stands as the only American city to be selected by the European Institute of Urban Affairs as one of the "world's most successful cities."

A public transportation mecca, Portland does not follow the trend of the world's most car-dependent nation. Car use here is growing at the slowest rate anywhere in the country, and Portland drivers are considered the most courteous to boot. Why drive when you can take a 500-foot-high commute over Interstate 5 on the Portland Aerial Tram, one of the first urban trams in the country? Everyone loves Portland's triumphant public transit asset, the Free Rail Zone zone on the Metropolitan Area Express (MAX) light rail through Portland's bustling downtown and Lloyd Center area. In the last couple of decades, city planners have looked to European transportation systems in cities such as Amsterdam for inspiration to continue Portland's legacy of being a bike-friendly city. The city's thriving bike scene and its conscientious urban-growth planning have earned it a high ranking from the League of American Bicyclists. For those who are content to travel by foot, a 2009 study by the American Podiatric Medical Association picked Portland as one of the top 10 best walking cities in America.

In addition to the city being an easy place to get around, it is also a place where the population moves in other ways. Portlanders use their mind to travel, as they are one of the most well-read cities in the nation. In addition, more than a quarter of the population is suited up with a bachelor's degree, so get ready to rumble. . .especially when it comes to pub quizzes (see page 133).

Creativity abounds in Portland, especially since the dot-com boom brought a massive influx of young designers. Even after that economic bubble burst, Portland's artistic population has continued to rise, and the last decade has seen a renaissance in the local art scene. *American Style* magazine ranks Portland the number 10 art destination among cities with populations of more than 500,000. Portland is also one of the best places for independent filmmakers to make a living, with the state of Oregon boasting more than 34 film festivals. GrassRoutes has devoted a section of this book (see the "Film Buffs" chapter, page 135) to the best movie houses in Portland. The artistic inhabitants of the city also account for the attractive restaurants, tasteful shops, and head-turning public art that make Portland the treasure that it is.

Artistry isn't limited to the highbrow, either. Matt Groening, creator of the animated television series *The Simpsons*, grew up in Portland. Characters of the show appear regularly on street signs in the mid- and northwestern parts of the city.

The creative nature of Portland's residents extends to the city's music scene. Having played a large part in the grunge rock evolution of the late '80s and early '90s, Portland continues to nurture blossoming bands. Most recently, the city has contributed to the indie-rock movement with bands like the Decemberists and the Shins. Portlanders have an ear for good rock 'n' roll, but that's not all they listen to (see page 155 for a local Portland Playlist).

Portland residents are also concerned with the welfare of animals. The Humane Society of the United States placed Portland third among the 25 largest U.S. cities for animal friendliness and caring. A high concentration of wildlife rehabilitators, Canadian seafood boycotters, vegetarian dining options, and establishments with cage-free egg policies contributed to this high ranking. And for your furry travel friends, Portland is the best all-around city for dogs in America, according to *Dog Fancy* magazine. Annual events include the Doggie Dash and the Pug Crawl fundraiser for the Oregon Humane Society. Doggie day-care businesses are never hard to find, and with 33 city-maintained parks, every dog can have his day and then some.

A surprising and distinguishing feature of Portland is the abundance of strip joints. It is believed that there are more of them per capita in Portland than in any other city in the United States. Portland is liberal with nudity laws, which is sure to be a contributing factor to the statistic. Mary's Club is the most noteworthy of these establishments, as it was the first topless club in the country. (As an added bonus, Mary's connects with a surprisingly scrumptious Mexican restaurant next door.)

Portland is also exceptional in the number of microbreweries that call the rosy city home. The total is somewhere around 60, with home brewers also contributing to the microbrew culture, as evidenced in the many local beer festivals throughout the year (see the "Calendar" chapter, page 220).

Portland is leading the way in sustainability by making a strong commitment to public transportation and thoughtful urban growth strategies. The overall conscientious mentality has earned the city acclaim in many aspects of urban life, from business to recreation to just getting around. Portland is an example of a community addressing the concern in the world for restoring the quality of public life.

The public agenda of the city is a clear display of environmental sustainability, and individual Portlanders take eco-conscious living seriously as well. By seeking out alternative transportation to work (many workers can be seen on bikes in their business suits during the morning commute), choosing to reduce consumption, taking advantage of recycling, and opting for organic and local foods whenever possible, the personal choices of city residents showcase individual responsibility and dedication to the environment.

Although the principles of sustainability are embraced citywide, it should be noted that the Eastside is where the movement thrives. With less traffic and congestion than downtown, more bike commuters can be found passing by locally owned stores, organic restaurants, and creative enclaves. Pioneering businesses like The ReBuilding Center (see page 107) and the Farm Cafe (see page 169) are plentiful. A walk on the east side of town will reveal lawns turned into gardens, free boxes galore, and a general atmosphere of conscientious living. DL

Portland Lingo

You may hear some words and phrases around town and not have a clue what people are talking about—here are a few:

The Beav: Beaverton, a nearby sprawl with some terrific hole-in-the-wall restaurants.

Classed up: An upgrade on anything, from meals to outfits to cars to gadgets.

The Coov: Vancouver—and no, not Vancouver, Canada. This Vancouver is the next town up, right over the state line in Washington.

Crust punk: Unlike hard-core or regular punk, crust punk is all about long electric guitar riffs and dark, pessimistic lyrics, and it's big in PDX. If you see black clothing with dental floss used instead of thread to sew big, showy stitches, you can bet there's a CD or vinyl of Initial Detonation, Gallhammer, or Aus-Rotten nearby.

DIY: Do-it-yourself culture is Portland's MO.

The Falls: Multnomah Falls near the Gorge (Columbia River Gorge).

Freddy's: Fred Meyer, a local grocery chain that goes way back in the City of Roses.

Portland's living room: Another way of referring to Pioneer Courthouse Square.

Rannoying: *Rain* plus *annoying* equals *rannoying*. When it's just too wet out, this state has a way of lingering, and the term gets used with increased frequency.

The Schnitz: The historic Arlene Schnitzer Concert Hall.

Sales tax: No definition 'cause there is none!

Spendy: Overpriced things and overposh places. A shop could be too spendy, but an entire street could also be too spendy. If you're paying more than you think you should, it's spendy.

Stumptown: A popular slang term for Portland twinged with guilt from all the trees chopped down to create the expanse of the city, thus leaving stumps. Other city nicknames include PDX, P-town, City of Roses, and the lesser used Little Beirut, Bridgetown, and Rip City.

The mountain is out: This phrase denotes a clear day when you can see Mount Hood from a plethora of city points.

WiFi: The definition of wireless Internet evolves in Portland. Whole neighborhoods have wired up for free, and Pioneer Courthouse Square, PGE Park, and several other public places also have free WiFi signals. Cheers to the future!

Pronunciation Tips: You'll recognize lots of Portland street names if you've ever watched an episode of *The Simpsons*, but there are some streets that need extra attention when it comes to pronunciation. *Couch*, the essential living room furniture, is not pronounced like "ouch" but more like the "coo" in cuckoo bird. *Glisan* is like my high school football coach: glee-san, not gli-san. And the ever-important river flowing through town has the stress on the middle syllable: wil-LAM-ette, not WIL-amet. Mispronouncing these is as bad as pronouncing Houston Street in New York City like the city in Texas—a big no-no unless you are trying to stick out like a sore thumb! *SB*

Climate

"Temperate" and "seasonal" are the best words to describe Portland's ideal rose-growing weather. With many of the same characteristics of a Mediterranean climate, Portland's winters are mild and wet, and summers are hot and dry. The average yearly rainfall is 44 inches, with the rainy season lasting from November to April, so pack a raincoat if you're planning to travel to Portland during those months. Winter lows average 35° F with snowfall uncommon. June to September marks the driest season, with temperatures averaging 80° F, although heat waves exceeding 100° F do occur.

Geographically, Portland is located at latitude 45°60' North, longitude 122°60' West and has a total land area of 134.3 square miles (347.9 square kilometers).

Getting Here

Tips to Get from A to B

Portland is an international destination without the frenzy of a major metropolis. Here are some options for travel that include everything from flying to walking. Even we conscientious travelers of the globe must, at times, make use of transportation options beyond walking! Weigh time, cost, and energy usage to determine which transport choice best suits your needs and the needs of the planet. There is something about time-consuming transit that provides a smoother transition to the next spot, though it may take a bit longer. Choose efficient routes to avoid wasting unnecessarily fuel.

By Plane

Portland International Airport (PDX)

7000 NE Airport Way
888.257.0126
www.flypdx.com

Flying into Portland International Airport (PDX) is a breeze. This place never seems to be crowded, the people who work there are helpful and courteous, and the MAX train runs right outside the baggage claim area, ready to scoop you up and deposit you in the city center. It's no wonder this airport has won accolades for being the most convenient airport for business travelers. There are plenty of chain-restaurant options in each terminal, which are priced higher than usual, so I recommend bringing a bagged lunch or waiting until you are released from the security line to get some real grub. Although you cannot bring more than three ounces of liquid with you, and you may even have to relinquish gels like lip balm to airport security officers, you can still bring an empty water bottle to fill at a water fountain once inside the terminal and avoid spending extreme amounts of cash on bottled water. Security regulations change with great frequency; check with the Federal

Aviation Administration (*www.faa.gov*) to see what the current restrictions are. Once you depart the airport, you can hire a shared shuttle on the spot, or in a pinch, you can take a taxi ride for around $40, which will get you to most places in the center of Portland. *SB*

Seattle-Tacoma International Airport (Sea-Tac)

Main terminal: 17801 International Blvd
787.5388, 800.544.1965
www.portseattle.org/seatac/

This modern airport is a hub of international travel, with many direct flights to Asian countries. An underground tram comes every two minutes, easily connecting the terminals. At the end of the baggage claim area is a pleasant fountain with huge local rocks and a sculpture garden with historic planes flying from the glassy ceiling. It is a courteous airport (if there is such a thing), and there are plenty of ways to reach downtown Seattle, where you can then easily make your way by train, bus, or car to Portland. United, Southwest, and Alaska Airlines as well as its subsidiary Frontier Alaska have main hubs at Sea-Tac, but most major airlines fly to and from this airport. *SB*

By Train

Amtrak

800 NW 6th Ave
227.1234
www.amtrak.com

Portland's Union Station serves travelers with a choo-choo link to the rest of the country and beyond. Hop aboard an Amtrak train for a romantic trip with guaranteed adventure, as stops are often delayed or slightly off schedule. But you will reliably get here, and you'll be rested and possibly even well-read when you arrive. *SB*

By Bus

Greyhound

550 NW 6th Ave, by Union Station
800.231.2222, 243.2361
www.greyhound.com

Greyhound operates its Portland bus lines into and out of its station located next to Union Station. There are a number of departure and arrival times. Call up the company directly or check out the web site for detailed schedules. *SB*

By Car

Ride Share
www.craigslist.org

Craigslist is the online community board of much of the United States and the world. To search the Craigslist of your city, choose from the city list on the right-hand side of the page. For the car-less or those seeking to be conscientious carpoolers, Craigslist has a special section under "community" called "rideshare." Often people who are looking for a ride or willing to accommodate passengers will post here. Send a few e-mails back and forth and have a chat on the good ol' telephone to make sure that you are comfortable with the person with whom you will be traveling. *SB*

Highways

Portland is located along the Interstate 5 corridor that runs the length of the West Coast, so it is easily accessible to the road tripper. For those arriving from the east, Interstate 84 will get you here. Traffic is not intimidating in the city, so don't be scared to exit off the safe confines of the highway, find parking, and begin your City of Roses exploration. *DL*

Getting Around

Here's the lowdown on your intracity transit options. Remember, powered transport is plentiful, but city blocks are small in Portland, and your own two feet are a viable mechanism to move from one place to the next—this is a walking city. To speed things up, a bicycle is another great alternative, as the city has bike routes aplenty (see the "Bike About" chapter, page 68).

Portland is mostly on a grid. The Willamette River separates Portland into east and west, and Burnside Street separates north and south. Streets running north to south are generally numbered, with numbers increasing as you head east from the river on the east side and west from the river on the west side. Streets are alphabetical as you head north from Burnside (Burnside, Couch, Davis, etc). Check out the maps on page xxiv to help get your bearings. I recommend toting a Portland street-finder map as well.

TriMet

203.7433
www.trimet.org

The public transportation arm of Portland is TriMet. In charge of the bus line, MAX light rail, and streetcar, TriMet keeps the city running and is constantly working on sustainable initiatives, such as alternative fuel for its buses and community development projects. TriMet's online Trip Planner on its homepage (*www.trimet.org*) will draw from bus and train options to bring you to your destination efficiently.

A fare of $1.70 covers most areas (two zones) and can be paid in exact change right on the buses or bought from ticket vending machines at MAX stations. Fares can also be purchased at grocery stores around town. Transfers between buses and trains are good for one hour on weekdays and two hours on weekends. *SB*

Free Rail Zone

www.trimet.org/fares/fareless.htm

TriMet's Free Rail Zone covers downtown and extends over the Steel Bridge into the Lloyd District. You get a free ride on all lines, buses, the MAX, and the streetcar as long as you stay within those boundaries! *SB*

Bus

www.trimet.org/bus

With the largest web of lines among Portland's public transport options, there is most likely a bus to get you to where you want to go. This is always a great way to see a nice slice of the city's inhabitants, as buses draw all walks of life. TriMet has fueled many of its buses with biodiesel and is working on more hybrid options as well, so the already sustainable choice of mass transport is becoming even more environmentally friendly. *SB*

MAX Light Rail

www.trimet.org/max

The MAX is a way to get to those outer-limit destinations. The MAX Red Line will bring you and your luggage from the airport to downtown Portland, and the Yellow Line will shoot you up to events at the Expo Center. If the burbs are calling your name, the MAX also has lines to Beaverton, Hillsboro, and Gresham. *SB*

Streetcar

www.trimet.org/streetcar

The Portland Streetcar travels between Legacy Good Samaritan Hospital in the northwest, Portland State University in the southwest, and the South Waterfront. With much of the line contained within the Free Rail Zone, taking the streetcar can be an affordable option for those staying in the downtown area. Riding the streetcar all the way to the South Waterfront will take you to the new aerial tram that connects the waterfront and the Oregon Health and Science University (OHSU) Center for Health and Healing with the OHSU Marquam Hill Campus. *SB*

TriMet Trip Planner

www.trimet.org/go/cgi-bin/plantrip.cgi

This web page is one-stop shopping for local transit info and resources. All of your questions are answered here when it comes to Portland's well-oiled network of public transportation options. *SB*

Portland Aerial Tram

www.portlandtram.org

Oregon Health and Science University (OHSU) and the city partnered to construct and operate this prominent structure, which crosses over I-5, and opened its use to the public at the beginning of 2007. Meant to provide a transportation option for OHSU patients, students, and researchers, it has also become a destination of its own for the sheer quirkiness of being an aerial tram and for the view it offers. Take a ride if you want to revel in this unique experience, and get up the southeast hill without guzzling gas or resorting to voodoo to find a parking spot. *SB*

Zipcar

www.zipcar.com

For the savvy ecotourist, the Zipcar car-sharing service offers an array of fuel-efficient vehicles available at hourly and daily rates. The service does not claim to be a cheaper alternative to renting a car, but it does claim convenience (usually there is a Zipcar to be picked up within a five-minute walk from your current location), affordability (you pay by the hour, not by the day), lower age requirements (21 years of age and older), and sustainability (with sport hybrids and ultra-low emissions vehicles). Membership is required (a $35 one-time fee), and the application process can take up to one week, so planning ahead is required. You can join the network online, make reservations, and pick up your car at a designated spot. Drop it off whenever you're done, 24 hours a day, 7 days a week. Gas, insurance, and designated Zipcar parking spaces are all included in the rental price. Best of all, this service is becoming more widespread, so you can use it in other cities where you travel. The company offers discounted plans for businesses, groups, and drivers who need to use the service more frequently. *DL*

Ptown Scooters

3347 SE Division St
241.4745
www.ptownscooters.com
Tues–Fri 11a–7p, Sat 11a–4p

Rent or buy electric and low-emissions scooters here.

Google Transit Search Portland

www.google.com/transit

This awesome resource is easy to use: just plug in your location and destination and you'll get all applicable mass transit options with schedules, fares, and stop locations. Yessiree, Bob.

Green Cab and Green Shuttle

234.1414
www.greentrans.com

Call for a cab for yourself or a van for you and eight of your friends, and these guys will show up in a jiffy in green vehicles.

Top Picks

If you have only one crazy, cramped day in this city

I've chosen 11 of my top Portland spots, in part because 11 is my favorite number and also as a nod to Spinal Tap fans who admire guitar amps that go the extra digit for maximum sound projection. Here are the 11 places that typify the dynamic, sustainable city of Portland.

Pix Patisserie (see page 187)

The alluring and passionate chocolate concoctions at Pix Patisserie are sinful in all the right ways. There's a reason the Pix bakers have won competitions, even against the French. If you don't partake in cocoa, Pix can tempt you with a long list of other desserts. Bring a friend when you go; he or she will be forever adoring.

Laurelhurst Park (see page 42)

In a city where green space is highly valued, this park outdoes all the rest. Let's make a list: It's beautiful and there are plentiful trails (paved and unpaved), sport courts for various games, picnic setups by a pond, and hilly views. On any given day, there may well be a GrassRoutes contributor frolicking there—we just can't help it!

Kennedy School (see page 137)

At this school, anything's game. The idea of watching a great cult flick while sipping a beer and just relaxing without moving an inch would have been too thrilling to entertain during high school algebra. Luckily, we can all fulfill our dreams of beer in the schoolhouse on the comfy sofas at Kennedy School. Stop studying, we command you!

Ten 01 (see page 166)

Yum, yum, and yum. Duck, charcuterie, local line-caught seafood, veggies covering the plate . . . I can barely form complete sentences reminiscing about my meals at this beautiful restaurant. The best part is you can enjoy it on the cheap by coming early for the exquisite happy hour menu. I almost don't want to say any more.

Mississippi Studios (see page 157)

Portland has a vibrant music culture, and Mississippi Studios is where many new artists pop up, performing and realizing the full extent of their potential. Seeing an intimate show here is your opportunity to say "I saw it first."

Palio Dessert and Espresso House (see page 29)

Palio is a snug spot where you can linger for hours in a Windsor chair with a good book and a slice of cake. The quality coffee served here, right smack-dab in the middle of Ladd's Addition (see page 33), is top-notch, and that is really saying something in coffee-crazed Portland.

Hollywood Theater (see page 137)

The beautiful mosaics and historic feel of the Hollywood Theater bring back memories of the classic movie-going experiences of old. You'll find silver-screen showings of all sorts, from throwbacks to the past to the most cutting-edge digital productions, featured at the many film fests here.

Vendetta (see page 67)

I used to think that bars were where ghosts duked out unresolved issues. But I've never felt any ghosts getting revenge at Vendetta—this place is just too friendly. The cozy feel of the place makes drinkers and nondrinkers at home, and there's a garden in back for warm summer evenings full of bubbly conversation. Tasty bites and an über-cool atmosphere, complete with shuffleboard, round out the picture.

Powell's City of Books (see page 35)

There's just nothing like a city block of books. I know I am biased being a writer, but trust me, no matter what your passion, you'll find something that ignites it here. Powell's is what comes to mind to many when they think of Portland, and that's because there's no bigger, more proudly independent bookstore in the country. On any topic, there are new and used titles from all different perspectives—this is one amazing cross section of wordy ideas!

¿Por Qué No? Taqueria (see page 45)

Soccer, beer, a great mix of people, and delectable, authentic Mexican food. Oh, baby! It's no surprise there's often a line out the door at this

Mississippi Avenue eatery. The community comes together here on special game nights—no better place for a taco and a team to root for.

Mt. Scott Community Center and Pool (see page 40)

When I was driving up to Portland to first research this book, I never thought I'd be in a whirlpool within a half an hour of getting into town. My extended family brought me with them to an impromptu pool night and ever since I've been smitten with this pool—rather, series of pools—and jealous of all the lucky folks who live within walking distance of its southeast location. Whether you are in the mood for the wild whirlpool, the warmer dipping pool, the waterslide area, the bouncy diving boards in the deep end, the shallow wading pool, the hot tub, or just the regular lap pool, there's no shortage of watery places to play.

Up Early

All things early bird, plus morning treats

Sometimes I simply wake up early with extra gusto. I remember vacations in my adolescence when I rose before anyone else and snuck out for a private walk, a personal view of the place where I found myself. A morning walk such as this, or a nice long breakfast, can help you start your day off on the right foot. Take the time to enjoy the simple things as the world is just waking; follow your nose on a whim. I like taking it easy, stepping back for a moment from all the electronic systems, and just letting my feet go for a stroll. Here are some of my favorite ways to spend the first hours of the day in Portland. Some are great solo, but you can always bring a friend.

Petite Provence Boulangerie and Patisserie

4834 SE Division St, 233.1121
1824 NE Alberta St, 284.6564
www.provence-portland.com
Daily 9a–7p

There is a truly gluttonous array of pastries staring at you from the displays inside Petite Provence, but do what you have to do to get past them and snag a two-top table. French-looking woven-back chairs pepper the main dining room, and each table seems to be laden with another delicious morning feast. Berry French Toast, or the equally divine savory version, smothered with Gruyère sauce, grilled asparagus, and fine smoked ham are two tempting choices. If you are in the mood for something simpler, order the sublime pan-roasted oatmeal, swimming in sweet coconut milk and sprinkled with brown sugar— delish! This ode to a Paris matin makes a welcome morning meal for a hungry traveler. *SB*

ⅴ Zell's

1300 SE Morrison St
239.0196
Mon–Fri 7a–2p, Sat 8a–2p, Sun 8a–3p
When Saturday morning rolls around, bellies start rumbling and lines spill out the doors of the best breakfast spots in the City of Roses. Zell's is one step ahead, providing free coffee, mini scones, and a box of sidewalk chalk while you await your table. The scrambles and eggs Benedict are in Portland's upper ecehlon of eggy breakfasts The industrious staff makes sure the line keeps moving so you can order your Gruyère potatoes and prosciutto-mozzarella frittata quickly. Zell's is serious about giving back to the community in ways other than hearty breakfasts—its annual food and toy drive benefits local foster kids. *SB*

Tin Shed Garden Cafe

1438 NE Alberta St
288.6966
www.tinshedgardencafe.com
Mon–Tues 7a–3p, Wed–Sat 7a–11p, Sun 7a–10p
Under the zigzag tin roof, huddled around tables full of dishes with names like Everything Naughty and Everything Nice, there are no unsatisfied diners at this cafe. The dishes may boast strange names, but once you dive in, you'll be smitten enough to understand those crazy cooks. After a lingering walk down the colorful sidewalks of Alberta Street, a meal of sweet potato French toast with scrambled eggs and a side of fruit (the aforementioned Everything Nice) or biscuits, gravy, and sausage over the best potato cakes (Everything Naughty) will be well deserved. If you bring your vegan friends, the cafe will gladly adapt any menu item to the pickiest of requests, a service not always guaranteed in this hipster hood. *SB*

Tin Shed Garden Cafe

$$ Kornblatt's Delicatessen

628 NW 23rd Ave

242.0055

www.kornblattsdeli.com

Mon–Thurs 7a–8p, Fri 7a–9p, Sat 7:30a–9p, Sun 7:30a–8p

This traditional Jewish deli is snuggled up in the ritzy Pearl District. Munch on a house-brined dill pickle from the bucket on your table while you wait for your main dish. My cravings for blintzes, matzo ball soup, and whitefish sandwiches are always satisfied at Kornblatt's, one of the few places to find Jewish food. Friendly service and hot pastrami are sure to brighten your day. Come in the morning for a hearty matzo brei breakfast. It might not taste quite like my mom's or my Bubba's, but I do love the drippingly delicious ruben—*l'chaim!* SB

Bread and Ink Cafe

3610 SE Hawthorne Blvd

239.4756

www.breadandinkcafe.com

Mon–Thurs 7a–3p & 5–9p; Fri–Sat 8a–3p & 5–10p; Sun 9a–2p & 5–9p

A confluence of all the variations in the indie-hipster Hawthorne crowd, Bread and Ink Cafe is a key stop along this busy shopping street. The menu has a number of choices—more than the average local gathering spot. The local oysters and line-caught salmon lox are both divine. Try the flatbreads and blintzes or the tasty eggs Benedict for a filling morning feast. Don't be surprised to see students alongside professors, lawyers next to anarchists, and bookish types like myself mingling with busy moms, all happily amused by the plentiful people-watching opportunities. *SB*

Salvador Molly's

1523 SW Sunset Blvd

293.1790

www.salvadormollys.com

Sun–Tues 11:30a–9p, Wed–Thurs 11:30a–10p, Fri–Sat 11:30a–11p

Home base of one of Portland's hard-working caterers, Salvador Molly's new location is a breezy ten minutes from the Rose City's hopping downtown, but has the feel of a neighborhood gem. The delicious smells waft down the block, drawing you in. Here you'll find cocktails you may never have imagined and tamales that will haunt your dreams in a good way. I like to eat here before spending the day discovering and rediscovering Portland's great music scene. *RM*

Friends of Tryon Creek State Park Guided Nature Walks

11321 SW Terwilliger Blvd

636.4398

www.tryonfriends.org

Every week there's a new park and a new topic for these informational nature hikes. Take a second look at the world around you through the foliage, wildlife, and waterways. Check the calendar of events on the web site for this week's adventure with a naturalist. *SB*

Screen Door

2337 E Burnside St

542.0880

www.screendoorrestaurant.com

Tues–Sat 5:30–10p, Sat–Sun 9a–2:30p, Sun 5:30–9p

I've come to the conclusion that Screen Door is actually a huge magnet, drawing me and my foodie friends back repeatedly for soothing Southern-esque food and good company. The corner location lets in soft morning sunlight, coating our satisfied faces with a glow. Screen Door treads on dangerous ground with provolone cheese-topped grits and biscuits and gravy that ain't like any I've had south of the Mason-Dixon.

Blue Moose Cafe

4936 NE Fremont St

548.4475

Daily 9a–8p

This homey vegetarian cafe, located in a quiet, peaceful corner of the city in close proximity to Rose City Park, will please all taste buds. You'll be pleasantly surprised with the delicious soups and satisfying grain and legume dishes. None of the greasy fake meat products are needed here—even meat eaters won't miss a thing. Of all the breakfast spots in Portland, this is the one I find myself coming back to the most, spending hours with a huge bowl of coconut soup, toast, scrambled eggs, and a good book. *SB*

Mother's Bistro and Bar

212 SW Stark St

464.1122

www.mothersbistro.com

Tues–Fri 7a–2:30p & 5:30–9p, Sat–Sun 9a–2:30p & 5–10p

The owners of the highly recommended Mother's Bistro and Bar in shiny downtown Portland somehow successfully re-created the bounty their own mothers provided them. And what a good job they've done. I'm always surprised when eggs, biscuits, and gravy inspire me—after all, comfort food is supposed to be basic and best indulged in on a sofa rather than in a restaurant setting. But the options at Mother's make me dream of the first time I opened a steamy, flaky biscuit at my own mom's *tavola*. It's not just about breakfast here.

Try the Greek Frittata, the Breakfast Nachos, or one of the other fanciful morning plates. If you are like me and are looking for a tasty trip down memory lane, order the Bob's Red Mill Oatmeal and two fluffy scrambled eggs. You can even have a real New York H&H bagel—Mother's thought of everything! Come back for happy hour to enjoy the Mother of the Month (M.O.M.) dinner menu and great wine specials. *SB*

Genie's Cafe

1101 SE Division St
445.9777
www.geniescafepdx.com
Daily 8a–3p, coffee service begins at 7a

This friendly neighborhood place tames grumpy hipsters and their parents with delicious organic coffee, yummy omelets, and strong drinks served at any hour without judgment. Come in first thing in the morning and order a bacon Bloody Mary (with house-infused bacon vodka) if you want to keep the night going. If not, you still might want the real McCoy—even with all the vegans around, Genie's fries up these sizzling strips until the late afternoon. *SB*

Utopia Cafe

3308 SE Belmont St
235.7606
Tues–Fri 7a–2p, Sat–Sun 7:30a–2:30p

Tiny Utopia Cafe is a real find—if you can find it. It's nestled on the Belmont main drag, and if you know what you're looking for, you're that much closer. The French toast alone makes it well worth the search. I come in after the main breakfast rush to enjoy the huge helpings—try the molasses bread and the fabulous biscuits, and don't be bothered if you brush up against your fellow diners during your meal. *SB*

Francis Restaurant

2338 NE Alberta St
288.8299
www.francisrestaurant.com
Mon–Fri 7a–3p, Sat–Sun 7a–4p

Francis Restaurant serves a big breakfast. Big. I don't know what Francis's mother fed him, but the result on my table is more than I can handle without help, even if I am hungover and in need of some sweet relief. Never mind the line—even if there is one, I find it moves more swiftly here than at other spots. Rich foods are all over the menu, but they are created with a sophistication you wouldn't expect from this classically hipster joint. *SB*

Clinton Corner Cafe

2633 SE 21st Ave
230.8035
www.clintoncornercafe.net
Mon–Thur 8a–10p, Fri–Sat 9a–12a, Sun 9a–3p

A mandatory breakfast eatery in this chill hood in the southeast, Clinton Corner Cafe equates to great baked things. I can't even hear the word "Clinton" without thinking of the fresh-baked scones and muffins I've gobbled here on many a groggy morning. That's not to say the scrambles and hearty huevos rancheros aren't delish—I just have never saved enough room to order them. *SB*

Arleta Library Bakery Cafe

5513 SE 72nd Ave
774.4470
www.arletalibrary.com
Mon–Fri 8a–2:30p, Sat–Sun 8:30a–2:30p

Sometimes my friends find my obsession with dogs—especially poodles—to be insidious, but I promise I mean no harm. I just can't resist the urge to morph into a cooing, ear-scratching machine whenever I see a cute pooch. I feel the same urge at Arleta Library Bakery Cafe, another secretive Portland gem waiting to be stumbled upon. Just don't be surprised if you find yourself reaching to pat its head! Wooden countertops are covered with a menagerie of baked goods enclosed in fancy glass antique containers. Couples mutter about their delicious plates in between uttering sweet nothings, and families hum together before diving into a feast of biscuits and gravy—widely known to be among the best in PDX—and scrambled eggs. Check out the art showcased under the bookshelf at the far end of the cafe—there is always something intriguing. *SB*

🏛 Bijou Cafe

🚇 *132 SW 3rd Ave*

☎ *222.3187*

🕐 *Mon–Fri 7a–2p, Sat–Sun 8a–2p*

Airy and welcoming, Bijou Cafe has the power to create lifelong fans with a single meal. Start with strong coffee or vividly hued orange juice, squeezed right in-house. Follow that up with a freshly baked zucchini muffin, a plate of buckwheat pancakes (served with a generous pitcher of real maple syrup), or one of the breakfast hash platters (the oyster hash is a local favorite). Since Bijou is a beloved neighborhood haunt, get there early or expect a wait. If you're a party of one or two, see if you can't finagle a seat at the counter. Sitting there, you can either spread out a newspaper and eat in silence or chat with the server behind the counter a bit while you wait for your order. Any way you do it, Bijou is a must for breakfast lovers. *MM*

🅢 Marquam Nature Park

🚇 *SW Marquam St and Sam Jackson Park Rd*

🚶 *www.portlandonline.com/parks/finder/ (search "Marquam Nature Park")*

🏕 The 176 acres of preserved woodland along Portland's outskirts draw me out of the city grid. Weaving along trails shaded by sweet-smelling cedars and big-leaf maples gives me a shot of nature, and some days that is just what the doctor ordered. The main trail is part of an extended swath of urban forest, and a welcome center details the history of the area and its botany. *SB*

🚇 Broder

📷 *2508 SE Clinton St*

$$ *736.3333*

🚲 *www.broderpdx.com*

Daily 9a–3p

Portland may not have the most diverse population, but it truly does have some of the most diverse and authentic world cuisine. For breakfast, slip halfway around the world and into Scandinavia at Broder. Breakfast spreads are laid out on cutting boards and on neat white square plates, European-style. But oh, the smoked ham, the aged cheese, and the fresh berry cups! Swedish pancakes, which resemble light and fluffy donut holes, are also served with crazy-good homemade jam. Whole-grain bread with a dense, complex texture comes out of the oven frequently—you might catch a whiff of it while you are dining. Traditional potato pancakes shouldn't be overlooked in favor of their sweeter and more famous counterpart. *SB*

Hash Restaurant

8728 SE 17th Ave
239.3966
www.hashrestaurant.com
Tues–Sat 8a–3p

I can't really guess why, but corned beef and I are kindred spirits. And the steak hash, mushroom hash, and Danish fruit pancakes served at Hash Restaurant are my soul mates, too. I wish I could make up my mind! Good thing breakfast is served all day at this palace of good food, sourced from local, sustainable farmers and artisans. The simple, cool feel of this modern restaurant provides an elegant backdrop for the food experience here; even a basic fried egg is made with artisan skillfulness, timed to perfection, and served with never-soggy sliced fruit and an ample potato pancake. Each month there's a new artist featured here, so it isn't just the food that will inspire. *SB*

Portland Yoga Studios

Is it safe to say that yoga is an epidemic in PDX? I can't go out without seeing an interesting, muted-shade yoga outfit, a biker packing a yoga mat in his cargo, or a lone parkgoer performing a sun salutation. There are oodles of places to find yoga gear, yoga mind, and yoga body, in whatever measure you so desire. Here are the top two locally owned spots of all the yoga fanatics I've talked to. After experiencing their range of classes, I understand why they are so highly recommended. Class times vary, so check the web site or call ahead to get the scoop on the latest offerings.

The Yoga Space

2853 SE Stark St
929.6161
www.theyogaspace.com

With well-educated instructors; a balanced array of prenatal, hatha, and vinyasa classes; and a mission to cultivate balance and sustainability, The

Yoga Space is a lovely place for a yoga break. You can drop in on any class (with a few exceptions)—just pay a few bucks more than you would with a 10-class pass. *SB*

Yoga Bhoga

1028 SE Water Ave, #265

241.5058

www.yogabhoga.com

Inside this calm and relaxing studio decorated with modern Zen art, I took the most clearly instructed beginners' yoga class I've ever attended—the breathing and basic pose techniques were easy to learn and remember. Opt for acro yoga (you don't need to bring a partner) or yoga for back care, unless you're a yoga veteran and want to attempt one of the serious advanced classes. *SB*

Coffee Time

Sipping a morning cup in many ways

Speaking as a true coffee lover, but only a part-time coffee drinker, I can say that when I choose to have a cup, I like a good one. Coffee-crazed Portland is populated with roasters as obsessed as I am with quality java. All locally owned and very much entrenched in the community, these stops are frequented by a cross section of local people who are in the know about the importance of fair-trade and organic brews. Find coffee, tea, and snacks at these admirable cafes, and avoid the chains at all costs. Even a regular cup at a locally owned coffee shop has a much more positive effect on the community in the long run than an organic cup at a chain. Each of these spots has its own vibe, an indicator of what the spirit of the surrounding neighborhood is really like. Whether you're on a strict diet of only two cups a day or you like to come and go with morning bevvies like I do, there's something for everyone at Portland's coffee meccas. And while famed Stumptown is an incredible coffee haven, there are many outstanding roasters sprinkled across this city.

Ladybug Organic Coffee Company

8438 N Lombard St
715.1006
www.ladybugcoffee.com
Daily 7a–7p

Easygoing and friendly are the two adjectives that describe this cozy NoPo coffee shop. Order at least one of the all-organic pastries baked fresh each morning, but keep in mind: It might be hard to split. If you want a whole mouthful of goodness, you're in luck—rarely are even the fanciest of drinks here oversweetened. *SB*

Random Order Coffeehouse & Bakery

1800 NE Alberta St
331.1420
www.randomordercoffee.com
Daily 6:30a–8p

Admittedly, I am a sucker for extra frills. Not Baroque-style gilded everything, but the odd special touch here and there always catches my eye. Random Order Coffeehouse & Bakery is full of sweet details: feathered ripples on the top of each coffee beverage, candles on every table when the sun hides behind the horizon, easy and reliable WiFi, and both indoor and outdoor seating areas. Consider this my living room away from home. *SB*

Sip

3029 SE 21st Ave
308.3581
www.myspace.com/getyoursipon
Mon, Wed–Sun 10a–8p

It might be more appropriate to put this cute Airstream trailer restaurant in the "Food Carts" chapter, as it has the ability to roam at whim. Sip is an all-organic coffee and smoothie trailer, complete with strange-sounding steamed tonics and more neon-green wheatgrass shots than I could ever take. But the coffee here is so stupendous, it keeps me coming back again and again, even on days I plan to go write at a brick-and-mortar cafe later. *SB*

Barista

539 NW 13th Ave
274.1211
www.baristapdx.com
Daily, 7a–6p

Seriously serious coffee drinkers must know Portland well, since there is so much good java up here, but do they know about Barista? This new-to-me coffee haven brews up consistently good espresso. The dozen or so drinks I've had here have each been served at a perfect temperature and with the sophisticated flavors that can come only from a high degree of technical skill. Each sip is a testament to the talent here. After all, there are many steps from bean to steam—but that's the fun for the folks at Barista. *SB*

James John Cafe

8527 N Lombard St
285.4930
Tues–Fri 7a–3p, Sat–Sun 8a–3p

This tiny little treasure on North Lombard is my new inspiration for community-involved business. I came here on a dreary morning and found loads of smiling faces eating full breakfasts and sipping Stumptown coffee. Everyone seemed to know each other's name, and every inch of the place had a deeply ingrained local feel since it's always full of St. John residents. It's hard not to wake up pleasantly when you start out here. *SB*

Muddy's Coffeehouse

3560 N Mississippi Ave
445.6690
www.muddyscoffeehouse.com
Mon–Wed 7a–6p, Thurs–Sat 7a–9p, Sun 7a–3p

Named for the owner's beloved albeit usually dirty pooch, Muddy's Coffeehouse is a home away from home. Organic coffee and homespun meals keep you company while sitting pretty on a Windsor chair or a sofa in the house. Bring a book and a laptop, and wax creative while getting some seriously delicious soup to go with your alone time. There's always art on the walls and something sweet to munch on after your breakfast or lunch. *SB*

⚲ Albina Press

🏬 *4637 N Albina Ave*
🖥 *282.5214*
🌀 *Daily 6:30a–8p*

One of the posher coffee joints in Stumptown, Albina Press gets my attention not only with its one-minute near-perfect espressos, but also with its surprisingly diverse magazine and newspaper collection (some in French!). To while away the time in line I play eeny, meeny, miny, moe with the delectable pastry collection and look at all of the interesting people swaying to and fro in this busy spot. Even if you are here for a much-needed dose of caffeine, pause and enjoy the fact that the folks behind Albina's bar are coffee artists. *SB*

🐦 Stumptown

🖥 *3356 SE Belmont St (one of several locations)*
🖐 *232.8889*
🍺 *www.stumptowncoffee.com*
Mon–Fri 6a–9p, Sat–Sun 7a–9p

Easily the most famous local coffee brand around Portland, Stumptown's name echoes the old-time nickname for this city based on the number of tree stumps left over from heavy logging. Now Stumptown has a more caffeinated connotation, and nearly all the myriad beans it serves are fairly traded or organically grown. Grab one of the recycled-paper coffee-making guides strewn about to learn how to properly prepare the beans you buy here at home. In addition to trying one of Stumptown's many superior house beverages, I recommend picking up some whole beans as a hostess gift or a present for your sweetie who couldn't come. *SB*

🏬 Cupping at Stumptown Annex

⚲ *3352 SE Belmont St*
💲 *467.4123*
🚌 *Daily 11a–3p*

After getting tipsy at one too many wine tastings, you'll appreciate a change of venue and bevvie at these coffee cuppings, hosted by Portland's pillar of caffeine, Stumptown. Follow closely as one of the trained connoisseurs takes you through each step of the cupping, from examining the beans, to sniffing the prepared coffee, to actually tasting the stuff. You can guarantee you'll come away with a newfound respect and understanding for what it takes to

Palio Dessert and Espresso House

blend beans from all over the globe and why it is important to go the extra mile to find organic and fair-trade beans. Latin American and African varieties are abundant, and each has a personality all its own. Taste away! *SB*

Palio Dessert and Espresso House

1966 SE Ladd Ave

232.9412

www.palio-in-ladds.com

Mon–Thurs 8a–11p, Fri–Sat 8a–12a, Sun 8a–11p

When the rain comes down in this lush city, what's better than a prime slice of cake, a hot beverage, and a good book? Palio Dessert and Espresso House (a Top Pick, see page 15) is the perfect neighborhood nook for regulars and travelers alike to get comfy in an armchair, tune in to a classical music mix, and dive into their favorite pages. Palio shops for its cakes at all the best places, so relax and sweeten up in this cozy library of a cafe smack-dab in the center of lovely Ladd's Addition (see page 33). *SB*

Bipartisan Cafe

 7901 SE Stark St
 253.1051
www.bipartisancafe.com
 Mon–Fri 6:30a–9p, Sat–Sun 7a–9p

Just when you thought you had seen every possible form of coffee resale business, here comes Bipartisan Cafe, the politically forward coffee head-quarters. Come to watch presidential debates—commenting and debating is encouraged—or for a quiet read through the *Wall Street Journal* or the *Oregonian*. Public places like this that support interaction and dialogue over the big issues are a win-win in my eyes. That, and Bipartisan serves a mean cup of joe. *SB*

Coffee Plant

 724 SW Washington St, 295.1227
 5915 SW Corbett Ave, 293.3280
www.coffeeplant.net
 Daily 7a–6p

Serving Stumptown in a more upbeat atmosphere, Coffee Plant is anything but commercial. Each worker bee adds his or her talents to the mix, and the result is a great scene complete with latte art, chill music, and an escapist mentality. Vegan, gluten-free pastries actually taste like something—and that something is not cardboard. I go for the coffee cake every time and opt for the free jazz concerts sprinkled throughout the diverse calendar of live music. *SB*

Pied Cow Coffeehouse

 3244 SE Belmont St
230.4866
 Mon–Thurs 4p–12a, Fri 4p–1a, Sat 12p–1a, Sun 12p–12a
 On the bottom floor of a brightly colored old Victorian house, the Pied Cow Coffeehouse is a funky (emphasis very definitely on the funky) and hip spot

that serves vegan desserts, strong coffee, and hookahs for those who want to relive the summer they backpacked through Morocco. Check out the specialty coffee drinks or order a cocktail from the bar to accompany your sweet confection. Don't leave without trying the lavender steamer or the hot toddy. The Pied Cow has a very distinct handmade feel; the Nick Cave altar and the garden gates made out of old bedsteads add to the appeal of the space. During the warmer months make sure to request outdoor seats, but any time of year expect a bit of a wait at this Portland institution. *mm*

Pets and Poodles

Furry and fuzzy things

Studies show that pets make their people happier and even live longer. In my own research, I know this to be true. Dutsi, my poodle, goes to the senior center regularly to cheer folks up, and when he returns I get the same joy from his uplifting presence. Whether you are into dogs, cats, or feathered friends, pets with personality are an asset to our lives, so here's the Portland guide to pampering your chosen pet.

 Green Dog Pet Supply

  4605 NE Fremont St
528.1800
www.greendogpetsupply.com
Tues–Fri 10a–7p, Sat 10a–6p, Sun 10a–5p

The folks behind Green Dog Pet Supply have some serious love. They love their animals, they love yours, and they love to educate each customer about what they mean by "green" pet supplies. They look for chew toys made from recycled materials and foods and treats made with organic ingredients and without chemical preservatives. They stock durable, long-lasting toys and source as many things as possible from local vendors and producers. Step inside the Fremont Commons Building, and enter a place designed to pamper your pet peacefully. *sb*

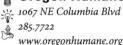

Oregon Humane Society

1067 NE Columbia Blvd

285.7722

www.oregonhumane.org

If you're a dog lover and you're living in Portland, or even if you're an ambitious tourist, you can volunteer your time at the Oregon Humane Society. This place is also a wonderful location to adopt a pet of your own, and there are great pet training classes at affordable rates whether or not you get your pooch or kitty here. If you find a lost pet, this is the first place you should call. *SB*

Dog Parks in Portland

I admit I am a bit crazy about dogs—I just love them, what can I say? But it turns out that Portlanders rival my level of pet insanity. There are so many dog clubs, dog parks, and pet and pooch palaces here, my head spins! Here are some of my favorite Portland dog parks where you can make new furry friends and human friends who bring their dogs for a run. Be aware that locals aren't fazed by the rain and somehow clean off their dogs after muddy romps, so the parks are usually attended even in a downpour. There are some 48 dog parks within the city limits, and you can find out the details of all the parks online at *www.portlandpooch.com/dogparks.htm* or *www.portlandonline.com/parks/finder/* (check the "Dog Off-Leash Area" box under the "Amenity/Activity" section). *SB*

Brentwood Park, SE 60th Ave and Duke St

Fernhill Park, NE 37th Ave and Ainsworth St

Gabriel Park, SW 45th Ave and Vermont St

Lents Park, SE 92nd Ave and Holgate Blvd

Normandale Park, NE 57th Ave and Halsey St

Sellwood Riverfront Park, SE Spokane St and Oaks Pkwy

Sewallcrest Park, SE 31st Ave and Market St

Woodstock Park, SE 47th Ave and Steele St

Furever Pets

1902 NE Broadway
282.4225
www.fureverpets.com
Mon–Fri 10a–8p, Sat 10a–7p, Sun 10a–6p

Nothing says "I love you" like a huge, Doberman-sized hunk of chicken jerky. At least that is the thinking at Furever Pets, a top-end, all-natural, locally owned pet-lover kingdom. I got some organic puppy treats that my little guy loves here, and the staff threw in a whole bag of gifts and giveaways, including his new favorite chew toy that's also good for his teeth. Whether or not your pet philosophy includes kitty Halloween costumes or just the standard doggie bone, you and your best friend's needs will be met here. *sb*

Ladd's Addition

SE Hawthorne, Division, 12th, and 20th Sts

From a bird's-eye view, Ladd's Addition is Portland's most recognizable collection of city blocks, full of scented blooms and plenty of doggy pals weaving along the symmetrical streets. Configured in a lattice reminiscent of a classical garden, hedges perfectly trimmed, this complete neighborhood has five community rose gardens, Palio Dessert and Espresso House (see page 29), a video store, and Funky Church (see page 159), and more at its core. *sb*

Bookish

Reading retreats in every flavor

Technologies can come and go, but as far as I'm concerned, the beauty of a bound book will never fade. Providing not only a comical, moving, challenging, or inspiring experience, a volume of words impacts every aspect of life, from early learning to individual solace. I think about where I've been with a good book: in a new city, at a favorite cafe, sitting in my grandfather's rocking chair, on top of Whistler Mountain giving my legs a break from the steep slopes. Search for a book and watch as it in turn takes you on a journey. Make your own book, share the experience of reading, and take your books on your world travels. Portland is home to a great many readers and writers, and plenty of ideal reading nooks to discover.

Powell's City of Books

St. Johns Booksellers

8622 N Lombard St
283.0032
www.stjohnsbooks.com
Tues 10a–6p, Wed–Sat 10a–8p, Sun 10a–6p

Eeny, meeny, miny, moe, which subject do I need to know? Women's studies, Spanish language, anthropology? St. Johns Booksellers is a serious book place that is organized perfectly, like it was done by a Capricorn, and inclusive of many academic subjects. *SB*

Powell's City of Books

1005 W Burnside St
228.4651
www.powells.com
Daily 9a–11p

Even though online book sales have changed the way the industry sustains itself, Powell's City of Books (a Top Pick, see page 15) the largest independent bookstore in the country, remains a keystone. Filling an entire city block, and with several other topic-specific locations strewn across town, the city of books is an absolute must-see. It's on every Portland tourist's itinerary, but it's also frequented by local city dwellers.

Prepare to lose yourself on four floors of books color-coded by theme. Enter by the pile-o-books statue and zoom through the graphic novels to the staircase that dumps you at the intersection of travel and world philosophy—as good a crossroads as any. Up another flight is an array of religious works from every culture, and farther still is the beloved art floor, complete with a small gallery and stocked with imaginative titles. You may not be able to leave the store without a stack of new and used books, so get a hot chai at the ground-floor cafe and start reading before you even leave the place. *SB*

Broadway Books

1714 NE Broadway
284.1726
www.broadwaybooks.net
Mon–Sat 10a–7p, Sun 12–5p

Portland's Hollywood neighborhood is fed the written word by this comfortable and comedic bookstore. Literary laughs are sprinkled around the shelves, bringing smiles to roving customers like myself. I find the travel guide section interspersed with Jetlag's hoax guidebook series *Molvania: A Land Untouched by Modern Dentistry*, and I get caught laughing aloud to myself more than once. Get into the well-read scene in Portland with a trip here—whether you find a laugh or meet a local children's book author, it's easy to get caught up in words at Broadway Books. *SB*

 ## Great Northwest Bookstore

3314 SW 1st Ave
223.8098
www.greatnorthwestbooks.com
Mon–Fri 9a–6p

For all the big-name stores found around downtown, there are equally as many great indie businesses, some of which ascribe to a more polished look. Great Northwest Bookstore could be a jewelry store compared to a place like Reading Frenzy, but it has a clarity known only to places like Elliott Bay Books in Seattle, King's Books in Tacoma, or Powell's City of Books. Finding historical titles steeped in Western history and Americana may not sound like what I had in mind for the afternoon, but when I got caught up in a conversation with a friendly staff-person on the subject, I found I had a penchant for ghost-town tales. Find your own inspiration here. *SB*

Portland State Bookstore

1715 SW 5th Ave
226.2631
www.portlandstatebookstore.com
Mon–Thurs 8a–7p, Fri 8a–6p, Sat 9a–5p

Some people fondly reminisce about their college days. Although admittedly I had lots of fun, I don't need to relive that time—at least so I thought. When I chanced upon the Portland State University campus and entered the bookstore, I couldn't deny the flood of good memories of cheering for our team. On the other side of the sweatshirts and memorabilia, there is actually quite an amazing collection of books, and they are not all academic fact manuals, either. If you are into electronics, for instance, this is a great place to get help finding a precise guide to building the robot of your dreams, and if you are looking for local poetry, you'll be equally as lucky finding Portland writers featured throughout the store. You'll receive better than average service when the librarians are working here; otherwise, make your own way through the aisles of students and reading lists. *SB*

In Other Words
8 NE Killingsworth St
232.6003
www.inotherwords.org
Mon–Fri 10a–9p, Sat 12–6p

In Other Words has a beautiful collection of books about, for, and written by women. The store carries CDs by local and national touring female performers, zines by chicks, and art by women. It also frequently hosts live music and poetry readings. If you are new to the world of feminism, this is a perfect place to start to exploring since there is such a rainbow of perspectives welcomed here. Scout out the staff picks for great recommendations. There are positive body image books, inventive young adult books, and woman-centric fiction and nonfiction titles. This is the kind of place I come to get a cup of coffee and hang out for hours of inspiration. *RM*

Reading Frenzy
921 SW Oak St
274.1449
www.readingfrenzy.com
Mon–Sat 11a–7p, Sun 12–6p

This funky and unique "small press emporium" may be within eyeshot of Powell's City of Books, but it is another world away. All the titles here come from independent publishing houses, and some are even fresh off a desktop inkjet printer in the neighborhood. A bookstore crawl in PDX is not complete without a stop at Reading Frenzy, which is run almost entirely by volunteers with a penchant for raw literary creativity. *SB*

Pageturners Book Group, Northwest Library
2300 NW Thurman St
988.5560
www.multcolib.org/books/groups
Call ahead for times

Exchange perspectives on works of fiction new and old, from near and far. Portland is a city cluttered with bookish types like myself. By my estimation, there are more reading groups here than in any other city, but this library-run one features some pretty special titles and isn't swayed solely by certain talk shows (*ahem*). We all love the works of Hemingway, Joyce, Wilde, and Fitzgerald, but this group goes beyond simply discussing titles written by "dead white guys." Find your place in the circle of reading. *SB*

New Renaissance Bookshop

 1338 NW 23rd Ave
224.4929
www.newrenbooks.com
Mon–Thurs, Sat 10a–9p; Fri 10a–9:30p; Sun 10a–6p

The second I walked into New Renaissance Bookshop, I felt calmer. There is quiet instrumental music playing, the singing of chimes, and essential oils in the air. The shop has every book imaginable on the topics of spirituality and the occult, plus alternative calendars, gorgeous handmade jewelry, and music for meditation. I'm tempted to return soon for one of the workshops on the healing arts, reading past lives, and other paths toward self-betterment. *RM*

Independent Publishing Resource Center

917 SW Oak St, #218 (above Reading Frenzy, see page 37)
827.0249
www.iprc.org
Mon 12–10p, Tues–Thurs 4–10p, Fri–Sat 12–6p, youth only Sun 12–6p

Aside from my zine discoveries in Portland's northerly neighbor, Seattle, I have never seen such a collection of local and international zines. If you aren't already on the "zine train," let me fill you in. Zines are self-produced, small publications—the end product of the underground world of magazines where low-budget production, art, and noncensorship converge. The zines at Independent Publishing Resource Center are organized by topic, with a special rare zine section. Sitting and reading is encouraged, as evidenced by the plethora of armchairs cluttering the small space. I can't help but stay for the rest of the evening. Warning: It's easy to get completely immersed! *SB*

Get Active

Hikes, runs, rides, bikes, boats—anything and everything to get you moving

Whether you are simply getting from point A to B or you are seeking some good sweaty fun, getting active always has a refreshing result. I started on a swim team at a young age, and I have been known to go through ski bum phases every now and again. I've also been challenged by Pilates and yoga. When I gave my time to inspire a love for the outdoors among inner-city youth, I came to love ropes courses, bouldering, and outdoor climbing, starting as a novice and working my way up to several pitch climbs. Whatever thrill level you are seeking, from kayaking the Willamette River to jogging in Laurelhurst Park, Portland is the kind of place that offers all manner of sporty and nonsporty ways to jam.

Lower Columbia Canoe Club

17005 NW Meadowgrass Dr, Beaverton
Call Mark for membership info: 246.2918
www.l-ccc.org

This club is a staple of the outdoor recreation community in Portland. Membership dues are collected annually, and bimonthly potlucks are hosted at members' houses. Check out the club's trip schedule online and get in touch with a member ahead of time to join in. Regular day trips include the Wilson, Kalama, and Washougal Rivers, as well as a monthly Coordinator's Choice trip that could include some sticky class 4 and 5 rapids. If you live in Portland or will stay for a while and join the club, you'll receive a friendly monthly newsletter with all the updates and outing information. *SB*

Powell Butte Trails

SE Powell St at 162nd Ave (entrance)
Public transit: TriMet #9, Powell Blvd
823.7529
www.portlandonline.com/parks, (search "Powell Butte")

Whether you're interested in hiking, biking, or horseback riding, this wooded tangle of trails even has wheelchair accessible routes. From Ellis Street, wind around the Mount Hood Trail to the Orchard Loop Trail, where there is a beautiful picnic area most others don't know about. I bike here with my hubby if he can rouse me, and we enter via the Springwater Corridor from the 40-Mile Loop (see Marquam Nature Park, page 23), one of the most scenic inner-city bike paths I know of. Stables are located near the service road beyond the parking lot. Show up on two wheels whenever the mood suits. *SB*

Portland Rock Gym

21 NE 12th Ave

232.8310

www.portlandrockgym.com

Mon, Wed, Fri 11a–11p; Tues, Thurs 7a–11p; Sat 9a–7p; Sun 9a–6p

Portland Rock Gym makes muscle building more fun than ever. The walls are higher here than at other gyms, and there's even a tiles element that mimics the technical nature of popular climbing spots nearby. Bouldering here will certainly prep you for Rocky Butte or a trip to the Bridge of the Gods boulders (off Highway 14, ask for detailed directions at Portland Rock). Try your hand at the slab or the corkscrew slab, two matrixed climbs with taped routes for all levels. My only peeve is the lead climbing area is almost exclusively overhang, whereas my preferences are chimneys and arêtes. But luckily, there is an extensive bouldering section for me to practice those overhang moves, even if sometimes it feels hopeless. *SB*

Mt. Scott Community Center and Pool

5530 SE 72nd Ave

823.3183

www.portlandonline.com/parks/finder/ (search "Mt Scott Community Center")

Mon–Thurs 5:30a–9:30p, Fri 5:30a–9p, Sat 8a–7p, Sun 12–6p

There is nothing more relaxing than a whirlpool on a rainy day. Inside the spacious Mt. Scott Community Center is an incredible indoor pool area, complete with lap pool, two-story waterslide, and whirlpool. Get your suit on, take a sit in the locker room sauna, and splash down the slide before you do your laps. I like trying to walk against the whirlpool jets and taking breaks floating around in circles with the current. Each neighborhood in Portland has its own park or recreation facility, many of which have excellent pool facilities. For more information, look at the Portland Parks and Recreation web site: *www.portlandonline.com/parks/. SB*

Burnside Bridge Skate Park

Wonders of Walking Club (Hosted by REI)

1405 NW Johnson St
221.1938
www.wondersofwalking.com
Sat 9a
Cost: Free guest visit, $75 annual fee

This community walking club includes fun treks all over the city at every pace, from leisurely to judged racewalking. The most natural healthy exercise is more fun in the company of locals. The founder of the club is an expert on walking, a master racewalker, and she has started quite a group—fun, relaxed, and fit! *SB*

Burnside Bridge Skatepark

Under the Burnside Bridge, east side
www.skateoregon.com/Burnside/Burnside.html

No doubt this skatepark comes with its fair share of mysteries and histories; after all, it was the very first community-built skatepark—but keep an open mind even if you're jaded about this skating landmark. The cover of the Burnside Bridge still shades some great local skaters, and during the summer there are sometimes full-on parties in motion, with out-of-towners here to watch the hard-core skaters successfully ride the whole park. SB

 Laurelhurst Park

SE 39th Ave and Stark St

www.portlandonline.com/parks/finder/ (search "Laurelhurst Park")

Laurelhurst Park is an idyllic respite from the hustle and bustle of the city commotion. Hours can pleasantly disappear adventuring here, wandering up knobby knolls, around winding pathways, past a dog park where Dutsi frolics, and by the duck pond. I walk by the big houses near the Oak Street entrance and check out the homey architecture before taking my dog off leash and gearing up for some horseshoes with friends. The tennis courts here are especially nice, and picnics can vary from those on blankets on lawns to those enjoyed with the shade and backrest given by an enormous old tree. The neighborhood to the north of the park doesn't follow the usual grid pattern, but rather wiggles and intersects—each street lined with *Leave It to Beaver*-esque houses. SB

Leif Erikson Trail

In Forest Park, NW 29th Ave at Upshur St

www.portlandonline.com/parks/finder (search "Forest Park")

Popular with Portland's active crowd, the Leif Erikson Trail is fun even when runners are speeding by. My slow jog may not be the fastest on the trail, but the scenery is so beautiful I am glad I convinced myself to take to the hills and run around the northwest industrial district and into the trees. Even though the city is within eyeshot, the wilderness surrounds you in the most sumptuous and satisfying way. Maybe I would jog more often if this trail were in my backyard. I have heard that the trail is great for a bike ride as well, and the length (a total of 11 miles) makes sense for a two-wheeled adventure. SB

Wilshire Park

416 NE 33rd Ave

823.2223

 www.portlandonline.com/parks/finder (search "Wilshire Park")

Daily 5a–12a

Wilshire is a party of a park. Play for hours on end in the horseshoe pit, after splattering your face in barbecue sauce. Jog off the gallon of lemonade and the stack of brownies you just downed on one of the paved trails, or gather up your buddies for a volleyball match. All the games you could ever want at a picnic with friends and family are here—it's an inner-city playground for all ages. *SB*

Nearby Skiing and Snowshoeing
Exit 16 off I-84 E to Hwy 26 toward Government Camp/Timberline Rd
Portland has it good, with a longer snow season than any other western ski area in the continental United States. You can even ski through June some years on the tippy top of Mount Hood. Reasonable prices for lift tickets make up for the corduroy one must deal with during early months of the season and the occasional icy day when only hard-core snowshoers will be satisfied with the brisk gusts. I like to take to the trees in the late winter months, and it's thrilling to ski a potentially active volcano. Two resorts are where most of the snow falls: Mount Hood Meadows (337.2222, *www.skihood.com*) and Timberline (622.0717, *www.timberlinelodge.com*). Rent equipment at the Mountain Shop (288.6768, *www.mountainshop.net*)—whether you are snowboarding, downhill skiing, cross-country skiing, or snowshoeing, this place has it all.

At Highway 26 when you pass through the tiny hamlet of Sandy, take the chance to buy a National Forest parking pass at one of the ski shops (more rental opportunities)—Mount Hood is a protected U.S. forest and therefore requires this pass to avoid pesky ticketing. *SB*

Vega Dance+Lab
1322 SE Water Ave
235.1400
www.vegadancelab.com
Embracing both the bold and the timid, Vega Dance+Lab's dance class offerings suit many types. Whether you're nervous about your hip-hop skills, you have a hankering for an upbeat workout, or you want to take your moves to the next level and try out a new technique, Vega has a class for you. Just throw away your fears and move your body to the music with the help of some incredibly talented instructors. Drop-in admission is affordable—just check the schedule online and show up. Whatever you do here is bound to turn up the heat! *SB*

Center for Movement Arts

1734 SE 12th Ave
236.1007
www.cmadance.com

The Center for Movement Arts offers a relaxed and comfortable atmosphere where you can hone your dance skills. Try ballroom, jazz dance, or the Limon method of modern dance, or take a Pilates mat class to stretch out and strengthen up. The professionals here inspire confidence, and I can't think of a more delightful way to build muscle. *SB*

Portland Parks and Recreation Main Office

Portlandia Building, 1150 SW 5th Ave
823.2223
www.portlandonline.com/parks

Portland's incredible knack for organization spreads beyond its zine libraries and beautifully situated neighborhoods—the spectrum of well-attended festivals are highlighted on clear web sites and pamphlets created by this city-run department. Come directly to the office to get all your up-to-date calendars, forest yoga class schedules, fishing license information, bike trail maps, pools, and who knows what else! It's one of the first places I go when I get into town—I need to get caught up in some citywide gardening project or join a pickup game of soccer before I get too sucked into the restaurants and galleries. *SB*

Do Lunch

Outstanding midday eating of every sort

Lunch is my favorite meal of the day. When I lived in Switzerland, it was an event, with several courses and mandatory attendance by the entire family. In fact, people in some parts of the world consider lunch the largest meal of the day, followed by a siesta. Portland offers many types of lunches—savory vegetarian treats at Paradox Cafe, Lebanese at Mezza Middle Eastern Cuisine, or Ethiopian at Small World Cafe. Even though I've avoided the restaurant chapters typical of other guidebooks and instead incorporated food into various sections, I had to dedicate a spot for lunch. From business power lunches to lazy afternoon munching, it's a state of mind. Let's do lunch!

Blueplate

308 SW Washington St
295.2583
www.eatatblueplate.com
Mon–Fri 11a–5p

I didn't grow up drinking soda, and I rarely drink it now. I scrap that when I go to Blueplate and travel back in time at this classic soda fountain counter where they suds up nonalcoholic drinks like the Chai Bomb soda with cinnamon and the Purple Haze with hibiscus. Delish! And the food—like dense, indulgent mac and cheese, and Blueplate's famous and traditional sliders—perfectly pairs with these sweet (and not-so-sweet) sodas. A must-eat. SB

$ ¿Por Qué No? Taqueria

3524 N Mississippi Ave
467.4149
www.porquenotacos.com
Mon–Thurs 11:30a–9p, Fri 11:30a–10p, Sat 11a–10p, Sun 11a–9p

Yum, yum, and yum. This is one of my very favorite eateries in P-town and a Top Pick (see page 15). I come to cheer on the national football teams of South America, and even though I know little about the players, I am accepted into the crowd after a few toasts with Negra Modelo. The tacos here are made from delicious and sustainable ingredients like line-caught fish, local grass-fed meats, and organic veggies from the farmers market. SB

$ Horn of Africa

3939 NW Martin Luther King Jr Blvd
331.9844
www.hornofafrica.net
Mon–Fri 10:30a–3p, 5–10p; Sat–Sun 5–8p

Discover the flavors of several distinct regions of Africa at this authentic and spicy-smelling eatery. I love the aromas; they always make me hungry. Buy the fresh *injera* at the market next to the restaurant and try your hand at an Ethiopian stew, or just get a feast to go and eat lunch outside. SB

Chef Naoko Bento Cafe

1237 SW Jefferson St
227.4136
www.chefnaoko.com
Tues–Sat 11:30a–3p

Delicious, organic *bentos* (lunch boxes) are handed out to the lucky folks who flock here. The Umi Fish Ginger Bento is a repeat order of mine, as is the Farmers Veggie Bento smothered in rich red tomato sauce. I usually take mine to go, but the small cafe has huge windows for people watching if you dine in. Chef Naoko genuinely wants to pass around her healthful cuisine to the community—her School Lunchbox Program benefits local school children. SB

Ya Hala Lebanese Cuisine

8005 SE Stark St
256.4484
www.yahalarestaurant.com
Mon–Sat 11a–9p

More than I'd like to admit, eating heavy restaurant food catches up with me and I just want a big simple something. A nice plate of tasty veggies and spicy salads, for instance, rather than more fabulously rich fare. Ya Hala Lebanese Cuisine and the various fresh meze plates served there quench my desire for a fresher, lighter lunch. In the spring, the Foul Mudamas is especially good with local fava beans and mashed garlic. And I never leave without ordering the house-made stuffed grape leaves, made Lebanese style with tomatoes, rice, and spices. SB

Food for Thought

1825 SW Broadway (in the Smith Student Union Bldg)
725.2970
Mon–Thurs 7:30a–5:30p, Fri 8:30a–2p

Run by Portland State University students, Food for Thought has a pure vision to bring healthy, sustainable food at affordable prices to the community. Vegetarian lasagna, sweet carrot soup, and a rich chocolate cupcake for dessert cost me about $10. The produce is gathered fresh from the campus farmers market (see page 57), and the menu changes seasonally. Just note that Food for Thought is open only when school is in session. SB

Little Red Bike Cafe

Small World Cafe

 416 SW 4th Ave
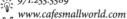 971.255.5589
www.cafesmallworld.com
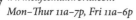 Mon–Thur 11a–7p, Fri 11a–6p

Visualize a big plate of garlicky greens, handsome purple cabbage slaw, saucy lentils, and a pile of fluffy rice. Now imagine it delivered to you! If you are hanging downtown in an office, hotel room, or other place with four walls, call Small World Cafe and they'll usher it over. The healthy menu is excellent for people with food allergies, those with a picky palate, or anyone in need of a soulful belly hug. *SB*

 Little Red Bike Cafe

 4823 N Lombard St
289.0120
www.littleredbikecafe.com
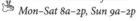 Mon–Sat 8a–2p, Sun 9a–2p

Nothing's more delicious than the honest, homespun recipes at this loveable little cafe. I could tell on my first visit that this place was entrenched in the local scene, and for good reason—strawberry pie, flavorful grilled tofu and pineapple skewer bento lunches, sinful devil's shortbread, and dressed-up baked polenta are all a part of it. At Sunday brunch, the wasabi deviled eggs with smoked salmon were a tasty treat not to be forgotten, but even better was the blood orange chocolate French toast that came to the table! Portland is so lucky to have such a pleasant place to remember fondly—these flavors are oh-so-memorable. *SB*

$ **Paradox Cafe**

3439 SE Belmont St
232.7508
www.paradoxorganiccafe.com
Mon–Sat 8a–9p, Sun 8a–3p

With a mostly vegetarian menu (the cafe also serves hamburgers to accommodate meat-eating folks) and a low-key atmosphere, Paradox Cafe is the place to go when you want to take the pace down a notch. Chill out over some sweet corn tamales or an unconquerable breakfast burrito, read your Free Will Astrology horoscope in *Willamette Week*, and try not to get too freaked out by the overabundance of mirrors by your booth. For a contemporary architectural foray, take a peek right across the street at the impressive Belmont Street Lofts, erected by well-known developer Randy Rapaport. Belmont Avenue is the more laid-back version of Hawthorne Boulevard, a busy and eclectic local main street, so hang here to avoid crowds. *SB*

$ **Laughing Planet Cafe**

3322 SE Belmont St (one of several locations)
235.6472
www.laughingplanetcafe.com
Daily 11a–10p

Rather than looking for some big plastic fast-food abomination, seek out a Laughing Planet Cafe to satisfy your hunger. This local chain, which serves organic gourmet burritos, can be found in nearly every neighborhood of Portland. Each order is full of fresh, organic ingredients, like the Che Guevara with plantains, sweet potatoes, and spicy barbecue sauce—not a combo you're likely to find at other burrito joints. All the to-go ware is compostable, and the workers can help you pick a hometown brew to try alongside your burrito choice. There's a good reason this place is a staple, and it isn't just the plastic dinosaur decorations or the piles of board games to play while you eat. *SB*

Blossoming Lotus

1713 NE 15th Ave

228.0048, ext 3

www.blpdx.com

Daily 9a–9p, deli only 4–5p

Blossoming Lotus may have relocated to the Eastside, but they didn't loose any of their creative vegan recipes in the move! Homemade sprouted buckwheat granola is much more delicious than it sounds, and with organic dried fruit and hemp milk, it's healthy and filling, too. Chances are you'll clean your plate if you order one of the tofu scrambles, with flavor combos like marinara sauce, herbs, and cashew sour cream or black bean chili with avocado goddess sauce. Even though the menus options are all vegan and gluten-free, you'd be surprised how tasty and satisfying they can be. Bring your family and friends to brunch after a nice walk around the indie shops of eastern Portland. *SB*

Dalo's Kitchen

4134 N Vancouver Ave, #207

808.9604

www.daloskitchen.com

Mon–Fri 9a–8p, Sat 10a–9p

Bubbly *injera*, sweet honey wine, and smoldering spices—Dalo's Kitchen is an exotic romance in the middle of the day. Ask the friendly folks behind the counter for instruction if you aren't versed in Ethiopian cuisine. My method is to slather at least a couple of different vegetable dishes on top of a whole *injera* to let the juices seep into the bread, then I try one of the fun appetizers, and when I come back to it, the *injera* is perfectly soaked. Order the vegetarian platter and you'll get a good combo for under $10. It's easy to get full here on the cheap and have a fun dining experience along the way. The dishes are healthy and the no-frills atmosphere begs for good conversation and laughs. *SB*

Red and Black Cafe

400 SE 12th Ave

231.3899

www.myspace.com/redandblackcafe

Daily 8a–11p

Worker owned and worker run since its inception in 2000, Red and Black Cafe is a royal renegade even in this edgy town. It evolves based on the needs and wants of its loyal customers and neighbors—hosting indie films, welcoming impromptu concerts and recording sessions, speaking up for workers' rights, and serving delicious vegan plates fit for kings and queens. I am in love with every salad I've ordered here, and my poodle Dutsi is happy to sit at the sidewalk tables and people watch with me after a meal. *SB*

Hush Hush Cafe

433 SW 4th Ave
274.1888
www.hushhushcafe.com
Mon–Fri 10a–6p, Sat 12–6p

Delightful Middle Eastern lunches are an everyday occurrence for the lucky people who work within walking distance of Hush Hush Cafe. Lord knows that's where I'd be every day if I were a downtown worker bee in the City of Roses. Order the classics—falafel, hummus, baba ghanoush, and stuffed grape leaves—or on cold days get the kafta kabob made with spiced sirloin beef or a fried veggie sandwich if meat's not your thing. Oven-baked spinach pies and cheese *sfiha* rolls are unique treats—my idea of lunchtime comfort food with foreign flair. *SB*

Mezza Middle Eastern Cuisine

5520 SE Woodstock St
777.6399
www.mezzapdx.com
Mon–Fri 11a–3p & 5–9p, Sat 11a–9p

It's no secret that Middle Eastern is one of my favorite styles of dining—it's often an uphill battle for me to select a mere few such eateries to decorate these pages. Before a week is out, I have usually eaten at most Middle Eastern spots in a given city when I am in the throes of exploring. Mezza Middle Eastern Cuisine was one of my first Lebanese meals in Stumptown, and it's still one of my favorites. For lunch, the family-style cooking is a vacation of a meal, with some recipes passed down generations in the Semaan family, the owners of Mezza. Order Mezza's mixes of skewered lamb, chicken, and kafta kabobs, or choose a few of the salads and appetizers like minty fattoush

salad, bulgar tabbouleh, and refreshing tzatziki. Don't skip the drinks—
if you've never tried *tout* (mulberry juice), *ward* (sweet rose water drink),
or *jellab* (date and rose water drink), this is a great place to do it. I'm now
addicted to these traditional bevvies. *SB*

Jade Teahouse and Patisserie

7912 SE 13th Ave
477.8985
www.jadeteahouse.com
Tues–Sat 11a–9p, Sun 12–6p

I consider this teahouse the one that makes me want to put on a pink angora
sweater. It's a special kind of place that brings out the schmaltz in me and
makes everyone who enters feel just a wink prettier. Perhaps it's the sweet
pastries all lined up behind the glass cases, or maybe it's the cute Parisian flair
that charms me. I order green cake or a matcha-iced brownie from owner-
bakers April and Lucy, and even though the *banh mi* are pricier here than at
most traditional Vietnamese sandwich shops, the atmosphere alone makes
them worth $6. On top of that, the baguettes are made fresh each morning in
the kitchen, together with the drunken chicken marinade and the zesty Vietnamese meatballs. It's easy to love this place, and it's tempting to return again
and again for teatime—with pastries, of course. *SB*

$$ Besaw's

2301 NW Savier St
228.2619
www.besaws.com
Mon 7a–3p, Tues–Fri 7a–10p, Sat 8a–10p, Sun 8a–3p

In 1903 on their way to the Lewis and Clark Centennial Exposition (which
would be held two years later), two Canadian loggers got sidetracked. They
stayed in Portland and opened a saloon and gambling hall, hammering their
last nail in the walnut bar. Today, the bar still stands surrounded by cheery
neighbors who come to enjoy Besaw's fabulously comfortable feasts. The
restaurant serves breakfast, lunch, and dinner, but an early lunch of the signature seafood soup and a colossal hamburger is what attracts me like a magnet. Large salads with plentiful chunks of chicken, feta, or house-smoked
salmon are healthy and filling. Standards like the Reuben and ham-and-Swiss

sandwiches are made with perfect balance. The restaurant is open all day but doesn't serve breakfast after 11am. Regardless of when you come, Besaw's is bound to cheer you through and through. *SB*

$ Pepino's Mexican Restaurant

3832 SE Hawthorne Blvd
236.5000
www.pepinos.org
Daily 11a–10p

Pepino's is a spot down on Hawthorne where you can grab a stack of fresh and satisfying tacos for 99 cents each on your way to a relaxed lunch nook. Something always mystified me about the off-limits teachers' lounge back in middle school, so there's a corner of my living room set up like what I imagined it to be. As often as possible I bring a pile of roommates and Pepino's takeout to my very own teachers' lounge. If we get to talking and it becomes movie time, we forget popcorn and swap it out for a carne asada mouthful of joy or Pepino's unbeatable pork carnitas. Stock up on the yum factor without breaking the bank or contending with lard and MSG. *—EMILY CRABTREE FROM LACTACIOUS (SEE "PORTLAND PLAYLIST," PAGE 155)*

$$ Typhoon!

2310 NW Everett St (one of several locations)
243.7557
www.typhoonrestaurants.com
Mon–Fri 11:30a–2:30p & 4:30–9p; Sat–Sun 12–3p & 4:30–10p

Typhoon! fills the hearts and bellies of Portland's plethora of Thai food enthusiasts and has been awarded a top spot on many "Best of Portland" lists. In the gourmet line of Pearl District restaurants, this bustling lunch stop has open-air seating for nice days and an extensive tea list to accompany the myriad classic Thai dishes. Unique curry blends are as plentiful as they are tasty. I like to try the daily specials, which are always outstanding and make the decision process far simpler. Enjoy the exquisite art hung around the restaurant as you dine on a steamy bowl of fish soup or a noodly stew. *SB*

American Dream Pizza

4620 NE Glisan St

230.0699

Mon–Thurs 8a–10p, Fri 8a–11p, Sat–Sun 9a–10p

This pizza parlor is decorated by creative customers who try their hand at pizza box art while digging into their custom slices. I like to do up my own design while sipping an Island Red beer from Roots Organic Brewery across the river (see page 67). Choose from four different sauces and heaps of toppings—I recommend the pesto-based Goddess Athena slice, featuring chicken and artichoke hearts. American Dream Pizza also delivers free of charge, so if you want lunch without moving an inch, just pick up the phone. RM

Thanh Thao

4005 SE Hawthorne Blvd

238.6232

Mon, Wed, Fri 11a–2:30p & 5–10p; Sat–Sun 11a–10p

Thanh Thao, right across the street from two smoke shops, serves up a slice of counterculture with tasty salad rolls and scrumptious barbecue. The cuisine is classic yummy Thai comfort food, and the service is always quick, so it is safe to come here when your stomach has already started speaking to you. I have been coming for years to have the coconut soup, but you can choose from 25 main dishes all priced under $6. RM

Thai Noon

2635 NE Alberta St

282.2021

www.thainoon.com

Mon–Fri 11:30a–10p, Sat 12–10:30p, Sun 12–10p

With a front-row seat to Alberta Street on a warm and happy summer day, Thai Noon is my fail-safe choice for a solid Thai lunch, a Portlander's favorite nationality of food. I usually order up one of the curries, departing from the traditional for a healthier meal by substituting organic brown rice for the usual white. Thai Noon might serve as a gateway to a Last Thursday night (see the "Get Inspired" chapter, page 86)—a bit of sanity before diving into the masses and clowns. Thai Noon serves up clean, fresh, and simple cuisine, and that is a priceless commodity in my book. RM

$ Hoda's Middle Eastern Cuisine

3401 SE Belmont St

236.8325

www.hodas.com

Mon–Fri 11a–9:30p, Sat 12–9:30p

After picking up *The Arabian Nights* from one of Portland's great independent bookstores, head to Hoda's Middle Eastern Cuisine to act out your new role as an Arabian prince or princess. Embrace the perfectly blended hummus or the most delectable stuffed grape leaves. *Hoda* is an Arabic word meaning enlightenment, and this comes through the restaurant's unparalleled Middle Eastern fare. Come for kebabs, grilled meats, hearty salads, or shawarma, but don't miss the plethora of homemade side dishes, including *labne*, a hard-to-find pressed cheese that makes fast friends with a crunchy falafel-stuffed pita. My drink of choice here is *jallab*, a mellow date-and-rose water combo that will make your belly sing songs of praise. SB

$ Detour Cafe

3035 SE Division St

234.7499

www.detourcafe.com

Daily 8a–4p

At Detour Cafe you can munch on an affordable meal (most around $7) that will also be amazingly fresh, made with organic ingredients and served with bread baked in-house. Bringing delicious and sustainable meals to those who can't break the bank, Detour has terrific breakfast scrambles, as well as spectacular sandwiches and salads for lunch at any time of day. The Bortfeld chicken sandwich hits the spot, and the Spicy Beef Salad is a treat for the deserving. Have breakfast for lunch by ordering some cardamom toast with your meal—its subtle flavor is the perfect accompaniment to any menu item. Detour's maple scones are great for the road, too. DL

Farm to Table

Edible bounties direct to your tavola

Connecting with the course of the food we eat is a wonderful step toward sustainable living. How can we look at produce or a list of ingredients the same way after having the experience of talking with the local berry farmer or cracking open brown and speckled eggs from free-range chickens? We can choose not to eat processed foods even if we aren't super-rich, and it is possible to think a little bit before chomping down to make sure what we are eating is as natural as we are. Escape to the countryside without leaving Portland's bustling blocks. At each of these neighborhood markets, a generous spread of local comestibles is offered up to hungry shoppers. Dream up your own inspired menus from the heavy-laden tables of mostly organic produce.

Hollywood Farmers Market

NE Hancock at 45th Ave
www.hollywoodfarmersmarket.org
May–Thanksgiving, Sat 8a–1p

Complete with all the fancy foodstuffs of other markets, this friendly neighborhood market has a jolly vibe that makes food shopping a joy. It's easy to find the fruits and veggies you are in search of, as well as some unexpected friends like native Oregon ground cherries, green-striped zebra tomatoes, and neon-lime tomatillos. Get ready to share your new discoveries with whomever you encounter—it's hard not to gloat when you are packing perfectly ripe tayberries! If you are interested in getting market updates, the free weekly e-newsletter *The Local Dirt* is a great resource; just sign up for it at the market's online homepage. *SB*

Hillsdale Farmers Market

SW Capitol Hwy and SW Sunset Blvd
www.hillsdalefarmersmarket.com
Year-round, Sun 10a–2p

Carrying more than just the staples, Hillsdale Farmers Market offers a cornucopia of raw ingredients and fine artisan foods like Nonna's Noodles, and also hosts an array of canners, honeybee keepers, and local cheese makers. If you want to loll about and bask in delicious local foods on a Sunday, this is *the* place to do it. I found loads of locals doing just this, and I was happy to join in, especially when the live music started wafting around with the fresh, summery smells. *SB*

St. Johns Farmers Market

St. Johns Plaza at N Lombard and N Philadelphia sts
www.sjfarmersmarket.com
July-Sept, Sun 9a–1p

Portland's newest addition to the farmers market scene is not just another place to buy fresh veggies, rather it is a unique expression of the St. Johns neighborhood that represents a rainbow of tasty and local delights. Find pit fruit from Baird Family Orchard (*www.bairdfamilyorchards.com*) or Duycks Peachy Pig Farm (*www.peachypigfarm.com*), hormone-free meat from Lilikoi, and baked goods from Dovetail Bakery (see page 190). The community that has risen up around this weekly event is inspiring, plus it has yielded many a good recipe, which have been posted in an organized way on the market's web site. I'm off to make my own vinegars with my new-found ingredients: Should I infuse this batch with blueberries and basil or with fresh mint instead? *SB*

Portland Farmers Markets

www.portlandfarmersmarket.org

This umbrella organization runs five of the farmers markets around town, but each remains unique and well stocked. This is because Oregon is full of food! If you're visiting from out of state or from outside the country, blueberries and pinot noir are two products you might associate with the state, but prepare yourself to be blown away by the veritable cornucopia from Portland's nearby counties. Some of the best produce and artisan food products

I've tasted yet have come from the western part of this state—incredible cheeses, fantastic fruits yielding jams and pastries, an array of organic produce from local seed, grass-fed beef, and much, much more. One gander at the regular vendor list and you'll see what I'm talking about; this state and this city are serious about food, and Portland Farmers Markets are the evidence. *SB*

Portland State University Market
Mar 21–Dec 19, Sat 8:30a–2p (Nov–Dec 9a–2p)
SW Harrison and Montgomery Sts

Eastbank Market
May 7–Sept 24, Thurs 3:30–7:30p
SE Salmon St and 20th Ave

Ecotrust Market
June 4–Sept 24, Thurs 3:30–7:30p
NW 10th Ave at Johnson St

Downtown Market
Apr 29–Oct 28, Wed 10a–2p
Shemanski Park, SW Park and SW Salmon Sts

King Market
May 3–Oct 25, Sun 10a–2p
NE 7th and NE Alberta Sts

Wealth Underground Farm
www.wealthunderground.blogspot.com
Visit an urban farm in Portland's St. Johns neighborhood. The lush harvest is always going, and the growers are as colorful and interesting as the things they grow from their own seed. Find the farm's goods at St. Johns Farmers Market (see page 56) or e-mail *wealth.underground@gmail.com* to schedule a visit.

Food Carts

Amazing lunches to go

Keep your eyes peeled while exploring Portland at high noon on an empty stomach—one of these food carts will make your day. It is amazing to me just how many different kinds of food you can buy from a cart in this Pacific Northwest city. I'm used to finding carts offering hot dogs, salted pretzels, and gyros, but to find delicious pad thai, epic garden salads, and topped potatoes—I might decide never to eat at a restaurant again! Remember the days when you could get a beautiful and filling lunch for under $5 that didn't involve a drive-thru? Those days are still alive and well in Portland, one of the easiest cities on the West Coast to eat for cheap. I like taking my food cart finds to the nearest park for some inner-city nature-and people-watching to go with the meal. Look for carts mostly downtown but also near SW 5th, SW 9th, and SW 12th avenues between Stark and Oak streets. At the time I'm writing this, the very first funded, curated, and organized collection of food carts, called Mississippi Marketplace, is being assembled at N Mississippi and Skidmore streets.

FlavourSpot

 2310 N Lombard St
289.9866
www.flavourspot.com
Mon–Fri 6:30a–2p, Sat–Sun 8a–3p

Look for the big bold blue letters spelling out f-l-a-v-o-u-r and you are one step closer to a new obsession: waffles with stuff inside them. Simple sugared and buttered versions are a mere $2, but I highly recommend going all out for the organic maple spread and pork or veggie sausage for $4. My hubby stops here first when he comes to town for his standard order of two ham-and-cheese waffles—shaved Black Forest ham, that is, and smoked Gouda cheese. Early birds with a sweet tooth order a Lemon Pie: two waffles sand-wiching luscious lemon curd and fresh whipped cream. *SB*

$ The Real Taste of India

$\mathbb{V}$ *340 SW 5th Ave*

750.7435

www.newtasteofindia.net

Mon–Fri 10:30a–6p, Sat 11a–4p

Unless you are trying to steer clear of the cops, who always seem to be hovering here enjoying hot curry, you have no excuse but to park it and try some for yourself. Much conversation has been had over which food cart best represents Indian cuisine, and in my view this is the answer. Saag paneer, moist tandoori chicken, and irresistible veggie kebabs are inexpensive, delicious, and healthy. No donuts for these Rose City coppers! *SB*

La Jarochita

Parking lot at Oak and Stark sts and SW 5th Ave

Mon–Fri 7a–6p

$ Oh, baby! Lupe and Magdalena make the tastiest tacos in Portland, 'nough said. I've never tried something from La Jarochita I didn't love, even when I switched from the tacos to the tamales. With nothing costing more than $3 on the menu, you can't go wrong! Don't leave without a large horchata—just $1 for a little taste of heaven. *SB*

Garden State

SE 13th Ave and Lexington St

$ *705.5273*

www.gardenstatecart.com

Daily 11:30a–3:30p

Break out the gangster film marathon—I'm going to Sicily! I mean, quaint, antique-y Sellwood . . . an admittedly odd place for an authentic Sicilian food cart, but why question something this good? As with many of the best Portland eateries, Garden State sources much of its fare from nearby bountiful valleys (one of the reasons I just had to do the Applegate Valley Divergence; see "Detour" chapter, page 198). Devil's Chicken is a must if you can handle the heat from crusted black peppercorns, served with panzanella for $12. Soups vary each day, but the *arancine* are always there—little balls of delight stuffed with your choice of cheese or meat ragu and dusted in homemade breadcrumbs. *SB*

Taste of Poland

SW 4th Ave and College St (also parking lot at Oak and Stark sts and SW 5th Ave)

After an impromptu pub crawl where I ended up near PSU, alone and very tipsy, Taste of Poland may very well have saved me. The rich potato and cheese filling inside the steaming hot pirogis and the hearty kielbasa I ordered put me back together, and I was able to find a bus out of dodge. Funny, it wasn't even 3pm yet, but then again, you never know where or when a party will go down in PDX. *SB*

The Whole Bowl

SW 9th Ave and Alder St
4409 SE Hawthorne Blvd
110 NW Glisan St
757.2695
www.thewholebowl.com

Yes, rice and beans are crucial. But did you know how tasty they can be with a little tali sauce? *Comment t'allez vous*, you say? Tali sauce is a secret blend of lemon zest, garlic, and other tasty things that ups the ante and brings back loyal Whole Bowl eaters day in and day out (including those who keep an eye out for the cruising Whole Bowl van). Order a bambino bowl or a whole bowl—each is covered with fresh salsa, lettuce, and cheese (which can be left off). *SB*

Junior Ambassador's

4734 N Albina St
880.0851
www.juniorambassadors.com
Fri–Sun 2–8p

Serving delicious homemade ice cream everyone loves Junior Ambassador's. Everyone. And why not, when you can order Dorian Grey ice cream (infused with the Tao of Tea's Earl Grey), a Caprese Sundae of strawberry chipotle and avocado ice cream, or a Dinner Ice Cream of coconut curry, corn on the cob, salmon and cream cheese, or asparagus? Don't be scared off by these flavors if they seem odd—just order the Gingersnap Cookies and Basil ice cream and everything will be right again with the world. *SB*

Potato Champion

SE 12th Ave and Hawthorne Blvd
www.myspace.com/potatochampion

These frites make me want to scream and shout and jump around like a giddy teenager who just had her first good kiss. Each batch must be soaked in water first, to release some of the starch, and I guess these guys have been double-fried, thus the "frites" style. The sauces up the ante—Dijon mustard, veganaise, horseradish ketchup, and inventive rosemary truffle sauce are impossible to choose between. There's even poutine fit for your vegan compadres. *SB*

Todbott's Triangles

2827 NE Alberta St, and roving
342.2081
www.guzzas.org/botts.html
Tues–Sat 11a–7p

If you are new to Portland you might not know what a Todbott's Triangle is, but you'll do well to find out quickly if you are looking for a delicious and unique lunch break. Bringing the handy finger foods of Japan to the City of Roses, Todbott's Triangles actually sells *onigiri* and *omusubi*, two triangular, yet traditional foods. These rice packages are folded with origami-like precision in seaweed wrappers, some stuffed with smoked salmon and sesame seeds, others with colorful pickles. Todbott's is known as Portland's only "bicycart," on the food cart scene, but I expect there will be more of them as time goes on. Just ask the satisfied customers in between bites for tips on which triangles to start with. *SB*

Homegrown Smoker Natural Barbecue

NE 27th and Alberta St
http://homegrownsmoker.wordpress.com/
Wed–Sat 12–8p, Sun 12–6p

Look for the white tent with the rainbow lanterns set up on Alberta Street, and you are on your way to a new kind of barbecue adventure, a meatless one. You may hesitate at the thought, but the flavors in the tempeh and tofu-based creations at Homegrown Smoker Natural Barbecue are nothing to scoff at. Choose smoked soy curls, field roast chorizo, chronic tempeh ribs, or mini tofu steaks, each one comes happily drowned in barbecue sauce, made all the merrier with baked beans, chipotle slaw or "mac no cheese" on the side. Follow the "homegrownsmoker" twitter feed for current specials and new foodcart locations or events. *SB*

Food Carts Portland

www.foodcartsportland.com

Just when I started to bite my nails over the lack of free museum days in PDX, I happened upon this eye-opening site, which straightened me right out. Each city has its own thing—free museum days may be the MO in San Francisco, but food carts are the MO in Portland. And my complaining comes to a full stop. This online guide, although slightly outdated, is a helpful tool for finding the nearest cart to you, featuring any cuisine you desire. I picked my favorites to highlight in this chapter, but there are oodles more. *SB*

Hang Out

All the best chill-out spots, from cozy reading nooks to a relaxed microbrew with your buddies

Sometimes the best way to get the sense of a place is to slow down and stop attempting to see everything and do everything. Try a pub game, attend a laid-back concert, or pop into Portland's wildest coffeehouse to give new meaning to loitering. Portland is fast and slow, caught up with the relaxed West Coast vibe and unique, flourishing businesses at the same time. Bring friends or venture out alone for a moment off the treadmill of life's usual routine.

 Beulahland

 118 NE 28th Ave
235.2794
www.beulahlandpdx.com
Mon–Fri 8:30a–2:30a, Sat–Sun 9a–2:30a

Fun is guaranteed at this coffee shop-cum-alehouse. Steeped in the local scene, Beulahland is a regular fixture in most neighbors' schedules for live music, fun contests, and all types of shows, including community-viewing sessions of the Olympics, soccer matches, and other big sporting events. Friendly service and weekly specials make it even more alluring. The happy hour menu (available Mon–Fri from 4–7p) is über-affordable and offers up chicken-fried chicken fingers, "happy" nachos, and a veggie and meat version of the classic slider. House-infused vodkas add a touch of class and sophistication, while Pabst Blue Ribbon and pinball keep things carefree and whimsical. It's an intersection of fun and fancy at this Portland indoor playground. *SB*

⑤ Tom McCall Waterfront Park

1020 SW Naito Pkwy

www.portlandonline.com/parks/finder/ (search "Gov Tom McCall Waterfront Park")

This isn't Portland's oldest park, but it just might be Portland's favorite. The beauty of Forest and Washington Parks is hard to contend with, but this swath of green along the Willamette River is a winner for all kinds of occasions. I come here for lunch when I get to-go food or to relax after a tizzy of Portland Saturday Market shopping (see page 111). A slew of fun annual festivals take place here, so be sure to check the Portland Parks and Recreation Department web site to see what's on. *SB*

Moxie RX

4011 N Mississippi Ave
285.0701
www.moxierx.blogspot.com
Check web site for hours

The ultimate Portland juice bar and smoothie shack, Moxie RX is a dreary day's sunshine and a sunny day's cool glass of water. But there's much more than simple H_2O here. Chewables include luscious buckwheat and rice flour waffles and gourmet sammies. If you stop in, be sure to try the mini vanilla custard berry cake for me. *SB*

$ Vita Cafe

3024 NE Alberta St
335.8233
www.vita-cafe.com
Sun–Thurs 9a–10p, Fri–Sat 9a–11p

Portland makes it easy to accommodate all types of diners—and Vita Cafe is serious evidence of this. Vita Cafe does breakfast, lunch, and dinner in a way that satisfies both your taste buds and your conscience. If you aren't vegan, there is a good possibility you won't care what the food in front of you is

Moxie RX

made of—you'll be too distracted by the delicious flavor of it. Try one of the soothing soups on a chilly night, or choose the chicken-fried steak served with biscuits and gravy for a morning feast. Plus there's always free use of the backyard bocce ball court. *SB*

Rimsky-Korsakoffeehouse

707 SE 12th Ave
232.2640
www.rimskys.blogspot.com
Sun–Thurs 7p–12a, Fri–Sat 7p–1a

The delightful sound of active espresso machines chimes in over relaxing string music in one of Portland's most unique and well-loved attractions: Rimsky-Korsakoffeehouse. For 25 years this place has hosted nightly live classical music, served delicious nosh and bevvies, and provided completely creative art installations all over the property. Walk in the rust-colored front door as if visiting a friend, and head upstairs when nature calls to visit the underwater scene in the decked-out loo. Cool your fears of rumored haunted houses and possessed tables by feasting on one of the insanely good ice cream sundaes. *SB*

Pioneer Courthouse Square
SW Broadway and SW Adler St
www.pioneercourthousesquare.com

I love gathering places, and this one is downtown Portland's most prolific—it hosts some great annual events, daily food carts, and local skateboarders and lunch eaters. The curious history of the place dates back to the 1950s when the area was slated to become a parking lot. By 1974 the public space was opened and became touted as Portland's living room. The square's famous designers have gone on to create a number of special public places all across the country with the success they saw from this project. My main associations with the place are drinking beer in public during the microbrew fest (see the "Calendar" chapter, page 220) and people-watching during lunch hour. I can't get enough of the lime-soaked watermelon from the Pioneer Courthouse Square food carts. *SB*

$ A Roadside Attraction
1000 SE 12th Ave
233.0743
Daily 3p–1a

Portlanders pride themselves on their inventiveness—in what other city can you find a vegan strip club, an all-night donut shop where you can be married, and a city block full of books? A Roadside Attraction is one of Portland's pleasurable oddities. Finding it is akin to a successful search for the Holy Grail of public living rooms. Huddle with friends new and old under the low ceilings and relish a strong drink and a delicious organic snack. *SB*

$ Valentine's
232 SW Ankeny St
248.1600
www.valentineslifeblood.blogspot.com
Daily 7p–12a

Valentine's is not the typical Saturday-night bar scene downtown. The space has a mature, calm ambiance mixed with the creative playfulness of a clubhouse. The minimalist loft seating over the bar looks like a contemporary tree fort straight out of the pages of *Dwell* magazine. Valentine's is the perfect spot for a twosome, so my friend and I retreat to the bar and order paninis and wine, and find our own little spot to soak up the atmosphere. Even though this place has slower service (and sometimes only one person working as barista and chef), the artsy vibe and tasty food make it worthwhile. Films screen on the white walls, art hangs, DJs spin, and a primo happy hour menu completes the very happening picture. *NK*

Crowsenberg's Half and Half

923 SW Oak St

222.4495

Mon–Fri 7:30a–7:30p, Sat–Sun 8a–6p

What's not to love about this neighborhood treasure? Tasty Dovetail baked treats, shade-grown Courier Coffee (*www.couriercoffeeroasters.com*), and the apple-and-bacon grilled cheese marvel are perks for the taste buds; the select periodicals, cool crowd, and edgy art are eye candy. Hang out and stay a while—there's nary a place that's easier to get sucked into. Maybe it has something to do with the homemade cookies. *SB*

Mississippi Pizza Pub and Atlantis Lounge

3552 N Mississippi Ave

288.3231

www.mississippipizza.com

Mon–Fri 11:30a–11:30p, Sat–Sun 11:30a–1a

For many, the Mississippi Pizza Pub is a home away from home. It is the kind of pizzeria that feels like a real night out without all the energy of a big excursion—there's often live music, always games and conversations to carry on, and great pizza and beer to feed everyone. Hide out in the sultry back room, where the cocktails are strong and the music is louder—you'll hear everything from bluegrass to hip-hop. Ask the friendly pizza cooks for any special modifications, and you'll find that they are very amenable. *SB*

℣ Vendetta

4306 N Williams Ave

288.1085

Sun-Thurs 3p-1a, Fri-Sat 3p-2a

North Portland is ever changing, but one of the neighborhood's mainstays is Vendetta (a Top Pick, see page 15), where I come even when I should be doing research elsewhere. Everyone in the neighborhood seems to agree with me, whichever side of the gentrification debate they are on, and the cool, casual atmosphere of this half-indoor/half-outdoor chill spot is conducive to any mood or viewpoint. Vendetta's cozy feel and friendly atmosphere make it fun for drinkers and nondrinkers alike. It is just a great place to hang out in a bountiful garden without getting dirt under your nails. Look for the cursive R glowing neon red in the window—Vendetta is still too cool to have an actual sign. *SB*

Bridgeport Ale House

3632 SE Hawthorne Blvd

233.6540

www.bridgeportbrew.com

Sun-Mon 11:30a-5p, Tues-Thurs 11:30a-10p, Fri-Sat 11:30a-11p

Even if you aren't a beer fanatic like many Portlanders are, you can surely enjoy the pub atmospheres of this sudsy city. In the midst of the excitement of the Hawthorne hood, the Bridgeport Ale House has both food and beer in massive quantities. The happy hour from 3 to 6pm will tempt anyone who passes by to stop in for a Blue Heron brew. *SB*

$ Roots Organic Brewing Company

1520 SE 7th Ave

235.7668

www.rootsorganicbrewing.com

Mon-Thurs 3-11:30p, Fri 3p-12:30a, Sat 12p-1a, Sun 12-9p

Reggae and organic brews are the name of the game at Roots Organic Brewing Company. Whether it's sunny or rannoying, I'm cheered by the good vibes and tasty hops in here. Grab a Chocolate-Habañero Stout when you're in the mood for a romantic love potion with a sensational burst of heat. I can't get enough of the Burghead Heather Ale with its sweet and tawny golden flavor. The folks I toasted at the bar were enjoying their Island Red—another top-selling house brew—and they recommended the stellar bar food. Each day, there's a new special. Tiki Tuesdays offer $2.50 pints all day, and NFL Sundays pair the game with cheap pitchers and cheeseburgers. Oregon's first entirely organic brewery is tasty and fun, and it's certainly a place where sports lovers can out themselves in this artsy city. *DL*

$$ Dan & Louis Oyster Bar

208 SW Ankeny St

227.5906

www.danandlouis.com

Sun–Thurs 11a–9p, Fri–Sat 11a–2a

The Wachsmuth family have been oyster farmers and sailors for generations, and for over 100 years Portlanders have been packing into Dan & Louis Oyster Bar for the freshest oysters and most divine smoked salmon stew. The historic dining room and bar are a warm and cozy shelter from any kind of storm. The jalapeño-infused vodka makes the unique Bloody Marys a perfect pairing for smoke-flavored stew or fried clams. Come before 6:30pm and a dozen local oysters on the half-shell are just under $10. *SB*

Bike About

Two wheels and at least one gear

Getting around by a self-powered two-wheeled contraption is indeed a part of American history. There are myriad biker types: the spandex-covered weekend peddlers, the laid-back beach bikers, the art bikers with bizarre custom-welded frames, the hipsters with their single gears, the practical commuter bikers, and the odd bike historians, rolling around on antique cycles. Portland's biking community is diverse and proud, and the many eccentric bike events that happen around town are proof.

Revolver Bikes

6509-11 N Interstate Ave

 285.1084

 www.revolverbikes.com

 Mon–Fri 11a–7p, Sat 10a–6p

It's easy to understand where the Revolver Bikes guys are at with a mission statement as simple and clear as "bicycle living." Revolver is another Portland bike treasure chest, minus some of the pretension and edginess of other shops. I am clueless about many areas of the bike world, and I've never gotten lip for it here—just helpful service and handy gadgets to help me get rolling. *SB*

Bicycle Transportation Alliance

233 NW 5th Ave

226.0676

www.bta4bikes.org

It isn't just the quantity of great bike shops in Portland that makes the city such a great place to wheel yourself around—bike organizations, especially the Bicycle Transportation Alliance (BTA), provide the groundwork, with bike safety education, resources, and maps. If you are biking here, you should know about BTA. Enough said. *SB*

Veloce Bicycles

3202 SE Hawthorne Blvd

234.8400

www.velocebicycles.com

Mon–Fri 11a–7p, Sat 10a–5p

Whether you desire a practical commuter cycle or a high-end road racer, Veloce Bicycles will piece together your ideal frame using "a sophisticated ruler" designed to meet each customer's size and riding habits. Man-powered transportation meets high tech at this locally loved bike shack. *DL*

Bike Gallery

1001 SW 10th Ave (one of several locations)

222.7017

www.bikegallery.com

Mon–Fri 9:30a–6p, Sat 10a–6p, Sun 12–5p

With its four conveniently located Portland stores, Bike Gallery is always just a stone's throw away so you can fix that leaky tire and be back on the road. The business has remained family owned since it began in 1974, and it is dedicated to lending support to organizations for bicycle awareness. In addition to its comprehensive repair and fitting services, Bike Gallery offers a wide range of clinics, from basic repairs and maintenance to proper gear-shifting techniques. DL

 ## North Portland Bike Works

 3951 N Mississippi Ave
287.1098
 www.northportlandbikeworks.org
Mon–Sat 11a–6p

This collectively run nonprofit bike shop is committed to bringing all members of the community together with tons of workshops and volunteer opportunities. Women and transgender nights keep the shop open late certain weeknights (check the calendar on the web site for the exact schedule), and youth workshops are offered during the summer months—a great way for the younger generation to acquire serious bike know-how. Get active in your community and put some elbow grease into it! DL

 ## Coventry Cycle Works

 2025 SE Hawthorne Blvd
 230.7723
www.coventrycycle.com
Tues–Sat 10a–6p, Sun 1–5p

It can often be an uphill ride for enthusiasts of the unconventional recumbent (lounge-chair-looking seated or supine position) bicycle—excuse the pun. Coventry Cycle Works caters to the specific needs of recumbent riders, offering products and services that can be difficult to find elsewhere. Consult these experts for special repairs, accessories, and proper fitting (so you won't have to deal with "recumbent butt"). DL

BikePortland.org

http://bikeportland.org

The cycle culture in Portland reigns supreme. Most residents own bikes and a large portion of them use their two-wheelers regularly for both transit and adventure. Whether you have a secondhand mountain bike, a single-gear handmade bike, or a hemp-welded bamboo bike with cattle horns for handles, you will be in good company in this city of cyclists. This blog is one-stop shopping for your bike needs. It includes events, missing and found bike notices, and handy tune-up tips. DL

River City Bicycles

706 SE Martin Luther King Jr Blvd

233.5973

www.rivercitybicycles.com

Mon–Fri 10a–7p, Sat 10a–5p, Sun 12–5p

Advocates of bike commuting, these guys specialize in pro builds—hand-built wheels and fenders for all those rainy nonsummer days. A team of fitting experts and an indoor test track will ensure a comfortable and satisfying ride for your money. I highly recommend taking the time to admire the impressive display of historic bikes, which includes one made of bamboo! DL

Citybikes Workers' Cooperative

734 SE Ankeny St

239.6951

www.citybikes.coop

Mon–Fri 11a–7p, Sat–Sun 11a–5p

For no-nonsense repairs and maintenance, Citybikes, a worker-owned cooperative since 1990, offers a variety of tune-up options or a complete overhaul of your one-speed, three-speed, or you-name-it. Classes and apprenticeship opportunities are available for the amateur mechanic to take his or her skills to the next level. DL

Zoobomb

13th and SW Burnside

www.zoobomb.net

Every Sunday night is your chance to either participate or watch from the sidelines as an ever-growing group of wild and crazy cyclists take the brakes off and whiz down one of Portland's steepest hills. The gaggle of bikers, decked out in costumes and helmets, gather round, ride the MAX up to the zoo (see the "Washington Park" chapter, page 79), and turn on their bike lights for the ride of their lives. The organizers aim to bring back the fun of childhood to Portland adults. SB

The Sprockettes

The Sprockettes

www.sprockettes.org

What's a bike town without a minibike dance troupe? The Sprockettes are more than just a gimmicky act. This dazzling all-female group rejects the monoculture of the ideal body type, promoting a positive self-image for people of all shapes and sizes. They are also strong advocates of bicycle riding and community interaction, so grab your ride and go check them out (you can find a performance schedule on the group's web site). Like learning to ride a bike, you'll never forget a performance by these strong and talented ladies. *DL*

Ira Ryan Cycles

www.iraryancycles.com

Famed Portland frame-builder Ira Ryan is a crucial character on the two-wheeled scene. I've seen his designs at the handmade bike show in California, and when I was back exploring PDX I kept my eyes peeled for them. Sure enough, there are lots of Ryan frames rolling along Portland streets, and there are many places to test them out for yourself. See the web site for up-to-date details. *SB*

Explore

Places where the wide world is explained, nature abounds, and adventure is waiting

Curiosity can lead down many a path; we've all seen our friend Curious George get in over his head. But fostering a healthy curiosity about the world is important when we are very young and when we are adults. If we fill our imagination with programmed images and digital friends, we miss out on all there is to explore for ourselves in the big wide world. History and science, nature and adventure are waiting around the bend to expand our understanding. Seek out the big questions, ask your own, and most of all, enjoy the ride!

Crystal Springs Rhododendron Garden

SE 28th Ave and Woodstock Blvd

771.8386

Apr 1–Sept 30 6a–10p, Oct 1–Mar 31 6a–6p

Portland's treasured rhododendrons in full bloom are on beautiful display here, and there is even an opportunity to purchase some plants as gifts. The cost is $3 to enter the garden March through Labor Day (otherwise it's free)—well worth it for the flowers as well as the serene paths and fountains. *SB*

Oregon Museum of Science and Industry (OMSI)

1945 SE Water Ave

797.4000

www.omsi.edu

Tues–Sun 9:30a–5:30p

Located right on the Vera Katz Eastbank Esplanade, a waterfront bike path and footpath (see page 112), the Oregon Museum of Science and Industry (OMSI) is a family-friendly, hands-on museum. It has extensive permanent and rotating exhibits, a zero-gravity chamber, an IMAX movie theater, a planetarium that features awesome laser light shows, and a working submarine. OMSI is available as a conference center, a school, or just a day trip. Educational highlights make learning entertaining. Take a date to a laser Pink Floyd show after eating at Produce Row Cafe (*www.producerowcafe.com*) on 204 SE Oak Street and Oak Street in the central eastside industrial district. *RM*

Oaks Park

7805 SE Oaks Park Wy, in Oaks Pioneer Park
233.5777
www.oakspark.com
Park hours vary

Even if you aren't the "I love children" type, you will appreciate the glee lighting the faces of the schoolchildren who frequent this park throughout the year and especially through the summer months. Located right off the Spring Water Corridor and next to Oaks Bottom Wildlife Refuge (see page 78) this classic amusement park has been open for over 100 years. You are sure to encounter kiddos and have juvenile interludes, but outdoor ice-skating is one middle school memory I am happy to relive here. Roller-skate like it's 1988, get out your pent-up aggression in a few rounds of bumper cars, and forget your age. *SB*

Forest Park

NW 29th Ave and Upshur St
www.portlandonline.com/parks/finder/ (search "Forest Park")
Daily 5a–10p

Forest Park is a giant of a park. Covering the peaks above Portland's northwest neighborhoods, it is the third largest city park in the United States, and it includes a magical grove of old-growth trees to boot! Whether or not you believe it, these trees have a special energy about them, maybe from the countless decades they've stood in reserved observation. I like to plan my trip just before sunset so I can visit the trees before the sky bursts into color over the picturesque skyline. This place has helped me work through a number of life's conundrums—the stillness and beauty have an amazing effect. *SB*

$ Pittock Mansion

3229 NW Pittock Dr

823.3623

www.pittockmansion.com

Daily 11–4p, summer hours 10a–4p, closed in January

Admission: $4–7

Standing high above downtown Portland is the stunning Pittock Mansion, a monument of local craftsmanship and a relic from the famed newspaper family's fortune. The Pittock family's contributions to the city were many—the most famous result being the *Oregonian* newspaper. The estate was purchased by the city of Portland in 1964, and following a 15-month renovation led by an adamant and passionate history buff and volunteer, it became a community landmark for posterity. Motifs from French, Turkish, and English design emerge as you make your way through the elaborately decorated home. Each room takes on a life of its own. *DL*

Rocky Butte Natural Area

NE Rocky Butte Rd, at the far end of Fremont Ave

www.portlandonline.com/parks/finder/ (search "Rocky Butte")

Looking for a Portland panorama? Rocky Butte is the simple answer to all view-related questions, at least for those with a wide-angle lens and a desire to have nothing obstructing their view, even peripherally. Check out all the landmarks—the Gorge, Mount Tabor, the Willamette River—after climbing around the bend from the far reaches of Fremont Avenue. Have fun climbing up the cinder cone at the tippy top of this antique volcano. *SB*

Mill Ends Park

SW Naito Pkwy and Taylor St

www.portlandonline.com/parks/finder/ (search "Mill Ends Park")

Four hundred and fifty-two square inches—yes, inches—of pure wonderment, Mill Ends Park holds the Guinness Record for the world's smallest park. Dick Fagan grew tired of seeing a weed-infested hole from a failed light-pole installation outside his office window, so he planted some flowers and gave it the name of his column in the *Oregon Journal*. Named an

Portland Classical Chinese Garden

official park in 1976, Mill Ends has received many contributions, including a tiny swimming pool (for caterpillars, I guess) and a miniature Ferris wheel installed by a normal-size crane. Mill Ends also received its share of attention with concerts by the Clan Macleay Pipe Band and rose plantings by the Junior Rose Festival Court. *DL*

Widmer Brothers Brewery Tour

929 N Russell St
281.2437
www.widmer.com
Fri 3p; Sat 11a, 12:30p

Did you know that Portland has more breweries than any other city in the United States? Well, Widmer Brothers is one of many in the long list of fabulous breweries and microbreweries making suds in Stumptown. Try Widmer's famous Hefeweizen, widely available all over the West Coast, and some rarer flavors. If you need a bite in between pints, follow your nose to the brewery's pub, Gasthaus, across the street. Free tours will get you a small sample of suds, but bring cash for an extra pint or two before you continue down Russell Street for an impromptu pub crawl. *SB*

Lone Fir Cemetery

SE 20th Ave and SE Morrison St
friendsoflonefircemetery.org

One of the many things I missed in regular travel guides was where to find a cool cemetery in town. Lone Fir Cemetery, my offering for Portland, is in a quiet but totally fabulous neighborhood off Morrison Street. Seriously, this is a pocket of solace, especially epic with a light rain, and complete with plenty of winding pathways and shady sitting nooks to read or ponder. *SB*

Portland Classical Chinese Garden

239 NW Everett St
228.8131
www.portlandchinesegarden.org
Nov–Mar 10a–5p, Apr–Oct 10a–6p
Admission: $5–7

North of where the Burnside Bridge meets Chinatown in Portland hides one of America's treasured gardens. The Portland Classical Chinese Garden may seem oddly placed, but the serenity felt within is authentic. No matter the weather, there is always a beautiful sight to behold at this magical place—sit by the Knowing Fish Pavilion or circumnavigate the garden and find your way to a hot cup of tea at the Tao of Tea's second location, within the garden walls. Restore your inner balance with a trip to this special garden. *SB*

Oaks Bottom Wildlife Refuge

SE 7th Ave and SE Sellwood Blvd

www.portlandonline.com/parks (search "Oaks Bottom")

Daily 5a–12p

The Blue Heron-dotted marshlands we now know as Oaks Bottom Wildlife Refuge is the result of the people of Portland speaking out to protect one of their last wetland areas. Back in 1959, the land (spanning nearly 150 acres) was chosen as an industrial development area, but the citizens—understanding the importance of this floodplain environment—would have none of it. The city bought the plot, and it remains development-free; a place to witness the magical presence of migratory birds on their long flights north and south each season. Hiking trails are clearly outlined, and information at the park staging area tells you all about this thriving inner-city wildlife scene. *SB*

Architectural Heritage Center

701 SE Grand Ave

231.7264

www.visitahc.com

Wed–Sat 10a–4:30p

The Architectural Heritage Center presents a window into Portland's earlier generations with a collection of salvaged architectural materials among the most extensive in the United States. Motivated by the tragic destruction of historic buildings throughout the city, Jerry Bosco and Ben Milligan spent 25 years gathering the pieces now on display. The center also includes modern building exhibits and is home to a wealth of green architecture resources. The center hosts a comprehensive library, two classrooms, and two galleries in addition to the workshop space where green courses are held. A trip here will bring out the historical archeologist in you. *DL*

Portland Walking Tours

774.4522

www.portlandwalkingtours.com

Various times, starting points, durations, and prices

Take an award-winning tour from a neighborhood expert. Dig deeper into Portland's history, underground tunnels, and food scene with one of these themed walks through the City of Roses. On the Epicurean Excursion, you'll get to sample tastes from an array of restaurants as you tour the kitchens, dining rooms, markets, and bakeries. *Willamette Week* even called these tours "the best way to fake being native," guaranteeing that locals and travelers alike will learn something new. Have a laugh and discover some juicy insider secrets. *SB*

The Big Pink

Bancorp Tower, 111 SW 5th Ave
275.3654

After a few days hanging out in Stumptown, you're bound to hear the term "The Big Pink" used more than once. It might be mentioned by your friends planning a happy hour trip to the top-floor restaurant for epic views, it may be pointed out as a landmark, or you may hear it recalled as an example of a granite-covered building—this time in rosy granite with copper-tinted mirrored windows. The building really does look big and pink, and it is a fun place to explore. The modern elevators are fast and will take you to the top without charging you a dime—just don't interrupt a big corporate meeting by getting off at the wrong upper floor. *SB*

Washington Park

All the goods inside Portland's favorite park

Washington Park is the setting of such attractions as Hoyt Arboretum, the Japanese Garden, the International Rose Test Garden, the Oregon Zoo, and the World Forestry Center, but on a clear day, it is worth a visit just for its sweeping westerly view. Look out over the city toward Mount Hood for the best panorama in the city. If you come in May, roses will be included in the scene. There are wooded trails to aimlessly amble, and if you have a tennis racket handy, you'll be happy to know there are public tennis courts just across from the entrance to the Japanese Garden.

Portland Japanese Garden

$ *611 SW Kingston Ave*
223.1321
www.japanesegarden.com
Tues–Sun 10a–7p, Mon 12–7p

Entering this garden, located at the foothills of Washington Park, is like a jetlag-free passport to Japan. The deliberate growing practices yield what seems to me a mini world—a collage of entire environments represented in small, exact designs. The foliage in this serene garden is sculpted in the traditional style to enhance the ambiance with what is termed "borrowed scenery." For more than 40 years the plants have been trained to form imaginative landscapes. Volunteer docents are knowledgeable tour guides who will gladly take you behind the scenes of specific plants and the meanings of their placement. *SB*

World Forestry Center

40033 SW Canyon Rd
288.1367
www.worldforestrycenter.org
Daily 10a–5p

Drawing you inside with its dramatic Cascadian-style architecture, the World Forestry Center boasts tons of interactive exhibits about the importance of sustainable forestry practices, especially to the Pacific Northwest. The exhibits are primarily intended for family audiences, but that didn't stop me from testing my skills at the controls of the harvester simulator. You'll also find displays showcasing the planting and use of trees in many cultures around the world. Head upstairs to take a whirlwind tour through all the major cities, sneak a peek at the rotating art show, and catch a great view of the forest below. You can ride the sky lift up for a totally unique treeside perspective. *DL*

Oregon Zoo

4001 SW Canyon Rd
226.5161
www.oregonzoo.com
Daily May–Sept 9a–6p, Oct–Apr 9a–4p

Just hop on the MAX and within 20 minutes you'll emerge through a tunnel under Portland's zoo at Washington Park. With exhibits a step above the standard zoo fare, this center for community gathering also has a world-class amphitheater with a terrific summer afternoon concert series (see the "Calendar" chapter, page 220), spring and summer camps for kids, and late-night holiday fun at Halloween and in the winter. Don't forget to check out Steller Cove, an exhibit featuring sea lions, otters, and a tide pool—all natives of the Oregon coast. *RM*

Portland Children's Museum

4015 SW Canyon Rd
223.6500
www.portlandcm.org
Mon–Sat 9a–5p, Sun 11a–5p
Admission: $6–7

The Portland Children's Museum shares a parking lot with the Oregon Zoo, both of which are easily accessible by Portland's light rail, the MAX, for pennies on the dollar. The Children's Museum is an active experience with water play, puppet shows, and a pirate ship on which to climb. Fun activities for younger kids abound, but children over 10 might not be as enthusiastic. *RM*

Hoyt Arboretum

4000 SW Fairview Blvd
865.8733
www.hoytarboretum.org

The native plants of Oregon are a true spectacle. I've visited Hoyt Arboretum at different times of the year and always found something in full bloom. The lushness of the arboretum has an innately calming effect on me—I frequently visit this spot before starting a Portland exploration to get centered and connect with what's in season. The geography and plant names are labeled well if you are interested in learning about the details, or you can play guessing games with the many types of trees before settling down for a picnic at the gorgeous sheltered barbecue grounds inside the arboretum. *SB*

International Rose Test Garden

400 SW Kingston Ave
823.3636
www.rosegardenstore.org/thegardens.cfm
Daily 7:30a–9p

When the Lewis and Clark Centennial Exposition of 1905 prompted all locals to help plant 50,000 roses around Portland, it became the City of Roses. At the time, the only variety one could come by in that amount was the genteel Madame Caroline Testout rose, now one of the many highlights on the self-guided tour around the largest rose garden in the city. Begin at the shop and pick up a free brochure that will take you by marvelous fountains, Shakespearean blooms, and over 550 varieties of these most enchanting flowers. The paths are paved, and most of them come complete with an expansive panorama of the city. Because of the gentle climate, mild winters, and long growing season, roses love Portland and bloom from May through September. Take a tour with one of the knowledgeable volunteers if you want to know all the secrets and stories behind the blooms. Even when the flowers aren't in full swing, the peaceful atmosphere, lush foliage, and epic views make this a great place to visit any time of year. *SB*

Learn

Courses, classes, and seminars of all sorts, and places to take on new challenges

Flexing your brain muscle is a great way to enhance a vacation, staycation, or prolonged visit to a new place. Classes allow you to easily meet locals with similar interests. My grandmother took courses to stay young and she was never bored; at the ripe old age of 82 she took Chinese classes, having no background in the language at all. She always inspired me to see what I could learn.

The Herb Shoppe

2410 E Burnside St
234.7801
www.theherbshoppe.net
Mon–Fri 11a–7p, Sat 10a–6p, Sun 12–5p

Learning the wonders of our natural world isn't just a matter of going on a hike or taking a birding course. You can also learn the special secrets of plants, and the Herb Shoppe is an open book of this sort of know-how. Check the web site for current class offerings in herbalism, healing plants, and how to forage for wild medicinal flora. *SB*

The Attic Writers' Workshop

4232 SE Hawthorne Blvd

963.8783

www.atticwritersworkshop.com

For small classes with exceptional and accomplished writing teachers, sign up for a workshop at the Attic. You may find yourself being taught by a contributor to the *Oregonian* or *The New Yorker*, who just might be able to launch you on your own successful writing career. *SB*

Portland Rose Society

777.4311

www.portlandrosesociety.org

This collective of rose enthusiasts offers a wealth of information for anyone interested in roses or learning more about them. With loads of fun volunteer opportunities, the Portland Rose Society also hosts regular events and classes on rose feeding, new types of roses, and rose arranging. Check the web site for current class offerings and meetings. Because Portland is the City of Roses, this club seems to be forever planning some major rose-planting events around town. Take a peek at the web site to find the latest ways to get involved. *SB*

Free School Portland

http://portland.freeskool.org

The lessons we have to teach and learn are infinite. With the mission to give everyone access to all sorts of classes, Free School Portland is a virtual resource where you can check current class offerings at many locations and even opt to host your own class. Sign up for the newsletter by e-mailing *portlandfreeskool-subscribe@lists.riseup.net* or go online for the most up-to-date calendar. *SB*

Community Music Center

3350 SE Francis St

823.3177

www.communitymusiccenter.org

Class and recital times vary

For more than 50 years, Portland's Community Music Center has been teaching students to appreciate and master different forms of melody. If you aren't taking a class yourself, come and enjoy a free or low-cost recital from a chamber group, choir, or orchestra. Both private and group lessons are available in guitar, music appreciation, voice, piano, violin, and more, all for reasonable prices. *SB*

💲 Swimming Lessons

www.portlandonline.com (search "pools")

I have to make a point about the wonderful aquatic facilities in Portland, many of which come complete with water features and lap lanes, diving boards and saunas. Enjoy the watery paradise for yourself, and take the chance while visiting this city's great pools to become a better swimmer. Classes are available at the following Portland pools: Southwest, Sellwood, Columbia, Montevilla, Creston, Mt. Scott, and Peninsula Park. For less than $50, you can choose from 10 different group lessons for adults, teenagers, and young ones, offered both during the summer months (more regularly) and in the off-season. Whatever your ability, you can take it to the next level—after all, swimming is a great skill to have, and it's one of my favorite activities in the whole wide world! Easy-to-read PDFs are available online to view all the class offerings at whatever location is most convenient. All facilities are completely set up with handicap access ramps. *SB*

💲💲 Wine Education and Touring

Portland is situated at the gateway of one great winegrowing region. I sometimes wonder if we'll be farming food any more—we'll soon just be drinking wine all day with all the vineyards! Check out web sites like *www.anoseforwine.com, www.willamettewines.com*, and *www.oregonwinecountry.org* to discover inroads to nearby wineries. You'll find regular wine events and classes to get the know-how when it comes to vino. *SB*

📖 Hip Hop Soulsation Academy

10231 NE Clackamas St

253.7447

Learn the basics of hip-hop dance at this fun-loving school. Geared toward both kids and adults, the school offers weekly, monthly, and annual class passes, or you can call ahead and pay a drop-in fee. Get active with other future b-boys and girls in this laid-back and comfortable setting. *SB*

Sewing Lessons

Lots of great sewing classes are strewn across PDX. The following are some standout schools of stitch.

Palmer/Pletsch School of Sewing

700 SE 122nd St, located inside Fabric Depot (see page 94)
492.9455
www.palmerpletschsewing.com
Pick a one-day lesson or a several-week course in all types of sewing techniques. These are seriously crafty ladies! *SB*

A Common Thread

15230 SW Sequoia Pkwy
624.7440
www.acommonthreadsewing.com
This community-oriented group of sewing masters consists of great teachers who are very patient with beginners interested in gaining traditional skills. *SB*

Bolt Fabric Boutique

2136 NE Alberta St
287.2658
www.boltfabricboutique.com
Bolt Fabric Boutique (see page 98) offers really creative classes and also those covering the basics, like how to fashion your own functional canvas shopping bags. The boutique is a great place to find materials for your class projects—plus you get a discount on everything in the store with your class registration. *SB*

Knit Purl

1101 SW Adler St
227.2999
www.knit-purl.com
Mon–Wed 10a–7p, Thurs 10a–9p, Fri–Sat 10a–6p, Sun 12–5p
This fashionable downtown yarn shop always provides tea and water for its parched shoppers. Mingle with a full spectrum of yarns in all textures, and stop by for one of the ongoing drop-in knitting classes. Check the Knit Purl web site for class offerings and times for all manner of topics, from a difficult sweater pattern to baby hats to how to cast on. *SB*

Get Inspired

Museums, installations, awe-inspiring exhibits, and anything that aims to enthuse

For generations, lively performing and visual arts have woven the fabric of Portland. With a multitude of top-notch art galleries and movements, the City of Roses will inspire you. Film, sculpture, poetry, painting, and performance art are all alive and well here—there's no escaping this city's creative vibe!

Guestroom Gallery

 4114 N Vancouver Ave

284.8378

www.guestroomgallery.com

The two shows I've seen at this gallery make it my new favorite. Seriously, where did this stuff come from? The answer is, the Northwest is America's new art hotbed, and I predict that the next art greats will come from the movements astir right now. Photography is a major part of it (coming back from a boring stint when it was stuck in techno monotony), as well as medium-sized works, slowly scaling down to inky lithographs and unframed oils. Take your spot at Guestroom Gallery for an unflinchingly accurate showing of Northwest art talent in a chic space. *SB*

Last Thursday

NE Alberta St

Year-round, last Thursday night of every month

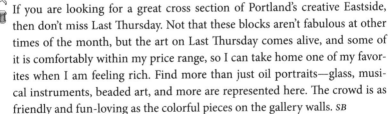 If you are looking for a great cross section of Portland's creative Eastside, then don't miss Last Thursday. Not that these blocks aren't fabulous at other times of the month, but the art on Last Thursday comes alive, and some of it is comfortably within my price range, so I can take home one of my favorites when I am feeling rich. Find more than just oil portraits—glass, musical instruments, beaded art, and more are represented here. The crowd is as friendly and fun-loving as the colorful pieces on the gallery walls. *SB*

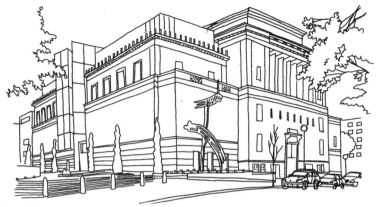
Portland Art Museum

/ Portland Art Museum

1219 SW Park Ave

226.2811

www.portlandartmuseum.org

Tues–Wed 10a–5p, Sat–Sun 10a–5p

The oldest art museum in the Pacific Northwest, Portland Art Museum's permanent collections are rich with Native American artifacts, African sculptures, and centuries' worth of paintings. Artist Kehinde Wiley, born in New York and based in Los Angeles, shows his modern takes on Renaissance portraiture, right down the hall from his original inspirations. Frequent events bring the museum to life on a regular basis. My favorite is Museum After Hours, which always features local wine and live music. SB

Working Artists

2211 NW Front Ave, #302

349.6075

www.workingartistsonline.com

Mon–Fri 11a–4p, and by appointment

As I walk into the quiet warehouse headquarters of Working Artists, the mood is definitely adventurous. The quiet hallway curves toward the entrance of a seemingly secret world. As I pop my head into the office looking for signs of life, the room lights up with colorful artwork strung along the walls. A friendly woman, busily typing away at a computer, greets me and then excitedly whisks me off on a tour of the facilities. A charmingly rustic staircase leads into the extending rooms, which include a low-key classroom, a large room where multiple artists share a studio space, a dance studio, and a gallery equipped for installations. Along with classes in belly dancing, collage making, and life drawing, this nonprofit's strongest attribute is the desire to educate and empower artists with business skills and resources to manage their careers. Working Artists is big on fundraisers and supporting community outreach—check the web site to find the next upcoming event or opening. *NK*

 Breeze Block Gallery and Goods

 1011 NE Alberta #B

282.0333

www.breezeblock.wordpress.com/

Mon 12–7p, Tues 12–4p, Wed–Sat 12–7p, Sun 12–5p

Breeze Block Gallery and Goods features stuff artfully made into other stuff—for example, Krylon spray paint cans morphed into stylin' desk lamps or harnessed onto working headphones with the tops beheaded. The possibilities are endless with this breed of sustainable design. *SB*

Grass Hut

811 E Burnside St

445.9924

www.grasshutcorp.com

Wed–Sun 12–7p

Entering Grass Hut is like discovering a magical little world filled with enchanted creatures and metaphors for mushrooms. This playful gallery will make you smile as your attention jumps from humorous paintings by local artists to silk-screened prints, colorful cards, and even creative underwear. The gallery has a nice selection of indie zines, including its own annual publication, *Pencil Fight*, which is filled with poems, writings, and inky images. Owners Bwana Spoons and Justin "Scrappers" Morrison use the space as their studio, gallery, and retail shop, and every once in a while they host Doodle Clubs that are open to the public to come and draw together. Let out your bottled-up ideas at this anything-but-crisp-white gallery. *NK*

⑤ First Thursday Gallery Walk

Various galleries and shops in NW Portland

Year-round, first Thursday of every month 6–9p

Like a choose-your-own-adventure book, First Thursday offers alternative opportunities for a fulfilling evening. Overall, the spirit of the night may entice you into entering aesthetic discussions at a bar, making new friends, taking home some artwork, or racing toward pen and paper to let out freshly inspired thoughts. From mattress stores to auto repair shops, it seems as though every business in Old Town and the Pearl District transitions into a gallery for one glamorous night each month, often celebrating with wine and cheese. This year-round event meshes old and young—from the very posh to scruffy creative types, the streets swell with bodies curious to view each other as much as the art world. Parking spaces fill up fast, so get there another way to avoid frustration.

Since galleries in the Pearl District close earlier, I like to start out near the Pacific Northwest College of Art (PNCA) on Johnson Street and wander along the bustling row of art vendors on 13th Avenue. Then I tend to zigzag through the streets of Everett and Glisan, popping into such galleries as PDX, Pullium Deffenbaugh, and Elizabeth Leach on 9th Avenue. From there, I cut toward 5th and 6th avenues in Old Town, and pause for a while at the Everett Station Lofts (a complex of 14 live-work galleries), Compound, and Motel. There are many routes to take and plenty of art to satisfy your visual needs— wherever you end up, you are sure to have an artistic adventure. *NK*

SCRAP

2915 NE Martin Luther King Jr Blvd

294.0769

www.scrapaction.org

Mon, Tues, Thurs–Sat 11a–6p; Wed 11a–7p; Sun 11a–5p

Visiting SCRAP is like going to a thrift store for art supplies—you never leave with exactly what you came for, but you always find goodies to spur your creative imagination. The School and Community Reuse Action Project (SCRAP) is a volunteer and donation-based organization. This nonprofit promotes sustainable reuse of materials and provides workshops, and offers it all up at affordable prices. Friends of mine find cork and foam cutouts to insulate the walls of their recording studio. I pick up stickers, zippers, three-ring binders, glitter, and beer cozies. Businesses around town often join together to support SCRAP, resulting in deals on services and products from cheap haircuts to recycled paint. During SCRAP's annual fundraiser, the Iron Artist Sculpt-Off competition (see the "Calendar" chapter, page 220), teams duke it out to see who can creatively promote waste reduction in the ultimate sculpt-off. Stop in and see where it leads you! *NK*

Orlo

2516 NW 29th Ave

242.1047

www.orlo.org

Open by appointment only

Orlo is like a rare old gem, partially buried under the settling dust of newer, glitzier galleries in the Northwest. This volunteer-run organization complements my curiosities by combining environmental issues with visual arts. Orlo puts together a quasi-annual publication called *The Bear Deluxe*, whose brown paper covers can be discovered in most grassroots coffee shops around town. Out of the Orlo headquarters comes schemes of gallery exhibitions, political puppet shows, hilarious video slams (like poetry slams but with camcorders and environmental themes), and Junk to Funk fashion shows. The organization also rents out a small amount of equipment, such as printers and projectors, for community use. This group is fun and intimate with an underground sort of feel. Check the web site for events and opportunities. *NK*

Launch Pad Gallery

811 E Burnside St, Ste 110

 231.7336

www.launchpadgallery.org

Wed–Sat 12–4p, Sun 12–3p, and by appointment

Launch Pad is one of the hippest, hottest galleries in PDX, a place where the artists go to check each other out. During each First Friday art walk there is a new show of cutting-edge paintings, sculptures, or installations. Shows are a mix of mediums, with artists of varied backgrounds and experience levels bringing art to the people in a new way. The alternative style of the gallery makes art more accessible for all. *SB*

Compound Gallery

107 NW 5th Ave

796.2733

www.compoundgallery.com

Mon–Sat 12–8p, Sun 12–6p

Compound Gallery resides within the Just Be Complex. This Japanese-owned retail store features plenty to delight your urban senses. Upon entering the space, you are greeted by an impressive selection of "serious" toys ranging from collectible figurines to mutant stuffed animals. Nearby is the DVD corner where you can peruse an international selection of live-action and anime flicks. Rows of vibrant sneakers line the front windows, directing your gaze toward hoodies and T-shirts enhanced with street graphics. Make your way upstairs and enter the airy loft-type gallery space featuring silk-screened prints, art books, and foreign magazines, along with rotating artists' works. During First Thursday, this colorful corner gallery drips with art aficionados. NK

Ogle

310 NW Broadway

227.4333

www.ogleinc.com

Tues–Sat 11a–6p

It's no wonder this gallery has a sophisticated eye for art—it sells high-end eyeglasses as well. This combination gallery and optical venue showcases cutting-edge work by local Portland artists. Whether the exhibit is small or large, the expansive windows and vast cherry-colored wood floors invite viewers into a warm and well-lit space. I observed coastal artist Anne R. Archer's works twice in the gallery, and both times she captured my sensory cravings with her unique fondness for mapping places in Oregon using found objects, natural elements, and painted images. Ogle is located in Old Town and is surrounded by 14 experimental live-work galleries called the Everett Station Lofts. The gallery is pleasant to browse during daylight hours, but I suggest visiting on a First Thursday to get the full effect. NK

📖 Regional Arts and Culture Council

🏛 *108 NW 9th Ave, Ste 300*
🎵 *823.5111*
💻 *www.racc.org*
🗓 *Mon–Fri 8:30a–5p*

This is the kind of place where dreams can come true. The Regional Arts and Culture Council (RACC) is a strong supporter of local artists, nonprofit organizations, and educational programs. It has funded many of the public sculptures and murals around the city. Look for RACC's walking tour brochure, featuring all the public artwork in Portland. The RACC web site is a great resource for art-funding opportunities, cultural events, job postings, and calls to artists. I took a fantastic grant-writing workshop the organization offered—it was cheap, informative, and most important, it inspired me to pursue my art-making intentions! *NK*

✒ First Fridays

🏢 *First Friday of each month 6–9p, Central Eastside area of Portland*
🎨 *www.firstfridayart.com*
🚌 Portland's Central Eastside Arts District comes alive in a new way on the first Friday of each month (weather allowing). A mix of shops, edgy design studios, and local art galleries, the scene is imbued with free wine, live music from street corners, and cool natives wearing chic clothes. Head to Bamboo Grove Salon (134 SE Taylor Street) for an unexpected show of style and art, while galleryHomeland (2505 SE 11th Avenue #136), 100th Monkey Studio (110 SE 16th Avenue), and Launch Pad (see page 90) are usually the most popular with exciting openings. Grab a bite in between your gallery perusals at Biwa (see page 173), the Egyptian Club (3701 SE Division Street), which often has local art on the walls, or Rontoms Lounge (600 E Burnside Street) for a stiff drink. *SB*

Create

From beads to seeds, fabric to photos, these spots will surely enable your creative side

I switched colleges my sophomore year to go to art school. I wanted to draw and paint and take photos all day instead of calculate chemical equations and study political systems. I changed my mind and went back to university, but what I learned from the experience was something that hadn't crossed my mind before: Everyone can create beauty, everyone can be an artist. I saw people who had never taken their pencil out of the lines on a steno pad draw impeccable contour figures after just a few months of focused study. Their eyes and their hands had become one unit. With a little drive anyone can contribute to the beauty in the world. I also feel that it is important to maintain a connection with handwork. If you haven't ever tried something like this yourself, the satisfaction of eating something you've cooked or better yet grown and cooked, or wearing a dress you've made or a scarf you've knitted is hard to top. Your hands are the greatest machines.

Dava Bead and Trade

 2121 NE Broadway
 288.3991
www.davabeadandtrade.com
Mon–Fri 10a–6p, Sat 10a–5p, Sun 11a–5p

Dava Bead and Trade has beads from around the world, in all shapes, sizes, colors, and variations. Find strands and singles, boxes and baubles, carved wood and handcrafted cloisonné. New findings, specialty metals, chains, and interesting necklace closures are highlights in the back section, so make your way there if you can stray from the tempting middle aisle. The staff consists of talented designers with inspiring stories of their own and a slew of amazing ideas—so engage one of them, and you are sure to get helpful assistance. *SB*

Dava Bead and Trade

Fabric Depot

700 SE 122nd Ave

252.9530

www.fabricdepot.com

Mon–Sat 9a–9p, Sun 10a–7p

Fabric Depot is one of the largest fabric and notion stores in the western United States, and when I go there, it is impossible for me to leave empty-handed.

Even when browsing the web site to find the correct phone number for this review, I couldn't help but make yet another fabric purchase. This time it was an incredible grass-patterned cotton quilting fabric that I ended up using on a quilt for my mother with an embroidered Basho haiku about grass on battlegrounds. Another trip yielded flannel fabric covered in bears that I used on an outdoorsy-looking simple quilt for my honey. The array of fabrics, continual sale prices, and unique prints get the creative gears going. Any aspect of a given project, from clothing patterns to quilts, is housed here and explained to you by friendly and helpful staff. I challenge you to enter this shop without coming out with a treasure chest of new and interesting projects of your own. *SB*

Yarn Garden

 *1413 SE Hawthorne Blvd*
 239.7950
www.yarngarden.net
 Mon–Thurs 10a–7p, Fri 10a–6p, Sat 10a–5p, Sun 12–5p

Truly a garden of colors and materials, this knitter's wonderland has three rooms of threads from all over the globe. Run your hands over the huge cashmere selection, or find something new like soy-silk or chitin, a soft yet strong yarn made from crab and shrimp shells. Every Wednesday morning at 11am a professional is in the house for a free knitting clinic. Bring your project with you and get friendly with other crafty people over some tea and scones at the in-store cafe, complete with comfy sofas. *SB*

Collage

 1639 NE Alberta St
249.2190
 www.collageonalberta.com
Mon–Fri 10a–8p, Sat–Sun 10a–6p

Although this store is primarily geared toward the scrapbooking craze, the crafty tools, hard-to-find art supplies, and complete rubber stamp collection can be used for any possible collage project, as the name suggests. Choose a wide brush marker in vermilion to go with some handmade paper and a marigold rubber stamp to make unique stationery, or pick up a poodle stamp like I did, which I use on absolutely everything now. Whatever your idea, talk it through with the creative salespeople while perusing the tidy booths of art-making treasures. I love the rolling tape dispensers and mini glue guns, as well as the varnish sprays that give a finished look to my projects. Get busy in the workroom or take a class—there are lots of ways to spend more time in this delightful space. *SB*

Mississippi Kitchen Supply

4035 N Mississippi Ave
284.1498
www.mississippikitchensupply.com
Wed–Sat 11:30a–5p, Sun 12–4p

Yes, yes, yes, I love to cook. Just thinking of this shop makes me want to skip out on writing and run to the kitchen! The gearheads at Mississippi Kitchen Supply sell only tools and equipment they'd proudly admit to stock in their own kitchens, and the atmosphere inside the store is directed toward serving and being a part of Mississippi's newfound community. Any place with staff who encourage you to ask questions like the helpful, honest folks here do makes me happy. *SB*

Ink and Peat

3808 N Williams Ave
282.2700
www.inkandpeat.com
Tues–Sat 11a–6p, Sun 12–5p

When the owner of Ink and Peat isn't creating jaw-droppingly gorgeous and modern floral designs or designing window displays for Portland's Street of Eames modern home tour, she's donating time and money for the betterment of homeless youth in Portland. Now doesn't that make you want to buy her flowers even more? Find her arrangements of wild irises, coxcombs, and golden lisianthus, or buy stems of unripe fig, double tulips, and peony roses to do your own arranging. Whether you are adding color to your dining room, your friend's office, or just your hotel room, these organic blooms are a reminder of the city's lushness. Ink and Peat also sells pretty gifts and decor items that will easily inspire a redecoration project, even if it is just a tiny corner of the house. *SB*

Trade Up Music

4701 SE Division St

236.8800

www.tradeupmusic.com

Daily 11a–7p

Need a noisemaker for an impromptu parade down Hawthorne Boulevard? Run out of money and forced to sell your guitar? Locally owned Trade Up Music is the best spot to find new and used instruments, sell a gently used piece of musical equipment, and get expert advice and repairs from local musicians. Also, you can get the lowdown on some lesser-known and possibly free concerts in Portland. As an added bonus, this is the kind of place where no one cares if you sit and play the mandolins and pianos for hours. —EMILY CRABTREE OF LACTACIOUS (SEE "PORTLAND PLAYLIST," PAGE 155)

Broadway Floral

1638 NE Broadway

288.5537

www.broadwayfloral.com

Mon–Fri 8a–6p, Sat 8:30a–5p, Sun 11a–5p

To go along with a rainbow of floral distraction, Broadway Floral is chock-full of silk ribbons, fun ornaments, and classy yard decor. Housed in a historic greenhouse structure in the cozy Hollywood District, the store's buds and blossoms are another cheery addition to this lovely hood. Arrangements in every shade, designed for many seasons and occasions, can be delivered by request, like the miniature cymbidium orchids with elegant ikebana-inspired lines. SB

Paperdoll

7909 SE Stark St

408.6867

www.paperdoll-co.com, http://paperdoll.ning.com

Tues–Fri 10a–6p, Sat 10a–5p, Sun 11a–4p

Paperdoll's walls are lined with handmade cards and invitations—examples that will get your fingers itchin' to make one of your own. With all the tools to do so, this quaint, small store is packed with pretty papers, rubber stamps, glitter, and even acrylic paint. If you need help getting started, Paperdoll offers classes like Watercolor Book Camp, Eco-Collage, and How to Make Your

Own Sassy Stationery. If you just don't have the time to make one of your own, the store sells elegant ready-made cards and invitations as well. I appreciate the chic selection of reusable gifts, and I'm a member of the Paperdoll Multimedia Girls Club, where members share projects, ideas, and suggestions online and at regular gatherings. Crafting can be so fun and so social. *NK*

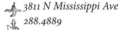 Bolt Fabric Boutique

2136 NE Alberta St
287.2658
www.boltfabricboutique.com
Tues–Fri 10a–6p, Sat 10a–5p, Sun 11a–4p

Bolt Fabric Boutique is the place to let out the *ooh* and *aah* in all of us—the ones we've been holding back until the moment was right. Cotton prints are selected from companies that are careful not to participate in some of the atrocities for which the fabric industry is known. Fabric patterns from Free Spirit, Robert Kaufman, and Japanese favorite Kokka fill the dainty shelves. Sit in the back and flip through designs from Amy Butler and Kaffe Fassett and if you don't already know how to follow a pattern, stay for a sewing class (see the "Learn" chapter, page 82). Don't miss Bolt's one-of-a-kind notions and button collections (which rival my Bubba's button jar!). *SB*

Pistils Nursery

3811 N Mississippi Ave
288.4889
www.pistilsnursery.com
Daily 10a–6p

Whether encountered on a stroll down Mississippi Avenue or as a predetermined destination, Pistils Nursery is always a worthwhile experience. From Turkish spike poppies to pineapple guava fruit trees, this little nursery is bursting with unique varieties of flowering flora. My favorite reason to visit is to inspect the selection of whimsical succulents and admire the fuzzy baby chicks for sale by the register. You can learn how to care for backyard chickens and get all the supplies you need for them, or you can just pick up some fake fuzzy ones from the gift section—it's that kind of flexible place. Along with bulk organic fertilizers, bee pollen, and secondhand gardening books, this place has the tools to get your country livin' on, right here in the city. *NK*

Portland Nursery

5050 SE Stark St

231.5050

www.portlandnursery.com

Daily 9a–6p

I was once asked what my last stop is before I depart a city I am researching for a guidebook. One of the first places I thought of was Portland Nursery, a shop I return to again and again each time I have to hop back on I-5 south toward Oakland, California. I fill my back seat with yellow plum trees, boxwoods, hydrangeas, an heirloom English rose, and a few fragrant lavender shrubs. When the plants arrive at my house, I have a nice "welcome home" garden project before diving back into my usual routine. Portland Nursery is a century-old establishment, and it's the perfect place to browse, whether you are a seasoned gardener or just want a unique exploration of native Oregon plants. It will continue to be one of my last stops before bidding good-bye to the City of Roses—although I'm never away for too long! *SB*

Office PDX

2204 NE Alberta St

282.7200

www.officepdx.com

Tues–Fri 11a–7p, Sat 11a–5p, Sun 12–4p

This isn't your ordinary office-supply store. Owners Tony Secolo and Kelly Coller happen to be award-winning graphic designers, so you are guaranteed to find visually stimulating and functional office goods. The pair fused a 1950s-era blue-collar space with contemporary designs that include modern Japanese aesthetics. Re-creations of vintage furniture, laptop bags, waterproof notebooks, ergonomic tape dispensers, and arrays of organizers will get you excited to head to work and finish your tasks with style. The selection of reference material for sale includes eco-design books, DIY manuals, and swanky international magazines. Office PDX also has a gallery exhibition space and partakes in Alberta Street's Last Thursday art walk. *NK*

Muse Art and Design

4224 SE Hawthorne Blvd
231.8704
www.museartanddesign.com
Mon–Sat 11a–6p, Sun 12–5p

For any creative endeavor, having good tools makes all the difference. Design to your heart's content after finding all the necessary objects at this local artists' treasure chest. For inspiration, stick your nose in a book at the free visual library, or follow it into the commission-free exhibit space, where customer artists are encouraged to show and sell their works. *SB*

Buy Me

A unique take on shopping, from artichokes to zippers

Andy Warhol really was on to something when he equated department stores with museums. Indeed, appealing to shoppers is an artful task involving a modern take on design and cultural signing. So whether you have a practical purpose for shopping, need a little retail therapy, or just want to gaze at the most up-to-date museums, these spots should fulfill your aims. While you shop, you can feel good knowing that you're supporting these conscientious enterprises and sending ripples of positivity across the community.

Mabel and Zora

748 NW 11th Ave
241.5696
www.mabelandzora.com
Mon–Sat 10a–6p, Sun 12–5p

Cool clothing never loses its charm. The pieces at Mabel and Zora are made to hold their shape and look good for the long haul. Each design is carefully selected by the fashion mavens who run this trendy shop. Have fun shopping and let these stylin' gals help you put outfits together—they are so good at it and are rarely pushy about the sale. The organic cotton jeans I found are still favorites and have traveled everywhere with me. The friendly folks here even threw in a handmade owl pin for my raincoat. *SB*

Pin Me Apparel

3705 N Mississippi Ave

281.1572

www.pin-me-apparel.com

Mon–Sat 11a–7p, Sun 11a–5p

They say it's what's inside that counts, but when I enter Pin Me Apparel I shift my thoughts toward outer beauty. The unique tunics and tops are so flattering, and the range of sizes allows many women to shop here. Local and small independent designers are showcased, and the dresses, skirts, flirty tops, and perfectly cut pants all push my desire buttons. Save up and visit this store when you've got a hot date or something fun to dress extra suave for. *sb*

Vegan Mall

SE Stark St and 12th Ave

Under the heading "Only in Portland" comes the world's first vegan mall, a concept few can imagine to be luxurious. But think outside the box and you'll witness cool fashions, epic body art, tasty cookies and cakes, and all kinds of indulgences. This collection of vegan shops focuses more on what vegan includes than what it excludes. Here are the store highlights: Herbivore Clothing (*www.herbivoreclothing.com*), Scapegoat Tattoo (*www.scapegoattattoo.com*), Sweet Pea Bakery, Food Fight! Grocery (*www.foodfightgrocery.com*), Seven Star Acupuncture Clinic, and more. You can find more information about all things vegan in Portland at *www.vegportland.com*. *sb*

Kitchen Kaboodle

1520 NE Broadway (one of several locations)

288.1500

www.kitchenkaboodle.com

Mon–Fri 10a–7p, Sat 10a–6p, Sun 11a–6p

If you're getting more and more interested in honing your culinary prowess based on the phenomenal dining experiences you're having around town, look no further than Kitchen Kaboodle for a veritable home chef's paradise. The helpful staff will guide you toward specific tart tins, rubberized muffin trays, and stainless steel gadgets for classy kitchens. Attend one of the many demonstrations and you're that much closer to mastering knife skills, making vegan cupcakes properly, or learning more about your current food fancy. *sb*

Greenloop

 8005 SE 13th Ave
236.3999
www.thegreenloop.com
 Tues–Sat 10a–6p, Sun 12–5p

Greenloop is a boutique that showcases the pinch of fashion that has gone eco-friendly. Greenloop's racks are stocked with designers like Blue Canoe, Eco-Ganik, and locals Anna Cohen and Sameunderneath, backed up by a popular online business that accompanies the store picks. Greenloop is not a place for bargain shoppers, but it's worth saving up for something extra special and, of course, green. Ensure that the seasons you're gearing up for keep on coming by shopping stylishly at this conscientious boutique. *SB*

Hecklewood

 114 NW 3rd Ave
922.1797
www.hecklewood.com
Mon–Fri 11a–6p, occasionally open on weekends

A rambunctious group of young and talented graphic designers, screen printers, and self-described Cascadian culturalist music fiends from Nowhere, USA found each other and got it together to create one of the top T-shirt stores around. You can't not look cool after donning one of Hecklewood's signature digs. Leopard print fitted tees for women are striking; I like to dress them up with a suit jacket on top. Men will be equally thrilled with the hat and hoodie collection, as well as the edgy printed wallets made of reused plastic. In addition to the great store, the Hecklewood crew has a rockin' mixtape project online, where you can listen to a new handpicked mixtape every couple of weeks. All this and Hecklewood has graphic prints on the walls that go up monthly, so there is always something fresh and inspiring to gaze at while you shop. *SB*

Fat Fancy

834 NE Emerson St (locations vary)
www.myspace.com/fatfancy

One blessed weekend a month, this underground vintage plus-size paradise opens its doors to me and my friends and anyone else who's in the know. And boy, are we happy to take advantage of the colorful, cheap spread and the cool community. It's also wonderful to see so many size 12's and up! There's stuff for men and women, all with an edgy style. E-mail ahead for more info: *fatfancy@gmail.com. SB*

Trillium Artisans

9119 SE Foster Rd

775.7993

www.trilliumartisans.org

Tues–Fri 10a–6p

Enter Trillium Artisans and behold a world where beauty is dualistic: It's pretty to look at and it's made in a way that benefits the environment. Find handmade and recycled goods and crafts at this inspiring gem of a shop. *SB*

Johnny Sole

815 SW Alder St

228.5844

www.johnnysole.net

Mon–Sat 11a–6p, Sun 12–5p

Portland's largest independently owned shoe store is known for its excellent collection of snazzy boots and ultramodern men's shoes. Embroidered cowboy boots, gathered leather knee-highs, and suede heels line the multilevel shelves at the two-story downtown store. Find bargains on stylish, high-quality footwear in the sale closet and a cool hand-printed shirt to match on the racks upstairs. And yes, these boots were made for walking, which is exactly what you'll want to do when you see how good you look getting from A to B. *SB*

Pinkham Millinery

515 SW Broadway

796.9385

www.pinkhammillinery.com

Wed–Sat 11a–5:30p, Tues by appointment

Dayna Pinkham's sought-after cranial creations push all my desire buttons. Her skills were honed under the tutelage of the European upper crust of milliners, and she's woven a Northwest edge and a modern flair into all the traditional styles. The felt collection will turn any proclaimed nonbeliever into a bona fide hat person, especially the elegant Turban Cloche and the witty

Boney Fedora Slouch. Bridal headpieces and custom hats for special occasions are created with mind-boggling variety and design. Take a second look at all those hatted Hollywooders, and you might well trace their head covering back to this Portland-only shop. Pinkham's hats also grace the runways of Seaplane's (see page 106) delightful local fashion shows. *SB*

Local35

🚌 *3556 SE Hawthorne Blvd*

💡 *963.8200*

🖥 *www.local35.com*

Sun–Wed 11a–6p, Thur–Sat 11a–7p

A cornerstone of the Hawthorne District, Local35 brings together area designers and adventurous labels from abroad. Hipster jeans and au courant sweaters and button-downs are neatly hung in front of art installations featuring local artists. The hottest styles don't come cheap, but the stuff on the sale rack is as cool as the front-shelf items and more realistic for many of us. Local35 has a large selection of men's clothes to help make any man's wardrobe more interesting and alive. *SB*

Oh Baby

 1811 NE Broadway St

🔔 *281.7430*

www.ohbabylingerieshops.com

🚌 *Mon–Sat 11a–7p, Sun 12–5p*

Whether you're svelte or voluptuous, Oh Baby has something to flatter every body. With styles conservative, flowery, and sultry, the shop's array of undergarments is sure to up the ante. The friendly staff is well versed in translating your personality into the perfect lingerie pick for you—and that goes for guys in search of romantic girlfriend gifts, too. When it comes to traversing this seldom-explored universe, the boyfriend or hubby is in good hands. Trust me on this one. *SB*

Una

 2802 SE Ankeny St

🖥 *235.2326*

www.una-myheartisfull.com

🕐 *Tues–Sat 11a–6p, Sun 12–6p*

There comes a time when you are in need of that dress of dresses. Honor that moment with a voyage to the far-off land of Una, where sheer beauty reigns supreme. Pull together your inspiration—and your pennies—and dive into a gilded sanctuary of soft romance. Una is a small store, but it's the kind of place that grows larger and larger as you browse through the racks, like carefully thumbing through a memorable novel. Dresses and whimsical blouses are carefully chosen from around the globe by a shop owner equipped with fashion's sharp blade and a graphic designer's keen eye. This is a place where that perfect dress is waiting to be discovered, and where you can access a world of small-batch, independent designers. *SB*

Trade Roots

 1831 NE Broadway
281.5335
www.traderootsinc.com
Mon–Fri 10a–6p, Sat 10a–5:30p, Sun 10a–4p

What do birch-bark boxes from Siberia and Indonesian wood carvings have to do with one another? Where do Nepalese yak-horn crafts meet billowing Moroccan skirts? The answer is Trade Roots, a store where all the products come from happy, healthy artisans who have been paid a living wage for their work. In addition to bringing together unique and affordable gifts, attention is paid to ensure that the environmental impact of the objects is minimal. Trade Roots has taken the care, so you can shop carefree. *SB*

Flutter

 3948 N Mississippi Ave
288.1649
www.flutterclutter.com
Mon–Sat 11a–6p, Sun 11a–4p

A miraculous thing happens when found objects are turned upside down and painted—they emerge as something new, usable, and desirable. In true homage to Duchamp's readymades (e.g., *Bicycle Wheel*), Flutter juxtaposes antlers and Buddhas, lace and statue hands, and strews them all about this fanciful shop in a way that gives them new life. Don't miss the jewelry case, and be sure to look above your head at the inventive light fixtures. *SB*

Seaplane

2266 Lovejoy St
234.2409
www.seaplanedesign.com
Daily 11a–6p

Seaplane is hands down the coolest boutique in Portland, and perhaps in the entire Pacific Northwest. Using clothing as a mode of self-expression and artistic whim, you will want to parade the streets for hours in your new outfit from this local designers' smorgasbord. Incredible necklaces are pieced together from found objects; frilly skirts layered with bleached aprons are strung together with seamless nuance. Every piece is a story, a centerpiece, and a flash of beauty. The staff knows the background behind each designer's work and can fill your ears with inspiring tales that will make you proud to splurge on any of these fine articles. Near the counter, look for journals made from re-bound old novels. I used mine to take notes while researching this very book and collected many compliments in the process. *SB*

Sameunderneath

752.9384
www.sameunderneath.com

One of those super cool Portland business concepts is a pillar of an innovative green movement in fashion. Sameunderneath items can be found at cool boutiques all over the country, but the main offices and design studios are right here in PDX. The hip styles are great for everyday wear, and creating more extravagant outfits is possible, especially during Portland's Fashion Week, of which Sameunderneath is a big part. Organic, sustainable fibers made by well-paid workers make these clothes look even cooler. Find the clothes online or at a local boutique such as Greenloop (see page 102). *SB*

Land Gallery

3925 N Mississippi Ave
451.0689
http://landpdx.com/
Thurs–Sat 10a–6p, Sun 10a–5p

Finally, the clever folks behind BuyOlympia.com, one of my very favorite web sites, has opened a retail store in their new hometown of Portland. You may know this local shopping site for its creative, edgy books and things—after all, it was a pioneer in the Buy Local movement, linking e-shopping with supporting local artists and craftspeople. Now you can peruse the upstairs art gallery on opening nights and meet loads of crazy-cool people—artists and iron welders, chefs and authors—the congregation that's come together around this place is uncanny. Downstairs is an array of incredible objects, fashionable stationery, witty posters and comics, and slick gifts, plus a fabulous sale section and the ability to see all the action in person. Rock on! *SB*

Re-Find

Take another look at what's been passed over . . . ahead is a treasure trove straight off a train from the past

There are enough DIYers, reuse freaks, and history buffs in Portland to sustain a healthy selection of stores specializing in resale. While away your time mulling over old record collections, perusing previously hinged doors, and purchasing a vintage treasure from one of many thrift stores. Use what we've got already circulating around rather than something new—if it's new to you, it's just as exciting!

The ReBuilding Center

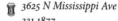
3625 N Mississippi Ave
331.1877
www.rebuildingcenter.org
Mon–Sat 9a–6p, Sun 10a–5p

Stepping through the epic earthen entranceway and into the ReBuilding Center will make you wish you were renovating a cute bungalow. This lofty, open-air facility is not just a place for items seeking a second life in your home, it is also part of a network of Our United Villages nonprofit community resource centers around the country that promote sustainable living, education, and community development. The ReBuilding Center is a warehouse of ready-to-reuse doors, lighting fixtures, lumber, windows, and more, stocked up, down, and around such cleverly named aisles as Looking Glass Loop, Appliance Alley, Carpet Square, and Miscellaneous Mile. If riding the bus with your newly purchased door would be a little awkward, a person can always use some more nails or a rainfall showerhead like the one I found. *SB*

The ReBuilding Center

Thrifting in PDX

More info: www.altportland.com/thrift/index.shtml

Portlanders take their thrifting seriously, and there are no fewer than 50 thrift shops within the city limits. My favorites? The bargain-basement clothing deals at Teen Challenge Thrift (3121 NE Sandy Blvd, 230.1910), the unique used books at Lombard Salvation Army (8426 N Lombard St, 286.9571), sewing supplies at the crafty thrift store Knittn' Kitten (7530 NE Glisan St, 255.3022), and the many random scores at William Temple House Thrift (2230 NW 23rd Ave, 222.3328). *SB*

Red Light Clothing Exchange

3590 SE Hawthorne Blvd
963.8888
http://redlightclothingexchange.com
Mon–Sat 11a–8p, Sun 11a–7p

When the thought of scouring the Goodwill racks puts a crick in your neck, turn to Red Light Clothing Exchange for a more easily digestible array of clothing of the vintage variety as well as trendy second-run releases. People watching is an added perk—Red Light draws hipsters like moths to a flame. If you're low on funds, you can hand over your wearisome duds to the captivatingly accessorized employees for, hopefully, a tidy sum, which is certain to be returned shortly to the store registers after a must-have boot acquisition. *SB*

Redux Reinventions

811 E Burnside St, Ste 110
231.7336
www.reduxpdx.com
Sun 10a–5p, Tues–Sat 10a–6p

If you like pretty things, clever crafts, sweet accessories, and creative reuse, than Redux is your new best friend. The first time I entered the shop, I immediately knew I had discovered something truly special. Find locally made art and accessories, not to mention fabulous and inventive jewelry, all of which fit the shop's slogan: "artware, reinvention, adornment." After you pick a new necklace with dangling antique chandelier drops, mosey over to the gallery walls to get a closer look—every month there's a new and fantastic show. *SB*

Stars Antiques Malls

SE Milwaukie Ave
239.0346
www.starsantique.com
Mon–Sat 11a–6p, Sun 12–5p

Just say no to shopping all new all the time. It takes energy to create and ship and store all these new manufactured things, and once in a while I recommend taking a break from that endless cycle. Instead, find new-to-you kitchen gadgets, dishware, and more at Stars Antiques Malls. This place is huge so you're bound to find at least a few corners of interest even if you don't think of yourself as an antiquer. *SB*

Portland Goodwill Outlet Store

1740 SE Ochoco St
230.2076
Mon–Sat 8a–8p, Sun 9a–7p

For the ultimate adventure in shopping, head to what Portlanders know as The Bins. It's a factory-sized Goodwill donation center where large bins of clothing, books, shoes, and knickknacks are carted in by the hour. Wear gloves and pick through the piles to find vintage and designer shirts and sweaters mixed in with broken dolls and old cutoffs. A trip here is a fun excursion where the possibilities are endless—I found a brand-new London Fog microfiber raincoat and some enviable Levi's. The best part is the price. For up to 20 pounds of clothing and knickknacks, it is $1.39 a pound. Above 20 pounds is 99 cents, and above 50 pounds is 69 cents. That made my coat and jeans a whopping $4.19 altogether. Yee haw! *SB*

Lady Luck Vintage

1 SE 28th Ave
233.4041
Mon–Fri 12–6p, Sat 11a–6p, Sun 12–5p

Lady Luck Vintage is a Portlander's top choice for vintage shopping. Such stores are found in great quantity along the east side streets of the city, but none is as totally '60s as Lady Luck. With excellent customer service and idyllic summer dresses aplenty, there is a reason this locally owned spot is touted as the best. The lady herself has sifted through thrift stores and estate sales to unearth these unique finds just for you. *SB*

Hippo Hardware

1040 E Burnside St
231.1444
www.hippohardware.com
Mon–Thurs 10a–5p, Fri–Sat 10a–6p, Sun 12–5p

When visiting Portland, it's easy to develop a crush on the city. For some people it's the restaurants; for others it's the shopping that's just the beginning. For those of you who fall hard for the array of charming bungalows that line the residential blocks, there is one way you can take a piece of the city home with you: Pay a visit to Hippo Hardware, the best architectural salvage store in town. Sleek bathtubs that look like Airstream trailers are lined up beside more buxom ones with claw feet. The light fixture section will leave you agog and, if you're anything like me, you'll lose hours rummaging through boxes of drawer pulls and light switch plates. Pick up a couple of old skeleton keys or an amber doorknob as a souvenir. *MM*

Weekend

Fun activities for Saturdays and Sundays, plus yummy spots for brunch

Weekends have a mood all their own. Laze around, relax with your loved ones, or explore something new. Portlanders like to get outside on the weekends and enjoy the glorious weather or one of the annual street fairs. A short weekend getaway is a great way to see this city. Americans don't get nearly as much vacation time as those from other countries, so take advantage of the weekends and create mini-vacations at these special spots.

 **Portland Saturday Market**

 SW Ankeny St and Naito Pkwy
222.6072
www.portlandsaturdaymarket.com
Mar–Dec 24, Sat 10a–5p, Sun 11a–4:30p

Shop to your heart's content among these local artisans, vendors, cooks, and musicians. Along with Powell's, the Portland Saturday Market is one of the most known attractions in the city. I come here to listen to great live music while enjoying my picnic-style lunch. Choose grub from myriad food stands, then weave through the expansive craft booth aisles toward Tom McCall Waterfront Park (see page 63), where you'll find benches to sit on and admire the city right on the river. *SB*

$$ Eleni's Philoxenia and Estiatorio

 112 NW 9th Ave
 227.2158
www.elenisrestaurant.com
Tues–Thurs 5–10p, Fri–Sat 5–11p

I am lying on a pristine beach in the Adriatic. Gentle waves wash ashore. Soft whistles rise with the ebbing tide as olive branches flutter in the wind. A kind sir finds me and offers an elegant feta and phyllo treat drizzled with sweet honey. In my other hand, I hold a glass of incredible Greek house wine. Now I am back on a rainy night off a concrete strip of turf in Portland. But my restful fantasy is still there, held up loftily by the strong renditions of Greek fare at Eleni's Philoxenia and Estiatorio—sautéed ground beef, mystifying phyllo creations and, of course, the seafood, with the nonspongy grilled calamari being most notable. Bring forth dreams of the most beautiful waters of Greece as you indulge in these delights at Eleni's. *SB*

Supper

Various locations
www.supperpdx.com
7:30p
Cost: $25 per person without drinks

The secret might be out about this communal candlelight dining experience, but the salt cod purée, grain salad, and toasty hearth-grilled meats are as mouthwatering as ever, whether you're trying something for the first time or you have deep culinary knowledge. Come sit at a long wooden table and be served large dishes that get passed around the table to those you know and those you don't. Take your friend who can never make up his or her mind, and you'll be free of all decisions, except for which local wine to pair with that day's three-course offering. Chat it up with your tablemates and have a good old-fashioned dinner with other Portland foodies. Check the web site for an e-mail contact so you'll get an invite to the next family supper. *SB*

Vera Katz Eastbank Esplanade

SE Water Ave and SE Hawthorne Blvd
www.portlandonline.com/parks/finder/ (search "Eastbank Esplanade")

This 1.5-mile riverside paved path leads walkers, hikers, runners, and bikers past four of Portland's famous bridges and by a collection of outdoor art. The riverbank you walk by has been reshaped to promote fish hatching and a rejuvenated habitat for native wildlife. Hundreds of trees and shrubs have been planted to reflect what this area was like before the city was here. Take notice of the inventive structures by local artist group RIGGA—these are permanent assets to the riverbank. The floating walkway leading to the boat dock is the longest of its kind in the country, and it transports you to the water taxi, a fun alternative mode of transit. All in all it's a great walk that gives you city and country all at once. *RM*

Industrial Cafe and Saloon

2572 NW Vaughn St

227.7002

Mon–Fri 11a–9p, Sat–Sun 8a–9p

Gearheads unite! Industrial Cafe and Saloon literally has gears hanging from the walls—a motif that sneaks its way into more than one menu item, including the buttermilk biscuits cut with gear-threading edges. But this place isn't as hokey as you might think, and the industrial chic look doesn't fatten the price tag. Expect huge, not particularly sophisticated plates of fried clams and eggs (when razor clams are in season, this dish is a must-order), vegetarian chili, apple French toast, and pancakes. Industrial Cafe has some of the quickest service for a weekend brunch, and the spick-and-span interior, with its fun marble and rusty metal accents, has an endearing effect, rather than making the place too cool for TV. *SB*

Vindalho

2038 SE Clinton St

467.4550

www.vindalho.com

Sun–Thurs 5–9p, Fri–Sat 5–10p

As soon as I entered this golden-hued restaurant, I felt the romantic vibe and I couldn't wait to read the menu because I just knew it would have more exciting offerings than the usual kormas and saag paneers. This incarnation of Indian cuisine is made with ingredients fresh from local farms. Recipes use cloves and cinnamon, black pepper, coconuts, and chiles to tell a story of place and a special weaving of traditions unique to the Spice Route. For vegetarians this menu offers more choices than most around town, but meat lovers will be just as satisfied, plus all meats are grass-fed, hormone-free, and sourced locally. Masala chicken wings, roasted beet salad with house-made paneer (a traditional Indian cheese), and madras lamb curry are my three top picks, but you'll probably find your own on this diverse and flavor-forward menu. *SB*

Mint/820

816 N Russell St
284.5518
www.mintand820.com
Mon–Sat 4p–12a

Finally, Mint/820 has heeded our pleas and is open both Saturday and Sunday for some of the very best cocktails and nosh in food-centric PDX. Owned and lovingly tended by Erika Polmar, the woman hailed as the best mixologist around, Mint restaurant and the adjacent bar 820 serve fresh and beautiful cocktails. House-infused liquors and syrups dapple inventive drinks like the Bella, with blackberry purée and sugared lemon juice, or the Ad Lib, with muddled cilantro. Most drinks are quite sweet, with the exception of the beet vodka and lemon Ruby. Chow down on the sweet potato fries or a Cuban lamb burger, both significantly cheaper during happy hour. Get a bit dressed up and live large in this swank atmosphere that at first seems snooty, but when you realize the bartenders are on a first-name basis with so many regulars, you'll see it's just an ultra-cool neighborhood place. *SB*

Rose City Park

NE 62nd Ave and Tillamook St
www.portlandonline.com/parks/finder/ (search "Rose City Park")

The feel of wood chips under my sneakers and the shade of larch trees make the paths of Rose City Park, located in the neighborhood of the same name, a great walk, rain or shine. This northeast neighborhood has a strong community feel, and you'll often find friends and puppy buddies meeting and talking on the trails. There are also picnic tables, a playground, and tennis courts for everyone to enjoy. *SB*

Beaterville Cafe

2201 N Killingworth St
735.4652
Mon–Fri 6a–2p, Sat–Sun 7a–3p

There are some eateries in Portland that could be lifted up by a giant hurricane and plopped thousands of miles away, and they would still feel like Portland inside. Beaterville is precisely such a place, echoing the PDX vibe with a strong resonance. Catering to the eclectic locals who swoon here on weekends, Beaterville doesn't get so busy that you can't get a good meal without being rushed. Enter through the white swinging back door in the middle of Beaterville's field of blue, and you'll be taken aback by the jumble of decorative styles and sensuous smells wafting from the kitchen. Don't expect service to be much more than abrupt. Your belly will forgive your waitress for not calling you "Honey." Vegans and vegetarians will rejoice at the number of suitable options, and for the price, it's hard to find a fuller plate on a dewy Saturday morning. *SB*

Saint Cupcake

407 NW 17th Ave (and other locations)
473.8760
www.saintcupcake.com
Mon 9a–6p, Tues–Thurs 9a–8p, Fri 9a–10p, Sat 10a–10p, Sun 10a–6p

Everyone loves cupcakes, and now everyone can enjoy them with all the varieties Saint Cupcake has blessed us with. Toasted coconut cream, lemon, chocolate, and endless classic and creative flavors are made for vegans and dairy lovers alike. Order coffee to enjoy along with your cupcake choice. Sometimes I need a sip of coffee just to make the cupcake decision! *SB*

Ken's Artisan Pizza and Bakery

338 NW 21st Ave
248.2202
www.kensartisan.com
Mon 7a–9:30p, Tues–Sat 7a–7p, Sun 8a–5p

The space is small here and fills up quickly, so hopefully the weather will be kind and accommodating for outdoor seating while you enjoy your savory slice. There is also a selection of sandwiches and pastries. I recommend topping off the visit with a *cannelle* (French for cinnamon)—these pastries are divine. Ken's Artisan Pizza and Bakery is a jumping-off point for exploring the goods of the Nob Hill shopping district or trekking up to Washington Park to catch the roses doing their morning stretches. *DL*

Slow Bar

533 SE Grand Ave
230.7767
www.slowbar.net
Mon–Fri 11:30a–2:30a, Sat–Sun 5p–2:30a

Serious burger lovers will rejoice at the rendition of this American classic at Slow Bar. Stacked atop a homemade bun are crispy onion rings, your choice of dressings, and a moist patty of organic, free-range beef. *Hooray!* Hunker down in the round red booths and you'll feel like the place is giving you a big, comforting hug. All of your usual bar food suspects are on the menu, but each is treated with special attention and a new flair. *SB*

Tastebud's Dining Room

3220 SE Milwaukie Ave
234.0330
www.tastebudfarm.com/dining_room.php
Wed–Mon 5–10p, Sat–Sun 9a–2p

It is new to me, but apparently many Portlanders have been waiting for a long time to enjoy Tastebud's cooking and baking at a brick-and-mortar location. You can still find Tastebud's supernal treats at New Seasons Market (see page 197) and at a few of Portland's farmers markets, but come in to the dining room for brunch or for a last-minute weeknight pizza, and you'll get much more of what I can only explain as edible love. *SB*

Simpatica Dining Hall

828 SE Ash St
235.1600
www.simpaticacatering.com

Catch much of the wildness of a secret, subversive dining society without the secrecy or subversion when you come to dine at Simpatica Dining Hall. Themes range from national recipes like Cuban fare complete with a pig on a spit to seasonal ingredients like juicy Early Girl tomatoes. Reserve a spot for Friday or Saturday night dinner, or gather at least eight of your friends together and make a brunch reservation—my personal favorite way to experience this incredible culinary paradise. *SB*

$$ Malay Satay Hut

2850 SE 82nd Ave
771.7888
www.malaysatayhut.com
Mon–Fri 11:30a–2:30p & 5–10p; Sat–Sun 12–3p & 5–10p

It's rare to experience the wonders of Malaysian cuisine on this side of the Pacific. It's rarer still to find such authentic black pepper duck, pompano fish, and stuffed handmade bean curd, in what looks to be part of a strip mall. But "the Hut" has been recognized nationwide for its supernal dishes, outdoing most other Malaysian restaurants in the United States with its flavorful classic dishes. Don't leave without trying the *roti canai*, a steamy and moist bread served with a buttery, spicy dipping sauce. My favorite menu item is the famous Buddhist Yam Pot, in which yam batter is broiled in a bowl shape and filled with steamed vegetables and an intoxicating sauce that will guarantee your satisfaction. The yummy blended drinks made from exotic fruits are also worth a try—just be aware that durian fruit is what you might call an acquired taste! This family-run restaurant has become so popular that two more locations have opened in Washington state. *SB*

Pine State Biscuits

3640 SE Belmont St
236.3346
www.pinestatebiscuits.com
Daily 7a–2p

Both my sun and rising signs are air signs, and I have a lot of influence from Aquarius, so if you know anything about astrology, you'll understand that self-control isn't always my strongest suit. This is truly evident at Pine State Biscuits where I can frivolously order bona fide breakfast feasts. As long as you aren't preparing to run in the Portland Marathon anytime soon, indulge once in a while in these delicious and hearty breakfasts. After a long night of dancing, or following a day or two of skiing, eating here is a grand slam. *SB*

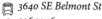 Dang's Thai Kitchen

$ 670 N State St, Lake Oswego
697.0779
Mon–Thurs 11:30a–2:30p & 5–9p, Sat 11:30a–2:30p, Sun 12–9p

Yes, there are boatloads of great Thai eateries in Portland proper, but heed my recommendation if you are a die-hard Thai food fan and trek to the nearby suburb of Lake Oswego for the best of the best. I think the menu is bigger than it needs to be because the family chefs do the staples flawlessly.

Thai fried rice, wide noodles, and pad thai are the mainstays, but I've never gone away disappointed. *SB*

$ Wong's King Seafood

8733 SE Division St, Ste 101
788.8883
www.wongsking.com
Mon–Fri 10a–11p, Sat–Sun 9:30a–11p; dim sum served until 3p

You might not expect a trek to a strip mall in far Southeast Portland to yield the best Hong Kong–style Chinese food in the city, but that's exactly what you get if you venture out to Wong's King Seafood. One of the only Chinese restaurants in town that serves a traditional Peking duck dinner, Wong's has rapidly become one of the hottest spots around for that dish, as well as dim sum and other authentic Chinese fare. Word has spread so rapidly about Wong's that despite its grand size, larger parties may find themselves waiting up to an hour for a table. Know that it's worth the wait and consider paying a visit during off-hours or midweek if you feel the need to hurry. For the ravenous in a rush, there's a take-out window next door to the dining room where you can get orders of succulent barbecue duck for the road. *MM*

Russell Street Bar-B-Que

325 NE Russell St
528.8224
www.russellstreetbbq.com
Sun–Thurs 11a–9p, Fri–Sat 11a–10p

They say the barbecue is all in the sauce. On Russell Street, the barbecue is all in the sauce, the meat, the sides, and even the low-emission smokehouse. First choose your meat: pork, sausage, chicken breast, brisket, or turkey, all hormone-free and grain-fed without antibiotics. Russell Street Bar-B-Que even serves wild grilled salmon and smoked tofu. Sauces are an array of geographic specialties like the tasty thin North Carolina vinegar version; the extra spicy Virginia Killer; or the Classic Virginia, a thick and sweet tomato-based sauce. Look on the counter for more heat—you'll find bottles of hot sauces from all over with such crazy combinations as tequila lime chipotle and chocolate chili. Every barbecue meal needs dependable sides, and the candied yams and "mess o' greens" fit the bill. Come with a big party so you can sample the whole lineup. *SB*

$ Burgerville

1122 SE Hawthorne Blvd (and other locations)
230.0479
www.burgerville.com
Daily 7a–11p

How can you support your values of sustainability while getting a drive-thru burger and shake? Look no further than Burgerville, where workers have health care and local chain locations are run on 100 percent wind power. Seasonal shake flavors include huckleberry, locally harvested before turning the vanilla ice-cream base deep purple. Burgers are made with locally raised country beef, and as an alternative to standard fries, which stand on their own with crispy flavor, you can choose sweet potato fries or hand-battered onion rings. All this with expeller-pressed canola oil used for all frying—nothing at Burgerville contains trans fat. So go ahead, break your no fast-food rule and head to this reinvented American classic. *SB*

$$ Papa Haydn

5829 SE Milwaukie Ave
291.8350
www.papahaydn.com
Mon–Thurs 11:30a–10p, Fri 11:30a–12a, Sat 11:30a–12a, Sun 10a–9p

On a weekend afternoon, nothing beats the lunch special menu at Papa Haydn for a blissful moment away. Parsnip ravioli, fine sandwiches stuffed with Italian salamis, squash risotto topped with mascarpone, and Gorgonzola fondue are stars in their own right, but these dishes are nearly overshadowed by Papa's specialty, the dessert course. You cannot order wrong, but I'll tell you about a few of the plates I've licked clean. Mayan Chocolate Torte is dusted with spice and rich fair-trade cocoa. The signature Boccone Dolce is layers of melty meringue interspersed with fresh fruit and dappled with dark chocolate. Cheesecake flavors are plentiful, and these cakes are as rich a rendition as I've ever had. A plethora of mousse tortes, pies, and Viennese buttercream-covered cakes on display across the back of this cozy restaurant give you a detailed idea of what you have to look forward to. A second location in the Pearl District has an entirely different feel but the same cakes. *SB*

Amnesia Brewing

832 N Beech St

281.7708

Mon–Thurs 2p–11p, Fri–Sun 12p–12a

On a rainy day, get warmed up inside Amnesia Brewing with a Desolation IPA and a bar seat with a view of the steel casks. On sunny days, catch some rays on the streetside patio, where there's space for several family reunion parties and bratwurst enough for everyone. The tofu brat is most excellent with a pile of kraut on top, or if spice is your thing, go for the Hot Bier of the Polish. All sausages are made locally with organic or hormone-free meats. Special beers are switched up each season so you can reach for a standard favorite like the Dusty Trail Pale or the Slow Train Porter, or venture into the great unknown with a new flavor. *SB*

$$$ Veritable Quandary

1220 SW 1st Ave

227.7342

www.vqpdx.com

Mon–Fri 11:30a–3p & 5–10p, Sat–Sun 9:30a–3p & 5–10p

On lazy late Sunday afternoons, the jet-setter air of Portland's quintessential fancy restaurant fades away. A full brunch menu caters to everyone's mood, with hearty quinoa and lentil veggie burgers, brioche French toast, and local Dungeness crab frittatas. Inexpensive and simple kid offerings include grilled cheese and pancakes. With each plate, the utmost care is taken not only to ensure fresh, mostly local, and organic ingredients, but also to represent a complementary spectrum of flavors. Sweet vinaigrette–tossed microgreens lighten up heartier dishes. Perfect guacamole and crème fraîche dazzle fluffy scrambled eggs. For weekend brunch, VQ, as it is lovingly called by locals, has a comfortable family feel and outstanding Pacific Northwest fare. And indeed, it is a veritable quandary deciding among the delectable menu choices. *SB*

Kiddlywinks

Take the kids!

There's a slew of kid-oriented things to do in Portland for parents of all dispositions: big kid adventures, more pristine kid-shopping sprees, messy adventures, and new challenges like learning to swim. Have fun!

Annie Bloom's Books

7834 SW Capitol Hwy
246.0053
www.annieblooms.com
Mon–Sat 9a–10p, Sun 9a–9p

My favorite kids' book selection is without a doubt inside these walls. And the best part is that there are regular free book events and readings that bring this cozy community shop to life. Annie Bloom's Books is what I imagine to be every parent's dream—great books for adults up front, and a safe and colorful children's section that will please tots and teens alike. Inspire the reader and learner in your young one without having to mention those words at all. *SB*

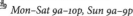 Grammy and Nonna's Toys

4940 N Lombard St
432.8732
www.grammyandnonnastoys.com
Tues–Sat 10a–5:30p

Encouraging creative play and featuring games and toys suited for both solitary and shared play, this store's products are all absolutely environmentally safe. The building set selection and science games, sets, and puzzles are out of this world, and the shop features arts and crafts projects that boys and girls will surely dive into. I bought a little weaving set here to play with, for myself. I guess I'll never really grow up. *SB*

 Missing Link

3562 SE Hawthorne Blvd
235.0032
www.missinglinktoys.com
Tues–Fri 12–7p, Sat 11a–7p, Sun 11a–6p

I suppose this isn't really a kids' store, but there are tons of puffy, bunny, kitty, shiny, blingy, funny thingys. And for that reason, I could see myself buying up an armload of these treasures to please a young one. Not the expensive ones, mind you—some sculptures here are collector's items that run in the hundreds and even thousands of dollars. But there are plenty of affordable and fun trinkets and toys with an artful slant for sale at Missing Link. *SB*

Grandma Leeth's Restaurant

10122 SW Park Wy
291.7800
www.grandmaleeths.com
Tues–Sun 10:30a–9p

Wonder what world comfort food is? Enter Grandma Leeth's Restaurant for a tour through global kitchen cleverness. The restaurant's namesake lives on through her recipes, which her family lovingly prepares for yours. Bring your child, and he or she will be supervised by childcare professionals and fed while you wine and dine with your sweetie. Here's to having dates even while rearing young ones! *SB*

Mt. Tabor Park

SE 60th Ave and Salmon St
www.portlandonline.com/parks/finder/ (search "Mt Tabor")

Out in Portland's southeastern backyard sits Mount Tabor, a beautiful landmark covered with goodies for those in the know. Savvy dog owners know this is one of the most interesting fenced-in off-leash areas, where your pooch can slalom through the trees and hike up the mountainside. Further up is a network of hiking trails—look for the reservoir, as that trail is easiest for younger children. It is hard to believe that Mount Tabor was once a volcano, back when triceratops hovered above the fiery plumes. Come early for a misty view of the city, or visit at dusk to catch a colorful sunset. If you happen to be in Portland when it is snowing (a rare occurrence), this is the best spot to sled. As if that weren't enough, Mount Tabor has free tennis courts, an epic playground, prime picnicking grounds, and perfect pavement for inline skating and skateboarding (or zooming downhill on a homemade vehicle as is done at the annual Soapbox Derby, see "Calendar" chapter, page 220). *SB*

☼ Rock 'n' Roll Camp for Girls

🏺 445.4991

✎ www.girlsrockcamp.org

♨ Kids can be inspiring, right? What about a 9-year-old whaling on a drum kit? Oh and by the way, she's never played the drums before five days ago. And that song she and her all-girl band were playing? They wrote that, all of it. The Portland Rock 'n' Roll Camp for Girls was founded in 2001 out of the DIY and riot grrrl philosophies. The Rock 'n' Roll Camp is a mostly volunteer-run nonprofit that aims to build girls' self-esteem through music creation and performance. During a five-day period, the summer camp provides workshops and technical training to create leadership opportunities, cultivate a supportive community of peers and mentors, and encourage social change and the development of life skills. Rock 'n' Roll Camp has spread to cities across the country and even the world, and it has grown to include a Ladies Rock Camp (for those of us who wish we had a Rock 'n' Roll Camp for Girls when we were kids), a year-round internship and after-school program, and even a record label. Who rocks? GIRLS ROCK! *JP*

Casual Night Out

Dining and delighting in a relaxed atmosphere

There's always a time when you just want to kick back and have a relaxed evening out. Portlanders are known the world over for their casual, hip flair. Go out, but go in comfort, with the divine purpose of repose.

$ Mi Wa

𝕍 6852 NE Sandy Blvd

🦝 493.7460

🏛 Daily 11a–10p

🚌 Pedal up Sandy Boulevard and you'll find yourself in an unlikely culinary mecca. Mi Wa is another simple-looking eatery featuring complex flavors in this far-out area of Northeast Portland. Order fresh and light *goi ngo sen tom thit*, a lotus stem, shrimp, and pork salad; sandwiches like *banh xeo*; and roasted, toasted squid *muc rang muoi*. Pho is on the menu, too, but I favor Mi Wa's incredible lighter dishes and fishy feasts. *SB*

$$ Sagittarius

2710 N Killingsworth St

289.7557

http://sagittariusbar.blogspot.com

Mon–Sat 4p–12a, Sun 4–10p,

Once I came in to this chill, mostly pink restaurant-bar-hangout, I got over any hesitation about the namesake zodiac sign. I may find most Sags to be hard headed, but not this one! Order veggie and meat burgers, or go out on a limb and try the "Wilky's Comet" burger, with a beer-battered, deep-fried meatless burger patty. Signature cocktails are a smash hit, especially on Mondays when Happy Hour lasts all day, plus many can be made "mock" for non drinkers. Pesto or rosemary mac and cheese, loaded salads, and hand-cut fries are the best orders from the fun-loving menu, (which includes items like octopus arm, young turk, and baby luau. SB

$ BeWon Korean Restaurant

1203 NW 23rd Ave

464.9222

www.bewonrestaurant.com

Mon–Thurs 5–9p, Fri 11:30a–2:30p, Sat–Sun 5–10p

Unlike the Korean barbecue joints around town, BeWon Korean Restaurant has a less hands-on approach to marinated meats. That and the nonmeat menu items set this place apart. Order sweet potato noodles, mushroom caps, and simmered pork and pancakes, and savor each dish with a more upscale spread of sauces and kimchis. SB

$$ Alexis Restaurant

215 W Burnside St

224.8577

www.alexisfoods.com

Mon–Thurs 11:30a–2p & 5–10p; Fri–Sat 11:30a–2p & 5–11p; Sun 5–10p

A big family-style restaurant is the place to go with your whole gaggle to try some new foods and have boisterous discussions about your comings and goings. Alexis Restaurant specializes in these festive occasions with family menus. Pay per person to try all the best dishes, most famously the moussaka (pronounced "moo-sah-ka," not "moo-say-ka"—Greek doesn't have a long *a* sound), a classic Greek lasagnalike comfort food made with lamb and potatoes. Get your kids prepared for some wiggly marinated octopus to go along with the toasty breads and filling appetizers, while you down some ouzo. *Opa!* SB

$$ Cha Ba Thai

5810 NE Sandy Blvd

282.3970

Mon–Thurs 11:30a–3p & 5–9p; Fri 11:30a–3p & 5–10p; Sat 12–10p; Sun 5–9p

In a less dense block of Sandy Boulevard, Cha Ba Thai is a wash of color and flavor that people count on for superb Thai food. Appetizers like fried tofu and spring rolls are both light, not oily like others you'll find. This warming spot has the best soups in town and also the best pad thai in Portland, GrassRoutes writers can agree. From the melted-down rice stew with tender chicken to the ever-present tom kha coconut soup—you can opt for the classic *gai* version with chicken or the veggie version with flavorful mushrooms—you can't go wrong with anything you order here. Don't pass up the whole steamed fish, spilling over with natural juices and Thai spices; it is a real crowd-pleaser. Plentiful curry and satay options are popular with all, bringing *sanuk*, or good fun-loving pleasure, to all who partake. Cha Ba is a few blocks away from the main drag but an immediate teleportation to Thailand. SB

$$ Nostrana

1401 SE Morrison St

234.2427

www.nostrana.com

Mon–Fri 11a–2p, Sun–Thurs 5–10p, Fri–Sat 5–11p

Housed in an airy yet warm barnlike structure, Nostrana is a happy meeting place of casual sophistication. Come for a beer and a snack-time artisan pizza, or an elegant Italian wine and guinea hen. The simple margherita pizza is best, with the option of arugula and duck egg piled on top. Meat and fish dishes are excellent—pork, lamb, and halibut are treated like celebrities and paired with understated veggies like puréed celery root or caramelized cipollini onions. Table bread and focaccia are baked fresh each morning and greet you at your table with a robust and nutty olive oil. Save room for Nostrana's superb panna cotta, my secret indicator of a real heavyweight Italian restaurant, and the inconceivably good flourless chocolate cake, which you may have to ask for, as it is often left off the menu. Nostrana's chef babies her main dishes, paying less attention to salads and small plates, but she has clearly mastered the fine palette of Italian flavors in a restaurant with real ambiance. *SB*

$ El Palenque

8324 SE 17th Ave

231.5140

www.elpalenque.org

Mon–Fri 11:30a–9:30p, Sat–Sun 12:30–9:30p

Salvadorian cuisine isn't always the first thing you think of for a casual weeknight outing with the gang, but El Palenque is one of the best places for a family feast. Papusas and Salvadorian creamy-style tamales are hearty and delicious. El Palenque's guacamole menu includes a Guatemalan mint version, a tequila concoction, and the tasty Salvadorian classic served with hard-boiled eggs. Everything is handmade in-house and reasonably priced. The restaurant also serves a full list of Mexican favorites. I recommend the family platters that include all of El Palenque's kitchen highlights and are certain to satisfy everyone around the table. *SB*

$$ Jo Bar and Rotisserie

701 NW 23rd Ave

222.0048

www.papahaydn.com

Mon–Thurs 11:30a–10p, Fri–Sat 11:30a–12a, Sun 11:30a–10p

Don't ever disregard a round sofa just because it's different. It's OK to sit close to the stove sometimes. It's OK to have dessert first. Be indulgent when the time is right. Throw out your mother's rules and adopt Jo Bar and Rotisserie for a luscious evening of food and good company at this purplish, reasonably priced wonderland of all things passionate. Perfectly roasted chicken with locally grown seasonal vegetables and a flight of wines or a round of well drinks will relax even the most stress-heavy shoulders. Stare into the eyes of those near and dear and share a rich moment without parting with all your dough. These dishes are made to rustle things up, in the best kind of way. *SB*

ⓥ Pok Pok

🏵 *3226 SE Division St*

☼ *232.1387*

ℝ *www.pokpokpdx.com*

Mon–Fri 11:30a–10:30p, Sat 5–10:30p

Pok Pok was once only a stand on Division Street, a perfect place to pop by when the weather was kind or for an incomparable papaya salad to go. The shack still remains and is complemented by the Whiskey Soda Lounge, located in the basement of the adjacent house, for dining inside the stylish wood-paneled rooms. Yes, Pok Pok is a Thai food restaurant, and it uses the freshest and most local ingredients possible, but you won't find pad thai on this menu. What you will find here is spicy Thai street food, the signature dish being *kai yaang*, a roasted game hen dish. The menu option I adore is *phat makheua yao*, with the most flavorful and perfectly textured eggplant I have ever eaten. The prospect of whiskey is also a draw; I've gone through a couple of "education" sessions here, learning the wonders of this strong drink. After the whiskey or cocktail of your choice, stay for dinner, and remember that the lounge is closed between 2:30 and 5pm. Bring a crew, chow down family-style to sample a variety of choices, and don't forget to order one or two dishes more than your number—these are not large servings. With an award for Best Restaurant of the Year from the *Oregonian*, at Pok Pok you can't go wrong. *SB*

$  Nicholas Restaurant

ⓥ *318 SE Grand Ave*

🏵 *235.5123*

www.nicholasrestaurant.com

Mon–Sat 10a–9p, Sun 12–9p

The first time I came here, I was in the company of a Nicholas Restaurant veteran. She found us seats in the tiny dining room and handled ordering, asking for the vegetarian meze for two, an order of Stephen's Chicken, a side of baba ghanoush, and the big bread. So good was that meal that to this day, more than 15 years later, I rarely deviate from that particular set of dishes. If you don't have a Nicholas Restaurant veteran to do your ordering, choose whatever strikes your fancy, but make sure to ask for that large, house-made pita. It will add a few dollars to your final bill, but if you don't ask for it, you'll

Pok Pok

be served some insipid, mass-produced pita that isn't worth your time, especially when such amazing freshly baked bread is available. Plan to sit back and take your time with your meal. The service isn't always speedy, but the relaxed atmosphere is the perfect setting for such flavor. *MM*

¡Oba!

555 NW 12th Ave
228.6161
www.obarestaurant.com
Daily 5p–late (bar opens at 4p)

Just walking into ¡Oba! makes me feel warmer—the colors, the smells, the "new" Latin menu, the friendly service, the inexpensive happy hours. Coming for dinner is a fiesta even without a good reason to celebrate—order the grape and almond gazpacho for something uniquely refreshing, and the mesquite-grilled gaucho-style prime rib or the Cuban pulled flank steak for meaty satisfaction. ¡Oba! is classed-up south-of-the-border dining. *SB*

$$ Andina Restaurant

1314 NW Glisan St
228.9535
www.andinarestaurant.com
Mon–Thurs 11:30a–2:30p & 5:30–9:30p; Fri–Sat 11:30a–2:30p & 5:30–10p; Sun 5:30–9:30p

An unexpected star in the exciting Portland dining scene, Andina is haute cuisine inspired by the Andes Mountains and Peruvian edible traditions. The elegant atmosphere of the dining room and the casual comfort of the bar area hint at the distinct ways to experience this incredible restaurant. Come between 4 and 6pm for the affordable and always changing Happy Hour menu, or for the delectable house cocktail menu, or to sup on a few tapas plates, or to savor the finer side of Andina with course after course of sublime plates. The sumptuous rack of lamb, always made to order, is paired with a creamy two-cheese and potato *timbale*, perfect for sopping up the meat juices. Pisco-brined chicken is pan-roasted with subtle pickled onions, or opt for the pork tenderloin with squash and gorgonzola ravioli and green apples— an instant favorite. Navigate the menus with the helpful servers and you'll go away with a prime knowledge of classic Peruvian cuisine. The incredibly long tapas menu allows for three sizes—small, medium, or large for big parties.

After one bite of the Yuca Rellena, a cheese stuffed yucca with mild pepper sauce, or the empanadas caseras de carne, a flacky pastry with slow-cooked beef, raisins and Botija olives, you may find it takes more than one trip to make it to the main course menu. In my mind, a trip to Peru wouldn't be complete without a Pisco Sour, and the one here is especially good with real cane sugar and a dapple of bitters on top. If pisco is too strong for you, don't worry, the cocktail list accommodates sweet, strong, sour, and savory tastes with a natural lime daiquiri, a vacation-y Ron-Yki-On made with roasted ginger-infused rum, and a "novoandino" cocktail called Sacsayhuaman made with habeñero-infused vodka and passion fruit purée. You could come just for the drinks, although, as you've heard, I don't recommend visiting without at least eating something. Experiment with the many uses for quinoa—even on the tempting dessert menu—an ancient grain from these mountains. *SB*

Corbett Fish House

 5901 SW Corbett Ave, 246.4434
4343 SE Hawthorne Blvd, 548.4434
www.corbettfishhouse.com
Mon–Fri 11a–10p, Sat 12–10p, Sun 12–9p, Happy Hour 3–6p daily

My dream come true is a place where I can nosh on gluten-free and sustainable fish tacos for under $4 at happy hour while sitting in the sun and sipping on a lemon drop. Corbett Fish House and its sister restaurant, Hawthorne Fish House, follow the Monterey Bay Aquarium's strict guidelines for sustainable seafood in order to keep the oceans healthy and our bellies satisfied. You'll do flips over the fish tacos, yummy calamari, and heaping bay shrimp quesadilla. Bring all your friends and smile because you are supporting a truly conscientious business and eating just about the healthiest version of fried food I can think of. *SB*

Pho Van

 *3404 SE Hawthorne Blvd*
230.1474
 www.phovanrestaurant.com
Tues–Sun 11a–9:30p

Pho Van is not your average Vietnamese kitchen. As far from a hole-in-the-wall as you can get in Portland, it is a palace of this intricate and time-honored food tradition. The grand size of the dining area isn't isolating because it is stylishly filled with antiques and art from the homeland. The menu features *cuon* handrolls made of rice paper, which you can fill with a mix of steamed and seared meats and veggies. Pho and vermicelli noodle soups are made with clear, flavorful broth, but aren't the only soothing soup options—on a rainy day one of the rice stick soups will seemingly bring sunshine to the day. The long menu incorporates many lesser-known Vietnamese dishes like fried rice pancakes and marinated pork sausage, or turmeric-stuffed shrimp, but whatever you try here you can expect to be fresh, and beautifully served at the very least. This is my favorite place for take out when I am not feeling myself, and for an in-restaurant culinary adventure on an especially wet and gray day. *SB*

Green Wok

11137 SW Capitol Hwy
246.1683
www.greenwok.org
Sun–Thurs 11a–9p, Fri–Sat 11a–10p

It might not be the most fancy or refined of Portland's many top-notch eateries, but this all-vegan Chinese menu is just what the doctor ordered if you've just come off a hiking trail, or are craving some sticky, filling General Tso's on a rainy day. Lunchtime and weekends are great, but for a quick and easy dinner with healthful ingredients and standout flavor, Green Wok is a winner. Some of the most popular orders are unexpected favorites like Bird-Nest Chicken, a tofu-based fake meat with fresh veggies served on a pile of crispy noodles, and the Tofu Hushpuppies, a pungent and fruity sauce on fried tofu served inside a crown of steamed broccoli. The lunch buffet is a mere $6.50, but Green Wok is affordable all the time, and a place where I am comfortable in my sweats without feeling inappropriately lax. *SB*

Queen of Sheba

2413 NE Martin Luther King Jr Blvd
287.6302
www.queenofsheba.biz
Sun–Wed 5–10p; Thurs–Sat 12–3p & 5–10p

Anytime I get the chance to sit back as chickpea, mushroom, and lentil stews soak into fresh *injera*, I get a deeper sense of relaxation. I'm sure it's because I know that just around the corner I will be munching down on the saucy, saturated dish, a traditional experience that is a must for a soul-satisfying midday feast. *SB*

$$ Ohana Hawaiian Cafe

6320 NE Sandy Blvd
335.5800
www.ohanahawaiiancafe.com
Mon–Sat 11a–9p

All around Portland are glimpses of a bountiful Hawaiian community, and Ohana Hawaiian Cafe attests to that fact. Completely authentic, with most ingredients sourced locally, this family joint is a perfect spot for a satisfying bite. The Hawaiian version of ceviche, called *lomi-lomi*, has delicate salmon and bold spices, and is a nice complement to one of Ohana's meat dishes. Whether you see it as a good or a bad thing, Hawaiian cuisine exhibits a determined propensity toward all things macaroni salad—this creamy side dish is a constant companion to every menu item. Kids are certain to enjoy the sunny atmosphere as well. *SB*

SubRosa

2601 SE Clinton St
233.1955
www.subrosa.textdriven.com
Tues–Thurs, Sun 5–9p; Fri–Sat 5–10p; Sat–Sun 8:30a–1p

What started as one of the West Coast's premier secret dining clubs is now open for dinner six days a week and on weekends for an enticing brunch. SubRosa has long been an inspiration of mine. The locavore mentality seeps into the soul of the menu, influencing the recipes with a touch of Portland spirit inspired by the chef. You won't be disappointed. *SB*

Chaos Cafe and Parlor

2620 SE Powell Blvd
546.8112
www.myspace.com/chaoscafe, http://parlourpdx.com
Cafe: Sun–Thurs 9a–4p, Fri–Sat 9a–9p
Parlor: Fri–Sat 7p–12a, Sun 4p–12a

The menu is tight and the price is right. Chaos Cafe is a bastion of subculture, linked up with the Parlor, which puts on free or low-cost concerts every weekend. Order from the all-organic menu and you'll be happily surprised at the bountiful plates laid before you: Homemade granola for a snack and the curried tofu and veggie plate are my standbys. The walls are covered with imaginative murals, and organic Hopworks ale is served in nice, big, chilled pitchers. *SB*

 Iorio

912 SE Hawthorne Blvd
445.4716
www.ioriorestaurant.com
Tues–Sat 5–9p

There's hardly an item on this menu that I don't want to start eating the minute I read about it: wild-caught calamari with a cornmeal crust, Oregon cheese plate, or real spaghetti and meatballs. Here you'll find only sustainable ingredients and accessible dishes done well. Why complicate things when you are so skilled at doing the basics right? *SB*

Pub Quizzes in PDX

Portland is a rainy place. There's no other way to say it. If you aren't regularly in Pacific Northwest weather, you'll quickly learn that the drops bring locals together under all kinds of shelters for all kinds of fun. Think art-house theaters, 24-hour donut shops, and pub games. Have some serious interactive fun at one of the many pubs in Portland to host quizzes. Pub quizzes usually start at 7pm, but call ahead to make sure before you jet out the door. Whether it's cartoon trivia, geography and politics, or jazz facts, everyone has a place on the team!

Mondays

CC Slaughters
219 Davis St
248.9135

Tuesdays

Biddy McGraw's
6000 NE Glisan St
233.1178

Bridgeport Ale House
3632 SE Hawthorne Blvd
233.6540

Wednesdays

Thirsty Lion Pub and Grill
71 SW 2nd Ave
222.2155

Space Room Lounge
4800 SE Hawthorne Blvd
235.6957

Sellwood Public House
8132 SE 13th Ave
736.0719

Roscoe's
8105 SE Stark St
255.0049

Thursdays

Belmont Inn
3357 SE Belmont St
232.1998

Hal's Tavern
1308 SE Morrison
232.1259

Various Nights

Green Dragon Bistro and Brewpub
928 SE 9th Ave
517.0606

Film Buffs

Movies a-go-go

A night out at the movies is a mandatory pastime in these parts. Portland's culture is silver-screen oriented, so skip the big movieplex and head to an art-house theater to see an old favorite or a new hit from around the block or across the globe. Portland's art-house theaters are mainstream—the culture is soaked through with film buff-ness. There are fabulous film festivals all year round (see the "Calendar" chapter, page 220), and you shouldn't expect to pay more than $5 for a ticket to the show. Also, there are more theaters than not that serve frosty microbrewed beer during the shows . . . who cares if it's raining?

$ Roseway Theater

7229 NE Sandy Blvd
287.8119
www.rosewaytheater.com

The Roseway Theater has been around since the 1920s, when each show began with an organ recital. In the same family-owned, independent fashion, this historic theater blacks all lights during shows and provides visitors with a neighborhood movie-theater feel. It's close to the airport in case you've got a layover or a long wait, and it isn't far from several great eateries farther down Sandy Boulevard. *SB*

World Cavalcade

Scottish Rite Center, 1512 SW Morrison St at SW 15th Ave
241.2575
www.worldtravelfilms.com
Film schedule varies

For over 30 years, World Cavalcade, hosted by the Scottish Rite Center, has brought the world to the screen with its intimate portraits of filmmakers and their travels. Go see the beauties and bounties of a journey to Slovenia, a coproduction including the film and a narrative story by the filmmakers themselves. For a full-scale trek, buy a ticket package to circumnavigate the globe without leaving your seat. After seeing these images and hearing the stories of such open-minded voyagers, preconceived notions and generalizations must fade away, with only admiration and curiosity remaining. *SB*

$$ Living Room Theaters
341 SW 10th Ave
971.222.2010
www.livingroomtheaters.com

A pioneering theater that has stepped completely and entirely into the digital age, Living Room Theaters offers as complete a cinematic outing as you'll find anywhere. Sample from a tapas menu of locally sourced goodies, sip cocktails or mocktails from the full bar, and watch high-definition art films from local and international directors. Before 4:30pm under 21s are allowed, and a daily menu is served from lunch through the times when the films start lighting up the walls. There are five or six theaters, so you've got gobs of choices and tastes. *SB*

Cinema Project
Screening locations:
New American Art Union, 922 SE Ankeny St
Northwest Film Center's Whitsell Auditorium, 1219 SW Park St,
232.8269
www.cinemaproject.org

Film festivals, cutting-edge art flicks, and a historical repertoire of silver-screen greats are brought to Portland viewers all year long by this important organization. Each season features an average of four themes ranging from Andy Warhol to "First Person in a Globalized World" to documentaries from Lebanese women. Whether you are a passionate film critic or have never been to see an obscure documentary, the moving images this project presents are so diverse and eloquent, there is sure to be something that piques your interest. *SB*

$ Avalon Theatre
3451 SE Belmont St
238.1617
www.wunderlandgames.com

The Avalon Theatre is the answer to the afternoon doldrums—or the whatever doldrums, for that matter. What makes this place unique is the incredible schedule and the awesome arcade. Movies run in two auditoriums all day, every day, so anytime is the right time for a good flick or a pinball demolition. Tickets are $2 for most shows, on occasion a whopping three, and you can get your candy and popcorn pile for less than any mainstream theater. Save up your spare change for the vintage arcade games. *sb*

Hollywood Theater

4122 NE Sandy Blvd

281.4215

www.filmactionoregon.org

With the help of Film Action Oregon, the Hollywood Theater has maintained its historic roots while inspiring Oregonian filmmakers young and old, novice and experienced. From the 1926 premiere of *More Pay—Less Work*, to the underappreciated Cinerama wide-screens of the 1950s, to the Forest Film Festival of today, this landmark theater has honored the film medium and served as a catalyst for engaging ideas. As part of the educational programs hosted here, special attention is paid to young documentary filmmakers. Watch the recognizable blinking sign illuminate the night air, waltz to the Wurlitzer, and catch a film from any decade in movie history, classic to current. *sb*

Kennedy School Theater

Kennedy School Hotel, 5736 NE 33rd Ave

249.3983; movie hotline: 249.7474 ext 4

www.mcmenamins.com

If only I had known about Kennedy School before I got through grade school—I never would have stayed where I was! Rather, I would have gone to "class" at Kennedy School, where beer and sofas overtake elementary school classrooms, and it's considered normal to spend the better part of the day lounging about watching art films. Popcorn pours endlessly from the kitchen, and there are no pesky children around to cry at the pivotal plot points. *sb*

The Academy Theater

7818 SE Stark St

252.0500

www.academytheaterpdx.com

The older, wiser cousin of Portland's teeming mass of great independent cinemas, the Academy Theater has the reclining seats and spaciousness of a

Hollywood Theater

sprawling suburban multiplex at art-house prices. The steady $3 adult price can be upgraded with a beer and pizza for a little extra dinero. Monday blues fade into oblivion with a $4 double feature. Before 8pm you can bring the kiddlywinks for just $1—just be careful not to overstimulate their young minds with violent or overly depressing flicks. *SB*

Bagdad Theater and Pub

 3702 SE Hawthorne Blvd
 *225.5555*
www.mcmenamins.com
Mon–Sat 11a–1a, Sun 12p–12a

The ever-present McMenamin brothers and brewmasters have created a slew of pubs, theaters, restaurants, and hotels across the city. A smaller incarnation of their usual grandeur, the Bagdad Theater and Pub is Moorish architecture-meets-hearty pints-meet-iconic Hollywood. Enjoy beautifully restored mosaic work on your way into the ornate theater. This is a great spot for hungry moviegoers—salads and sandwiches are served to you while you bask in the glow of the silver screen. I highly recommend indulging in the locally farmed marionberry cobbler while a thriller gets you scooting toward the edge of your seat or into the arms of your sweetie. *SB*

Laurelhurst Theater

 *2735 E Burnside St*
 *232.5511*
www.laurelhursttheater.com

Don't think for one minute that chillaxing around PDX isn't a full-blown tourist activity—at least for those interested in being authentic to the city. There are seriously inventive minds here, dedicated talents, and diverse innovation, but there is an undeniably chill vibe running through the current of this great city's culture. Laurelhurst Theater is a great place to be a tourist while taking a load off and just watching a good flick. One of the oldest silver-screen theaters in the city, it dates back to 1923, when it was a big draw for black-and-white classics. The pizza is yummy, and you can order a pitcher of beer to share with your buddies if it isn't a matinee all-ages screening. *SB*

St. Johns Theater

8704 N Lombard St

286.1768

www.mcmenamins.com

Quite possibly the best deal in Portland's movie land, this funky old theater near the bridge of the same name serves up cheap pizza and beer to go along with its cheap tickets, plus there are tables in the theaters. Talk about dinner and a movie! *SB*

Cinema 21

616 NW 21st Ave

223.4515

www.cinema21.com

A Portland classic, the locally owned and independently operated Cinema 21 plays host to some of the city's most ravishing film festivals. In addition, it often plays rare and unique films other theaters dodge. Check out the weird and wild cosmic-hex cult films of the 1970s or the brash films from today's urban youth and gay activists. This place will push your buttons (in a good way) and make you think. When you come up for air, no matter which direction you turn, there will be a great restaurant awaiting your tableside pontifications. *SB*

Clinton Street Theater

2522 SE Clinton St

238.8899

www.clintonsttheater.com

Daily from 5p

During the hot summer months, the Clinton Street Theater is a cool venue for catching a vintage flick or a big-screen replay. On a rainy night I had to keep my coat on, but the next time I went I brought a snuggly blanket in my bag and got so comfy it was hard to go home! It was worth bundling up and getting reacquainted with *Buffalo 66* and an overflowing basket of popcorn. As the smallest operational brewery in the state of Oregon, the walk-in-closet-sized space yields some high-class suds. Match a monstrous hamburger with your unique brew and groove to live music playing most nights in the attached cafe before or after the show. *SB*

Volunteer

Fun, quick, and easy ways to give back to the city

Volunteering is the best way to meet locals. Unite in a common cause to make a positive impact in some area or another, and you're sure to make fast friends. Portland is a city of eager volunteers, so it follows that there are some interesting opportunities for helpers. Roll up your sleeves!

Portland Radio Authority

222.5278
www.praradio.org

Portland Radio Authority (PRA) is the ultimate in free speech wavelengths. Volunteer to be a DJ or help with community outreach work. You can also send in your songs to *praradio@yahoo.com*—record deal or no—and they'll put your music in the mix. Click the DJ Application link on the web site to download a volunteer form, or contact PRA directly when you want to start broadcasting! *SB*

Portland Impact

988.4996
www.portlandimpact.org/volunteer
Hourly, daily, and ongoing opportunities

This wonderful organization does a plethora of good service for low-income elderly folks and families around Portland. It runs several housing complexes and it can always use your help. Put a smile on a homebound senior's face by fixing up his or her yard, or give someone in a shelter a haircut. Help distribute donated food or spiff up a room in one of the shelters to make it ready for a new tenant. There are many volunteer opportunities that will get you talking to lots of residents. *SB*

Friends of Trees

284.8733
www.friendsoftrees.org/events
Events year-round, usually weekends, hourly

Put on a sturdy pair of shoes and get ready to have fun with trees and neighbors. Portlanders are seriously tree-savvy, and this group brings together all kinds of people to plant trees and restore wildlife all around the area. Check the Friends of Trees events calendar for things to do most weekends of the year. You don't need to register or know anything about how to plant trees—just show up, as tools and guidance are provided. This is one of my favorite organizations in Portland, and it's certainly a fun way to spend a few hours while meeting some great people. *SB*

Parks and Recreation Department

823.2223
www.portlandonline.com/parks
Hourly, daily, and ongoing opportunities

One of the most popular ways to volunteer in Portland is with the Parks and Recreation Department—maybe that's one of the reasons it is so great! Choose to volunteer with kids and community centers, as a youth coach, or just for a day clearing parks of invasive plants. This organization is community based and supported by a genuine drive to improve the environment and community life. Check the web site for the time that's best for you to join in the cause—from the main page, click the volunteer link to see all the options. Search for specific programs like the Library Volunteer program, Community Gardens program, or Urban Forestry program. *SB*

Film Action Oregon

www.hollywoodtheatre.org/volunteer.html

Film Action Oregon, the force behind our favorite Hollywood Theater, keeps volunteers happy with free movie passes. Sign up to help with film festival events or as an usher at the Hollywood Theater. Take a closer look around Portland by delivering newsletters to coffee shops and boutiques all about town. *SB*

City Repair

www.cityrepair.org, volunteer@cityrepair.org
Varied opportunities

Citizen activists unite! There are hundreds of events and volunteer-based projects throughout the year that focus on socially integrating neighborhoods and giving a jolt of culture from the grassroots level. The idea has since spread beyond Portland to other cities. Bring back the local, community feel to streets and neighborhoods under threat of isolation. The types of jobs you may find yourself doing are so vast I cannot do them justice here, but go to the web site, get involved, and you'll have so much fun, you'll forget that you're working!

Oregon Museum of Science and Industry

239.7814
www.omsi.edu/info/volunteer
Varied opportunities
Whether you are greeting school kids or helping with Japanese-inspired summer camp, your time will be well spent at the Oregon Museum of Science and Industry (OMSI), whose aim is to make science education fun for all.

U.S. Fish and Wildlife Service

2600 SE 98th Ave, #100
231.6179, 1.800.344.9453
www.fws.gov
Daily and ongoing volunteer opportunities
Volunteering for the Fish and Wildlife Service can be a real adventure and a valuable learning experience. This organization will teach you to raise fish at a hatchery, band endangered birds at a wildlife sanctuary, or lead tours of preserves and parks. There are plenty of ways to lend a hand and events to inspire community action. *SB*

Multiple Sclerosis Society of Portland

297.9544
www.msoregon.org, volunteers@msoregon.org
Mostly short-term opportunities
This caring organization strives to alleviate the stresses and pains of MS through a healing community. Whether you participate in an afternoon social event or engage a patient one-on-one through the Good Neighbor program, your involvement will be greatly appreciated. *SB*

Free Geek

1731 SE 10th Ave
www.freegeek.org
Opportunities of various durations

This unique computer recycling center and tech support service connects computers with those who need them. Even if you aren't a tech-head, you'll find a place helping these cool cats out. *SB*

Other Resources

The many and varied volunteering opportunities abounding in Portland are always changing and evolving as new organizations and projects form. Here are a few places online to find current listings across the entire city:

Hands On Portland, *www.handsonportland.org*

KPSU, *www.kpsu.org*

Loaves and Fishes Centers, *www.loavesandfishesonline.org*

PortlandOnline, *www.portlandonline.com*

SCORE, *www.scorepdx.org*

Sisters of the Road, *www.sistersoftheroadcafe.org*

VOAR, *www.voar.org*

Volunteer.gov, *www.volunteer.gov*

VolunteerMatch, *www.volunteermatch.org*

Imbibe

Where to sip and swill with a local feel

Drinking, ah drinking. It is so wrong, yet it is so right. I go for places that offer mocktails and cocktails; it is rare that I am down for too much alcohol, but that doesn't mean I can't appreciate it. I love a good whiskey or bourbon; I just can't take more than one drink most of the time. But don't mind me, go and prove you're more robust at one of these ideal spots, and if you don't drink at all, no worries—most serve creative nonalcoholic bevvies next to their strongly intoxicating ones.

$$ Bar Mingo

811 NW 21st Ave

445.4646

www.barmingonw.com

Daily 4p–12a

This is one classy and warm place to loiter. Order a sensuous Italian red wine and sip away over an array of tapas. Sure, it is a bar, but I come here as much to eat as I do to chat with friends; Bar Mingo is a noshing destination. Antipasti is a must, always changing with what's in season like avocado and fennel wrapped with prosciutto. Substantial meat and pasta dishes also don't disappoint. *SB*

Moon and Sixpence

2014 NE 42nd Ave

288.7802

Tue–Thurs 3p–12a, Fri–Sat 3p–1a, Sun 4p–12a

British pubs are right at home in Portland with all the great microbrews and chill people to hang with. Moon and Sixpence is a favorite local joint, where great conversations are waiting to be had over a couple o' sudsy local pints. Amuse yourself with the long list of beers from deep in Europe—Czech pilsners and Belgian ales are as plentiful as microbrews. Warm, stick-to-your-bones food fills out the M&S experience. If you need a half-chicken dinner to set you right again, this is the place to get it, especially if you don't want to be bothered with the pomp and circumstance of trendier, shinier spots. *SB*

Teardrop Cocktail Lounge

1015 NW Everett St

445.8109

www.teardroplounge.com

Mon–Sat 4p–close

There doesn't need to be *one* good reason to love Teardrop Cocktail Lounge, because there are just too many of them. And my reasons have sexy names: Smokin' Herb, Ephemera, Sophia Loren, and To Boldly Go—all cocktails with the most interesting and enticing ingredients. Celery bitters, St. Germain elderflower liqueur, Dolin blanc vermouth, saffron, marshmallow root, and miso are all regular players in the cocktails. On especially chilly evenings, there's nothing quite like the TDL Toddy with Rittenhouse rye whiskey, agave nectar, meyer lemon juice, saffron, allspice, clove, star anise, and cinnamon. For a wake-up call, try Untold Stories with Ransom Old Tom gin, Pineau de Charentes, hibiscus-grapefruit bitters, yellow chartreuse, and house-made licorice root tincture. Even with all the creative contenders in the Portland bar scene, Teardrop's cocktails stand out. It also has a constantly evolving small plates menu to please and a wonderful wine list featuring some Willamette Valley finds. *SB*

Secret Society Lounge

116 NE Russell St
493.3600
www.secretsociety.net
Fri–Sat 5p–1a, Sun–Thurs 5p–12a

Sisters, tighten up your corsets. Folks, light your pipes and tip your top hats. Secret Society Lounge is located back in the Victorian times! Enter the deep red and black historically renovated hall and enjoy all the perks of Portland nightlife, from beers to buddies to booze. There's also a recording studio above the bar where many of the touring acts choose to lay down a track or two. *SB*

Red Fox

5128 N Albina Ave
282.2934
www.redfoxpdx.com
Daily 3p–1:30a

There's an undiscovered coolness to a watering hole like Red Fox. And a clear and present temptation of $1 cans of beer and $4 glasses of wine at all open hours, an epic coin jukebox, and a small but seasonal menu to keep me coming back like a boomerang. Kick it here with the North Portland crew. *SB*

The Goodfoot

2835 SE Stark St
239.9292
www.thegoodfoot.com
Upstairs pub, every day 6p–2:30a; downstairs lounge, Mon 8p–1:30a, Wed 9p–1:30a, Thurs–Sat 9p–2:30a, Tues and Sun special shows only; happy hour, every day 6–9p

The Goodfoot has two levels and two feels. Upstairs are big ol' hot sandwiches, ice-cold microbrews (and Pabst Blue Ribbon, too), pool tables, and that neighborhood bar feel that we all love. Downstairs features some of the best up-and-coming nationally touring and local jam bands, as well as some hip-hop and Friday's dance party, Soul Stew, with a sick DJ and a packed dance floor. It is a real smoky place, though, so if you're seriously opposed to smelling like an ashtray when you get home, you might want to skip this one. In my opinion, the music makes up for it. *RM*

Hip Chicks Do Wine

4510 SE 23rd Ave
234.3790
www.hipchicksdowine.com
Daily 11a–6p

The quickest way to get caught in the wine web of Portland and find a tasting event to pounce on is via Hip Chicks Do Wine. These winemaking women know about all the current wine events and are always planning their own. Try the merlot and pinot noir at the inner-city tasting room and come back in the evening during one of the bottle-opening parties for a thrill. *SB*

Gilt Club

306 NW Broadway
222.4458
www.giltclub.com
Mon–Sat 5p–2a; happy hour, weekdays 5–6:30p

Yum is the name of the game at the Gilt Club, where you can splurge on fancy foods without draining your wallet during the spectacular happy hour. The lush interior space hosts fine plates for just $5, including Alsatian *flammekueche* with melt-in-your-mouth caramelized onion and creamy *fromage blanc*. Steamed mussels and an Angus beef burger make a swanky entrance paired with Gilt's most famous drink, the spicy Moscow Mule. Served in a traditional pounded copper mug, this ginger-heavy drink heals your body, mind, and spirit. *SB*

Tugboat Brewing Company

711 SW Ankeny St
226.2508
www.d2m.com/Tugwebsite
Mon 5–10p, Tues–Thurs 4p–12a, Fri–Sat 4p–1a

The Tugboat Brewing Company is a sweet little jazz and indie music venue in southwest downtown Portland. This is the kind of place where you can listen to some obscure jazz musician while telling the bartender all your troubles. One of the coolest things about this bar is that there is a library's worth of books lining the shelves. Go read a book and listen to music, and you'll be all the smarter for it. *RM*

LaurelThirst Public House

2958 NE Glisan St

232.1504

www.laurelthirst.com

Seriously late nights of great loud local music happen most of the week at LaurelThirst Public House. It's a dream if you are in search of hearing the intersection of punk, pop, and folk Portland has come to be known for, but it's not a scene the weak of spirit will enjoy. With a list of sammies and salads, LaurelThirst offers more choices than your average pub, so if you need a bite, don't hesitate to grab one here before the show. The Tiananmen Turkey with cranberry sauce and cream cheese tastes better the later it gets, in my experience. *SB*

Mash Tun Brewpub

2204 NE Alberta St, #101

548.4491

www.themashtunbrewpub.com

Mon–Thurs 4p–12a, Fri 4p–1a, Sat 10a–1a, Sun 10a–12a

This pub isn't trying to put up a front—it is what it is, and that is good. Find comfort food en masse, with loads of beer in bottles and on tap to wash it down with. The bar food here isn't typical; it's extra delicious and made from locally sourced products. *SB*

Bye and Bye

1011 NE Alberta St

281.0537

Mon–Thurs 4p–2:30a, Fri 2p–2:30a, Sat 12p–2:30a, Sun 12p–2:30a

$$

With punk tunes pumping from the jukebox and wafts of nicotine seeping in from the backyard patio, Bye and Bye is southern comfort, hipster style. Food options include breaded or barbecue sauce–drenched tofu, vegan mac and cheese, black-eyed peas, and salty, spicy greens. The beer is organic microbrew and the namesake cocktail is served in mason jars. It's the kind of place that sucks you in—lord knows I'm happy to while away the hours hanging here when I'm in the mood for a pumped-up crowd. *SB*

Tanuki Izakaya

413 NW 21st Ave
241.7667
www.tanukipdx.com
Tues–Sat 4–10p

Here, *tanuki*, the mythical protective raccoon dog known to hang out at bars and eateries in Japan, comes together with *izakaya*, a place where sake is to be had. Good combo, I say. Order classic Japanese street food like *kushiyaki*, literally meaning cooked on a stick, including Pinoy sausage, marinated beef, and local bay scallops. Or class up your drinking and dining diversions with *hotate sudachi*, another succulent scallop preparation with spicy citrus broth and bergamot, chilies, and shiso, or *oi naengguk*, a Dungeness crab and cucumber salad with watermelon *dashi*. This place can name the farm where the meat or poultry in the dish originated, and seasonal menus are always changing with what is freshest. *SB*

H₅O Bistro and Bar

50 SW Morrison St
221-0711
www.h5obistro.com
Breakfast 6:30–11a; Lunch 11a–2p; Dinner (Sun–Thur) 5–10p, Dinner (Fri–Sat) 5–11p

Hovering around H$_5$O, an unexpectedly awesome hotel bar, I've had many liquid inspirations. I assume it was during an especially rainy season that the ingenious cocktail menu was thought up. Try the very Portland-esque "tea" (recipe follows) either at home or from the vantage point of the suave seats inside. If you're wanting vino, I'm sure you'll find something you like among H$_5$O'S 800-some bottles. *SB*

Rose City Tea

5 mint leaves
ice
1 orange slice
1 lime slice
¼ plum
black tea
garnish (3 grapes skewered, orange wheel, mint leaf, and plum slice)

Muddle mint, then add the fruit and a touch of ice. Add tea and shake. Strain over fresh ice. Garnish.

Happy Hour in Portland

Whether you're having a late lunch, an early dinner, or a really, really late breakfast, the best time to eat cheap in Portland is during happy hour (between the hours of approximately 3 and 6:30pm.) Since most restaurants have a special menu for this time of day, foodies can satisfy fancy food cravings on the cheap. Some places make such extravagant gourmet drinks that ordering virgin has become a common occurrence, so you can partake even if booze ain't your thing. Below are a few of the most fabulous happy hours in the Rose City.

Sagittarius (see page 124)
2710 N Killingsworth St
289.7557
http://sagittariusbar.blogspot.com

Pambiche (see page 177)
2811 NE Glisan St
233.0511, ext 3
www.pambiche.com

Mint/820 (see page 114)
816 N Russell St
284.5518
www.mintand820.com

¡Oba! (see page 129)

555 NW 12th Ave
228.6161
www.obarestaurant.com

Tugboat Brewing Company (see page 147)

711 SW Ankeny St
226.2508
www.d2m.com/Tugwebsite

Typhoon (see page 52)

2310 NW Everett St (one of several locations)
243.7557
www.typhoonrestaurants.com

Ten 01 (see page 166)

1001 NW Couch St
226.3463
www.ten-01.com

Saucebox (see page 170)

214 SW Broadway at W Burnside St
241.3393
www.saucebox.com

Teardrop Cocktail Lounge (see page 145)

1015 NW Everett St
445.8109
www.teardroplounge.com

Bluehour (see page 165)

250 NW 13th Ave
226.3394
www.bluehouronline.com

Doug Fir Lounge (see page 178)

830 E Burnside St
231.9663
www.dougfirlounge.com

Vault Martini (see page 179)

226 NW 12th Ave

224.4909

www.vault-martini.com

Andina (see page 129)

1314 NW Glisan St

228.9535

www.andinarestaurant.com

Listen

From festivals to open mics to performances—it is all here

Well-strung notes can carry every shade of emotion. I like to close my eyes and let my other senses go when I catch wind of some magical melodies. My mother used to say you can't listen with your mouth open, but some of these places promote listening while you eat scrumptious meals. Whatever your ears perk up to, it's essential to indulge in listening as often as possible. I encourage trying a genre of music or a type of performance you wouldn't usually look for—stretch your ears' horizons!

 Portland Center Stage

 Gerding Theater at the Armory, 1111 SW Broadway

274.6588

www.pcs.org

Showtimes vary

Portland Center Stage relocated in 2006 to the renovated Armory, a stone's throw away from Powell's on Burnside. Revamping this historic building was done in sustainable style, and the Armory was awarded LEED Platinum certification. Come here to witness live theater and moving performing arts. *DL*

 Holocene

 1001 SE Morrison St

239.7639

www.holocene.org

Wed–Fri 5p–late, Sat–Sun 8p–late (hours depend on performance schedule)

It's time to go dancing! Holocene will scratch that relentless boogie itch with its many nights of DJs spinning and people grooving. There are always gay dance parties here, and DJ Anjali often makes appearances with her bhangra and Bolly-wood mixes, bringing culture from across the planet right to my back door. The space has a large dance floor with incredibly high ceilings to accommodate all that heat. Check out Holocene's calendar—you may find listings for some great acts that stop by for a show, like Portland's own Horse Feathers. *RM*

$ Rotture

 315 SE 3rd Ave
234.5683
www.rotture.com
Daily 5p–2:30a

Located in the industrial district, this diamond in the rough has a diverse, queer-friendly bar, great weekend DJs, and a spacious patio overlooking the Willamette River. Deep, dark, and mysterious, these exhilarating shows have never let me down. There's always something going on either downstairs where DJs shadow over pool tables and a bar that specializes in stiff drinks, or upstairs where the whole city feels within your reach and the dance floor is rarely empty. *SB*

$$ Proper Eats Market and Cafe

 8638 N Lombard St
445.2007
www.propereats.org
Mon–Thurs 10a–10p, Fri–Sat 10a–2a, Sun 12–10p

Who knew that a vegetarian market would be one of the best places around to see live local jazz. That's just how Portland goes, I guess, with cupcake shops, antique stores, and city blocks full of books. Order veggie and vegan delights from the cafe and settle down to some homegrown tunes, then pick up your healthy gro-ceries or some snacks for the road on your way out. Fridays and Saturdays there are always touring and local acts—check ahead for an up-to-date calendar. *SB*

$ Powell's Books Events

Various Powell's Books locations citywide
www.powellsbooks.com/calendar

Nearly every day of the week Powell's offers a book event. Whether it is children's story time, an author reading, or a discussion group covering a new title, there is sure to be something you'll enjoy. Check out the online calendar for current information on who is coming to town. There are local authors and big names spreading themselves all over Powell's epic list of events. Get behind the pages of your favorite book. *SB*

Fez Ballroom and Lounge

318 SW 11th Ave
221.7262
www.fezballroom.com
Tues–Sat 9p–2:30a, schedule varies

The Fez Ballroom and Lounge is a two-story club with rotating DJs every night of the week. '80s night brings in a fun and appropriately dressed crowd. Special events and seasonal parties round out a calendar of theme nights that include everything from house to hip-hop. Many weeknights are free of cover charge. Fez is the only Portland club with that expansive, cool, European feel. *RM*

Oregon Symphony

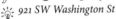
921 SW Washington St
228.1353
www.orsymphony.org

Tchaikovsky, Rachmaninoff, Stravinsky, Shostakovich, Sibelius, and Strauss. Do you know these names? Do they live in your heart? Try as I might, I can't avoid being a bit pushy here. Classical music is cooler than you think, and it brings me to tears quicker than watching the movie *Life Is Beautiful*. I am always bringing new friends to the orchestra and watching as their shoulders drop back, their eyes glaze over, and goose bumps cover their skin. Whether you are familiar with this foundational form of music or not, hearing the full symphony sound is sure to inspire and move you. Classical music isn't just for background sound at a cafe or a massage, it is intellectually stimulating, emotionally pulling, and a powerful experience that can be enjoyed universally. If this message is already your own banging drum, you'll be dumbfounded by this spectacular symphony's rendition of Mendelssohn's music for *A Midsummer Night's Dream*. And those who've never been to the orchestra will, too. Recently appointed concertmaster Jun Iwasaki has gotten off to a riveting start leading this already mellifluous group to new heights. *SB*

Portland Playlist

Here is Jamie Freedman's superb starting point for authentic, multidimensional, local music—some sounds to get you into the real Portland music scene, including different genres and periods. It isn't meant to be encyclopedic, just a taste for some of our favorite auditory pleasures homegrown in the Rose City. Happy listening!

1. The Shins: "Split Needles"
2. Jackie-O Motherfucker: "Hey! Mr. Sky"
3. The Dandy Warhols: "Bohemian Like Me"
4. U-Krew: "If U Were Mine"
5. Elliott Smith: "Sweet Adeline"
6. M. Ward: "Never Had Nobody Like You"
7. Pink Martini: "Sympathique"
8. The Decemberists: "Engine Driver"
9. At Dusk: "For a Reason"
10. The Joggers: "Horny Ghost"
11. MarchFourth Marching Band: "Getcha Now"
12. Lifesavas: "Hellohihey"
13. 3 Leg Torso: "B & G's"
14. The Gossip: "Standing in the Way of Control"
15. Blitzen Trapper: "Black River Killer"
16. Menomena: "Wet and Rusting"
17. Stephen Malkmus (of Pavement): "Dragonfly Pie"
18. Viva Voce: "Red Letter Day"
19. Mel Brown: "Chicken Fat"
20. Laura Gibson: "Hands in Pockets"
21. The Kingsmen: "Louie Louie"
22. Loch Lomond: "A Field Report"
23. YACHT: "See a Penny (Pick It Up)"
24. Modest Mouse: "Float On"
25. Foghorn Stringband: "Lost Girl"
26. Dead Moon: "Dead Moon Night"
27. Obo Addy: "Jama"
28. Bryan Johanson: "Strum und Jam"
29. Starfucker: "Florida"
30. Tomas Svoboda: "Sonata No. 2. Op. 121"
31. Cool Nutz: "I Heard That"
32. Dragging an Ox through Water: "Aces"
33. Sleater-Kinney: "Jumpers"
34. Liv Warfield: "I Decided"
35. Greg Sage & the Wipers: "Taking Too Long"
36. Lactacious: "Fire Song"
37. Raina Rose: "O Oregon"
38. Mo Mack & Company: "I Am a Pilgrim"

Arlene Schnitzer Concert Hall

1037 SW Broadway
510.248.4335
www.pcpa.com/events/asch.php

This gilded concert hall echoes of times gone by, yet still enchants modern audiences. "The Schnitz," as it is lovingly called, is Portland's primary concert hall for opera, orchestral works, and renowned artists and speakers. The space has exceptional acoustics that carry through to the upper balcony level. Renovated to its full elegance in 1984, the theater packs in thousands for Oregon Symphony performances and shows by the White Bird Dance Company. Just remember to keep your eyes on the stage—the beautiful Italian Rococo Revival architectural details are dazzling. *SB*

Portland Center for the Performing Arts

248.4335
www.pcpa.com

A network of five theaters that house six theater companies, including the Portland Ballet, Oregon Symphony, and several other musical organizations, the Portland Center for the Performing Arts (PCPA) is the spot to go for an evening of the arts. But this place is far from snooty. PCPA hosts ballets and operas, but it also brings acts like Sleater-Kinney and Pearl Jam. So a night at PCPA can beckon for a tux or some casual slacks. The theaters are scattered around downtown, and each has an air all its own. Opera and major classical performances take place at Keller Auditorium (222 SW Clay Street, 274.6560, *www.portlandopera.org*), major touring acts take over the Arlene Schnitzer Concert Hall regularly (see page 156), and all are kept up with the support and determination of this incredible arts organization. *SB*

Newmark Theater

1111 SW Broadway at SW Main St
796.0132
Showtimes vary

This intimate Edwardian-style theater is the baby brother of PCPA, and it's the perfect place to experience dance performances or improv. The yearly schedule of productions focuses on plays and dance performances. Pretend you are in Europe a century ago, attending a royalty-only viewing of some talented writer's new play. No matter where you sit, you'll be no farther than 65 feet away from the actors. A recent choral performance filled this acoustic gem with the symphony of voices of Portland's own Aurora Chorus (*www.aurorachorus.org*). *SB*

Albert Street Pub

1036 NE Alberta St
284.7665
Mon–Thurs 5p–12a, Fri 5p–1a, Sat 5p–2a

A staple of the Albany District, this neighborhood pub has music year-round. Choose from local suds, reasonably priced well drinks, and the ever-present free hot cocoa next to the stage as you get a happy earful of strummy music. Homey pig decor flies from the ceiling and can be found throughout the two side-by-side pub halls. Friendly bartenders complete the scene. *SB*

Jimmy Mak's

300 NW 10th Ave
295.6542
www.jimmymaks.com
Mon–Sat 4p–2a, music usually begins at 8p

Jimmy Mak's has a good collection of some of Portland's most respected jazz musicians as its regular players. It is always a good bet if you want to spend an evening in the Pearl and "be seen." Decently priced drinks and a low cover charge make it a cheap date for downtown. *RM*

Mississippi Studios

3939 N Mississippi Ave
753.4473, box office: 288.3895
www.mississippistudios.com
Box office: Tues–Fri 2–6p, showtimes vary

This is the premier place to see live music in Portland. The room seats no more than 130, with sexy red walls, bottled beer and wine, impeccable sound, and a list of some of the finest touring and local musicians in the country. If you love music, you will love this intimate venue in one of the hippest neighborhoods in town. You never know who is going to be on the schedule, from Rickie Lee Jones, to Hot Tuna, to Country Joe McDonald, to amazing locals Sneakin' Out and Storm Large. A trip to Portland wouldn't be complete without catching a show, and you can bet that even if you haven't heard of the band playing here, it's gonna be good. Above the music venue is a world-class recording studio, and if you ask nicely, they might let you take a tour. *RM*

Portland Fret Works

3039 NE Alberta St

249.3737

www.portlandfretworks.com

Wed–Fri 12–6p, Sat 10a–2p

Portland Fret Works is the place to get your guitar fixed if you're in town and you need a bridge pin or a strobe tuning real quick. The people who work here are guaranteed to do a great job with your ax. *RM*

Pacific Festival Ballet

4620 SW Beaverton Hwy

Box office: 977.1753

www.pacificfestivalballet.org, www.portlanddanceacademy.com

Master classes, performance opportunities (at the Schnitz, no less!), and season-long programs make a complete ballet school here in Portland. Each year new and talented dancers graduate, and every year there's another popular performance of *The Nutcracker*. Join in and learn how to make your body move like the instrument that it is. *SB*

Mississippi Records

4007 N Mississippi Ave

282.2990

Wed–Mon 12–7p

Music fiends of all flavors make regular visits to this used record and cassette-tape store. Skip out on CDs and iPods and get back to the classic sounds of vinyl and tape. As much as everyone loves the new technology, I've noticed personal music players separate people not only from one another but also from their environment. Take off your headphones, disconnect from your devices, and get into the sounds around you. Then head to this well-organized, inexpensive, and friendly record store to pick up something you can share with your friends. My last visit there produced a three-record addition to my collection with Miles Davis's *Sketches of Spain*, Pink Floyd's *Dark*

Side of the Moon, and an Aretha album. For under $10, I had a tune in my head, a party at my apartment, and an extra skip in my step. *SB*

Funky Church

2456 SE Tamarack Ave
Check pc-pdx.com and pdxstump.com for upcoming shows

The Funky Church is just that: a church that has been refurbished as a homey theater. Shows light up the stage four or five times a month, with mostly acoustic music, but occasionally there's a full band. The Funky Church is on the edge of Ladd's Addition (see the "Pets and Poodles" chapter, page 31), a beautiful and vintage neighborhood with alleyways and rose gardens. The Funky Church even has a bell tower and baptismal font.

Portland Baroque Orchestra

1020 SW Taylor St
222.6000
www.pbo.org
Office hours: Mon–Fri 9:30a–5:30p, showtimes and locations vary

To get the real sound of Telemann, Schubert, Scarlatti, Bach, Purcell, or any of the other Baroque composer greats, you have to hear their pieces performed on the original instruments. And that's just what this world-class orchestra plays. The evolution of tuning and shaping strings, brass, and especially the variations of the keyboard have changed the way the music sounds. Though there is always personal preference involved, as with all the arts, there's no question any listener will have a more intimate knowledge of the life of the music when hearing it in its nascent form. These composers have been my close "friends" from a young age, and I encourage even those who've never been interested in this music to give it a listen and open up to the tapestry of melodies. After all, counterpoint and the harmonies thought up by these guys have influenced nearly all music being played today. Get in the know! *SB*

360 Vinyl

214 NW Couch St
224.3688
www.360vinyl.com
Mon–Sat 11a–8p, Sun 12–6p

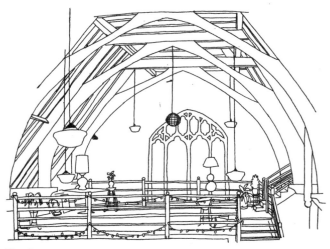

Funky Church

Stop what you're doing and perk your ears toward 360 Vinyl, the best underground and hip-hop record store to speak of. For DJ hopefuls or professionals, or little ol' me with my record player keeping me company while I make wild forays in the kitchen, the truth is that music will never be all boxed up with that impossible shrink-wrap. We'll still be making it, singing it, dancing to it, and proudly spinning it on our turntables. *SB*

Chamber Music Northwest

Box office: 522 SW 5th Ave
223.3203
www.cmnw.org

Bringing to Portland the refined joy of classical music, Chamber Music Northwest presents concerts all year long, in addition to an outstanding five-week summer festival. World-renowned musicians come to Portland venues thanks to this important organization. Chamber music transcends a specific time period. Rather, its defining feature is its intimate instrumental grouping of no more than eight players. During the summer festival, concerts are held at two college venues, Reed and Caitlin, and are built on themes explored through a series of performances. It is like having a vacation in the world of a single composer or time period—a very powerful way to listen to such impressive music. For instance, there has been a four-concert series on Shostakovich, where one concert is billed "Russian Music Before Shostakovich," another focuses on his early years, and so on. My favorite living pianist, André Watts, played a similar three-concert grouping, with David Shifrin on clarinet, comparing Beethoven and Brahms. Not only are the musicians of the highest caliber, but also the inventive method of organizing concerts makes Chamber Music Northwest one of Portland's most important musical and cultural assets. *SB*

The Blue Monk

 *3341 SE Belmont St*
 595.0575
www.thebluemonk.com
Tues–Sat 5p–1a, Sun 5p–12a

It wasn't even 5:30pm and the sky had already blackened, storming so strongly that we had to swerve around fallen tree limbs. We were trying to drive toward Belmont Street, cringing as we swaggered down the road past an eerie cemetery. When the weather persists like this in Portland, as it is known to do on occasion, there's no place I'd rather be confined than The Blue Monk. With wicked happy hour deals and an East Coast–inspired menu of classic spaghetti and meatballs and chicken parmesan with a gourmet twist, my belly is always satisfied. On über-indulgent nights, I order the bacon-wrapped scallops before heading into the jazz-filled basement for an intimate concert. *SB*

Music Millennium

 3158 E Burnside St
231.8926
www.musicmillennium.com
Mon–Sat 10a–10p, Sun 11a–9p

Think that the classic music store—where you can browse for hours, buy used, and check out the tunes before you commit—is dead? Music Millennium is living proof that the category still exists and can even thrive in the twenty-first century. This place captures the feel of a small-town independent record store perfectly, offering both new and used CDs, as well as an extensive vinyl selection and an entire room devoted to classical music (complete with a soundproof door to keep the strains of French horn and cello unadulterated by the rock 'n' roll). Scattered throughout the store are inserts for Music Millennium's picks for the 100 Greatest Albums. For someone looking to try something new, these are inspired suggestions. If you want to take a listen, the staff is happy to pipe in the sounds at the barber chair listening station. This is no pretentious or elitist joint; they just want you to find some great music. *MM*

$ Crystal Ballroom

1332 W Burnside St
225.0047
www.mcmenamins.com

The Crystal Ballroom is one of Portland's bigger venues, so your favorite indie bands are sure to come through here. Upstairs is a big box of an auditorium, and downstairs there is a smaller venue space that hosts some pretty epic '80s parties if you've packed your purple stretch pants. Look for upcoming events; concerts are scheduled well in advance. *SB*

Karaoke in PDX

I don't know to what I can attribute the karaoke craze in PDX—maybe it's the hipster thing, or maybe it's a perfect rainy-day activity and there are just a lot of rainy days. Whatever the cause, the result is fun any night of the week, as long as you dig blue curaçao, doo-wop, and Motown covers, and squeezing into a sticky vinyl booth with a gaggle of buddies. Here are some infamous spots for nightlong song battles:

Chopsticks III
535 NE Columbia Blvd
283.3900

Galaxy Restaurant and Lounge
909 E Burnside St
234.5003

Spare Room
4830 NE 42nd Ave
287.5800

Voicebox Karaoke Lounge
2112 NW Hoyt St
303.8220
www.voiceboxpdx.com

Spectators
Sit back and watch this

Major league sports and exciting sardine cans can be found here!

Trail Blazers
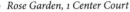
Rose Garden, 1 Center Court
Box office: 797.9619
www.nba.com/blazers

While Portland may not be a city known for its professional sports, it does boast an NBA powerhouse: the Trail Blazers. Head to the Rose Garden for a live view of the action, some beer, and some civic pride. DL

PGE Park

1844 SW Morrison St
Ticket line: 553.5555
www.pgepark.com

Despite its modern corporate name, PGE Park is over 100 years old and has echoes of the classic American stadiums. Come here for more than a healthy dose of patriotic nostalgia, but also to cheer on the Timbers (just make sure to wear either green or yellow or both) or watch the Beavers minor-league baseball team play. The tickets are cheap, the crowds are friendly and boisterous, and all in all it's a great place to watch sports. SB

Rose City Rollers

Portland Expo Center, 2060 N Marine Dr
736.5200
www.rosecityrollers.com

If you see the famous knuckle bumper stickers around town, you'll know what you're looking at—another serious Rose City Roller fan. These hardcore women bust it on the roller rink during a rough-and-tumble season against other Pacific Northwest teams. Get rowdy and be prepared to cheer at full volume! *SB*

Memorial Coliseum

 1401 N Wheeler Ave
 www.rosequarter.com
 Flower shows, school graduations, ice skating, and the biggest names in music all grace the stages and corridors of this coliseum. Check the web site for what's going on today, and head over for one of the large-scale events this snug city has to offer. Incidentally, Memorial Coliseum is also the venue for the yearly Grand Floral Parade, where you'll witness more roses and other flora in one spot than you ever thought possible. *SB*

Dress Up

Don your shiny shoes and head out to one of these fancy places—not all come with a huge price tag

There are those occasions when you just have to dress up, when something inside you wants to put your best foot forward and go all out. These are Oregon's top fanciest spots. While wild rivers, wine valleys, eclectic culture, and raw beauty are what most people know of this state, Portland is quickly making a name in haute cuisine, and for good reason. Food is the next thing to make this state famous, and some of these spots are why. Not all of them require big bucks, though some places are pricier. Remember, drinks are usually the culprit in amping up your dining bill, so if you are careful in that department, you can make the more expensive places affordable.

$$ Park Kitchen

 422 NW 8th Ave
223.7275
www.parkkitchen.com
Mon–Fri 11:30a–2p, Mon–Sat 5–9p
Under the sultry lights and amid the enticing aromas and muffled murmurs, Park Kitchen's subtle nobility shines through. The food is nothing less than

manna, but there's also some fun to be had. Menu items run from artistically sophisticated to indulgently satisfying, for example, the green bean tempura with bacon. *SB*

$$$ Bluehour

250 NW 13th Ave
226.3394
www.bluehouronline.com
Mon–Fri 11:30a–2:30p & 5:30–10p; Sat 5:30–10p; Sun 10a–2:30p & 5:30–10p

Bluehour is a quick lesson in French phraseology, and its meaning—a moment of heightened emotion—is well expressed in every aspect of the dining experience. In the Pearl warehouse district, in what is now a chic patchwork of high-end advertising agencies and booming new businesses, settle down for truffled potato pillows, flawless frozen banana soufflés, and braised local meats that practically melt in your mouth. The large, open room is always kissed by a regal arrangement of flowers. Romance is in the air at Bluehour, but it's an equally ideal spot to take clients in need of an impressing array of Portland tastes. *SB*

$$ Urban Farmer

525 SW Morrison St, 8th Fl
222.4900
www.urbanfarmerrestaurant.com
Mon–Fri 6a–11p, Sat–Sun 6a–11:30p

When you eat at Urban Farmer, you literally taste the city, because not all the farms are located outside city limits. These folks get many ingredients—from cheese to jam to wine to meat—from both farmers and producers in the nearby vicinity. With a menu that focuses on juicy steaks cooked to order (just how rare or well done is your preference) under the rustic lamps and warmed-up farmhouse ambiance, I easily fell in love with the grass-fed porterhouse from Painted Hills Farm my hubby and I shared. The menu is organized so that you can create your own meal from scratch—add to your choice of meat several vegetable offerings and a dessert to polish off the beefy romance. *SB*

Bluehour

 ## Ten 01

 1001 NW Couch St
 226.3463
 www.ten-01.com
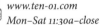 *Mon–Sat 11:30a–close*

Ah, the art of eating. I never tire of the search for a creative, inspiring, extravagant array of local edibles. At Ten 01 I am amid my fellow foodies—dedicated to cooking and eating, mixing and drinking—enjoying the fruits of their labor. Start with the cocktail and wine lists; if you like drinking while you eat, you will also be in good company. It's a well-known fact that Ten 01's bartender and sommelier are envied by other classy Portland restaurants, and luckily they let me share the recipe for my favorite of their epic drinks: the Mystic Wood. Happy hour is irresistible and affordable—braised lamb mac and cheese, chorizo burgers, and house-made charcuterie plates are all $5. Every detail has been thought of, and even the fries are dipped in truffle oil before they arrive at the table. There are an amazing array of menus, always changing with the seasons and the chef's whim. It's impossible to tire of eating here—even after three visits in a two-week period I was left wanting for more. It's no wonder that my new top pick was also named top restaurant for 2009 by the web site *Portland Food and Drink*. SB

Mystic Wood

(Recipe courtesy of Kelley Swenson, bar manager at Ten 01)

2 ounces rye whiskey (6-year-old Sazerac)
1 ounce cherry liqueur (Heering)
1 ounce apricot brandy (Rothman & Winter)
2 dashes Angostura bitters

Stir ingredients over ice and strain into a small chilled cocktail glass or champagne coupe.

$$$ Paley's Place

1204 NW 21st Ave
243.2403
www.paleysplace.net
Mon–Thurs 5:30–10p, Fri–Sat 5:30–11p, Sun 5–10p

Come to Paley's Place, a New England-esque whitewashed house dotted with smug porch diners and full of culinary magic and tell-tale tantalizing aromas. Let the Nina Simone tune playing drift along the breeze or, on a cooler night, dine inside by the fireplace. Sup on the daily offerings—the Paleys have direct relationships with many local farmers and purveyors, so they base each day's meals on what's freshest. Local Treviso, a grilled bread salad, comes with incredible house-cured sardines and a mix of arugula and frisée, the Spicy True Cod a la Plancha is one of the best preparations of this fish, together with a sauce gribiche. Handmade pastas, slow-cooked roasts, and inventive northwest fare is the MO here—finally captured in a new cookbook *The Paley's Place Cookbook*, Ten Speed Press, 2009. This intimate restaurant has been a favorite of Portland's discerning diners for years, and it consistently offers a superb and sustainable meal. *SB*

$$$ Higgins

1239 SW Broadway

222.9070

http://higgins.ypguides.net

Mon–Fri 11:30a–12a, Sat–Sun 4p–12a

Under the pressed tin ceiling and between the wall tapestries, onions turn into part of a sensuous salad, cucumber and jalapeño granita tops local oysters, and pears are poached in Oregon pinot noir to cover duck confit. Transformations are what this fine restaurant is all about, so sustainable flavors, created with organic, small-farm produce and meats, are the main dish. Each season brings a completely new menu, though autumn is my favorite time to come, when roasted root vegetables set the stage for maple-spiced hazelnut and farro salad. Vegetarian plates are as divine as the sustainably harvested seafood and free-range meats. Make a complete night of it by indulging in the wine pairings, salads, and desserts. After dinner, follow your nose around the neighborhood to find a concert or play, or just walk along the river while reminiscing about the otherworldly meal you just enjoyed. *SB*

$$ Phlox

3962 N Mississippi Ave at N Shaver St

890.0715

www.phloxpdx.com

Tues–Sun 11a–6p

Ladies, get ready for your ultimate night on the town by stopping by Mississippi Avenue to pick up a gorgeous dress at Phlox. For the summer months, choose a flowery wraparound or floor-length silk dress. Heat up the night with a frilly skirt before stepping out. The owner handpicks items from independent labels and even sells her own handmade line. This boutique is a cornucopia of girlie desire, stocked with the most artful, flattering, and feminine pieces perfect for wearing to one of Portland's many divine dining spots. *SB*

$$ The Farm Cafe
10 SE 7th Ave
736.3276
www.thefarmcafe.net
Sun–Tues 5–10:30p, Wed–Sat 5–11:30p

Off East Burnside is an itty-bitty farmhouse you might miss if you're not paying close attention. Take care to make a stop there, preferably with a loved
one with whom you feel comfortable gushing over a fine organic meal, tasty
drinks, and the best chocolate soufflé ever. I started one evening happily with
a Snowflake (which contains Frangelico and Kahlúa), served in a martini
glass with dark-chocolate shards covering the white liquid. That warmed me
up considerably so I could dive into crab risotto, slow cooked to perfection,
a few of the ravishing salads, and a pork dish that drove me, the nonpork
person, to exclamations of bliss. That was before we had the chocolate soufflé, a dessert so rich and creamy we had to have another round of Snowflakes
and take our sweet time. The Farm Cafe is a small place, but it doesn't feel
crowded. For the kinds of refined dishes served here, the prices are astonish-
ingly low. The food is warm and comfortable, cooked with good karma and
without a rush. Few things make me happier than another chance to come to
the Farm Cafe for a full-course meal. *SB*

Portobello Vegan Trattoria
2001 SE 11th Ave
754.5993
www.portobellopdx.com/wordpress
Tues–Sat 5:30–9p

Italian, Spanish, and French cuisines are finally accessible in their full-
flavored forms to those who aren't into animal products. Fight over the
tomato bruschetta appetizer, and then savor linguine with pesto or the signature portobello steak with polenta and braised organic greens. For dessert, don't miss the vegan cheesecake from Cherry Bomb Bakery, which once
upon a time had its own brick-and-mortar location. Serious indulgence. *SB*

$$ Wild Abandon Restaurant

2411 SE Belmont St
232.4458
www.wildabandonrestaurant.com
Wed-Mon 9a–2p & 4:30–10p; Sat–Sun 9a–2p & 5:30–10p

Have you walked along the Willamette River mystified by the beauty, and then started to hear a grumble coming from your belly? When you've got to get off your feet and into a grand meal, take yourself for a wallet-friendly dress-up dining experience at Wild Abandon Restaurant. The Willamette Dream Salad will allow you to continue your pretty ponderings. Oregon blue cheese is perched atop wild harvested greens and currants bursting with flavor, with a light bite of vinaigrette. The pasta dishes are the stars—ravioli and polenta lasagna, with noodles made from scratch in the kitchen, will give you comfort from the inside out. The ingredients are all local and all lovely. This may sound like a personals ad, but I am not messing about when I say these dishes are one fine lady of a meal. *SB*

$$$ Saucebox

214 SW Broadway at W Burnside St
241.3393
www.saucebox.com
Mon–Fri 4:30–late, Sat–Sun 5p–late

Enter Saucebox and come into the world of culinary power team Chris Israel and Bruce Carey. If you're not just stopping in for a swanky drink (and that wouldn't be a misstep; I name them the best cocktails in the city), wind around the bar, passing by Mr. Mumu, the DJ of Portland DJs, and into a mural-covered room with wall-mounted protruding statues in vibrant hues. Now calm down, sit, breathe, relax, take your eyes off the glass-enclosed closet where booze gets infused, and get to the menu. Can I butt in here and order for you? Well, I think I will, then. To get a mix of appetizers, order a Pupu Platter to split so you can sample the gooey goodness of the tapioca dumplings and the tasty sauce on the baby back ribs—this place is called Saucebox, after all. Following that same thread, the Javanese sauce on the roasted salmon makes it one of the best renditions of this favored fish I've ever had. Green curry with duck breast and other seasonal main courses are worth a try, but if salmon's on the menu, then look no further. Go ahead, take yourself on a mini-vacation to Saucebox, where it's possible that you could be dining in any great city of the world. *SB*

$$ Le Pigeon

738 E Burnside St
546.8796
www.lepigeon.com
Mon–Sat 5–10p, Sun 5–9p

Arrive at opening time and be seated behind seared foie gras with gingered rhubarb, scallops with duck fat hollandaise, and a modest pork osso buco. If you get to Le Pigeon after the usual rush, you'll be tested to wait as these dishes pass by your jealous nostrils. But I suggest you come to play—you won't be disappointed. Organic and local ingredients have never been so decadent, and yet the atmosphere is reminiscent of sitting on your grandma's wooden counter, snacking as she cooks an heirloom recipe. This is Portland's best place to impress your date. *SB*

Lauro Mediterranean Kitchen

3377 SE Division St
239.7000
www.laurokitchen.com
Sun–Thurs 5–9p, Fri–Sat 5–10p, Tues–Sat 11:30a–2:30p

It's incredible to see the variety of Mediterranean flavors wrought from local ingredients at Lauro Mediterranean Kitchen. The chef makes playground games of spices and lusty flavors, enticing diners to get a little closer or to close their eyes to savor the flavor. Order melon salad with olives and mint, goat cheese–stuffed chicken breast, Portuguese-style pork loin, and pudim flan for dessert. Nothing is too fussed up; instead, the flavors are bright and relaxed, and they will have the same effect on you. *SB*

Navarre

10 NE 28th Ave
232.3555
www.navarreportland.blogspot.com
Mon–Thurs 4:30–10:30p, Fri 11:30a–11:30p, Sat 9:30a–11:30p, Sun 9:30a–10:30p

In a city where the farm-to-table mentality is a well-known and well-loved method of eating, Navarre still manages to stand out. This is the younger cousin of the fine eateries around town that tout direct relationships with farmers—chef John Taboada simplifies the grandeur of this undertaking by enlisting Navarre as a member of the local CSA, 47th Avenue Farms. His small band of cool cooks work together as one in this small kitchen. The small plates offer myriad dining styles from cheap, quick bite before flick, to long drawn-out evening of culinary elegance. Staple menu items like filler-less crab cakes, foie gras preparations, homemade bread, and braised greens strengthen a sumptuous rotating menu that's based on what's on the farm. In spring expect lovely baby green salads, and desserts topped with house-made lavender jelly; when autumn comes around there'll be rabbit legs and but-ternut squash with handmade tagliatelle . . . Here's to the season's eatings! *SB*

Lovely Hula Hands

4057 N Mississippi Ave
445.9910
www.lovelyhulahands.com
Tues–Sun 5–10p

I first discovered this place when it was housed in a pink-painted house, and as it has evolved, it has only grown sweeter and more loveable. Aged cheese and local leeks and foraged mushrooms show up on a summer tart, and starters include line-caught cured salmon and green bean salad with Marcona almonds, cherries, and Teleme cheese. Handmade pastas and meat served directly from a small, sustainable farm make perfect main courses, but save room for elegant but rustic desserts like cherry clafouti with house-made toasted almond ice cream or vanilla bean panna cotta. I want to eat here every night—I'd never get tired of it, and I'd always eat a rainbow of local bounty cooked with a skilled, loving touch. *SB*

Stay Up Late

Where to find midnight snacks, 24-hour businesses, and casual late-night drinking, dining, and dancing

Staying up late to dance, dine, and relax is something everyone does at least once in a while. Here are the best places around to get in touch with your nocturnal side.

Acapulco's Gold

2610 NW Vaughn St

220.0283

Fri 11a–11p, Sat–Thurs 11a–11p

Acapulco's Gold is on the border of Portland's northwest industrial district and can be easily overlooked, but if you want a pitcher of citrusy margaritas; a giant plate of nachos with meat, grilled veggies, or soy taco meat; and a place with an authentic Tex-Mex feel, look no further. A large order of nachos can comfortably feed three, and you can stay all night laughing and getting a bit on the sloppy side. *RM*

Biwa

215 SE 9th Ave

239.8830

www.biwarestaurant.com

Daily 5p–12a

Yum, yum, yum. Southwest Portland has yet another shiny, glimmery asset in Biwa, an Asian street food eatery. Kimchi and yakitori are the specialties, but I couldn't resist ordering the classic Chinese pork and noodle soup. The dried seaweed in the slow-cooked broth added a complex, luscious flavor and made me want more. *SB*

Gil's Speakeasy

601½ SE Taylor St

234.8991

www.myspace.com/gilsspeakeasy

Mon–Thurs 11a–2a, Fri–Sat 10a–2a

Sundays at Gil's Speakeasy mean dollar beers for all, but on any night trigger-happy bartenders mix some of the strongest drinks in town. Stay busy with the antique shuffleboard set. *SB*

Ararat

111 NE Martin Luther King Jr Blvd

235.5526

Fri–Sat 6p–4a

By day, Ararat bakes up the best challah in town, but by night Russian techno music pulses through the restaurant-turned-club, making it one of the most fun nights to be had in PDX. An authentic cultural experience, this all-in-one doesn't candy-coat the ex-Soviet party scene. People here are serious about getting their groove on, but whether or not vodka is your thing—and there is a lot of it here—it's easy to join in the excitement. *SB*

$ Hammy's Pizza

2114 SE Clinton St
235.1035
www.hammyspizza.com
Daily 4p–2:30a, takeout until 4a

Imagine you're out having a blast, but all you want to do is go to bed and veg out with a pizza and a movie. Or say your body is all danced out, but your friend is vegan, and where will you find a vegan pie at this hour? Hammy's Pizza has both situations covered. Call in your order for salad, locally brewed root beer, breakfast pizza with eggs, or vegan pizza sprinkled with nutritional yeast and toasted cashews. Head off to Movie Madness Video (see page 193) to rent a flick, and the night will be complete. *SB*

$ Zach's Shack

4409 SE Hawthorne Blvd
233.4616
www.myspace.com/dogswithasnap
Daily 11a–3a

Eating a vegetarian hot dog never seems that glamorous to me. But now it's one of my schmaltzy memories of Portland, when my honey and I rediscovered our favorite snack from New York at Zach's Shack. Hawthorne Boulevard is the perfect place to eat a hot dog, too—there is ample people watching, or if you feel like keeping to yourself, you can grab a seat at the old-school Pac Man game table inside. The beef dogs in natural casing are like a mini-trip to Coney Island, but I am still smitten with Zach's stunningly flavorful veggie weenies. *SB*

$ Hollywood Bowl

4030 NE Halswey St
288.9237
www.hollywoodbowlpdx.com
Mon–Thurs 9a–1a, Fri–Sat 9a–2a, Sun 9a–10p

There's a staying power to the game of bowling. Disco dancers, hippies, beat boxers, goths, grunge kids, skaters, hipsters—everyone ends up at Hollywood Bowl on one night or another. And it's all laughs. Order a pitcher or two of beer or soda, and go for the strikes with your Portland crew. *SB*

Original Hotcake House

1002 SE Portland Blvd

236.7402

Daily 24 hours

The Original Hotcake House serves stacks nonstop, 24 hours a day, 7 days a week. On weekend nights there is a small cover charge to pay for the security guard, so go to this classic Portland diner knowing there will be a truly mixed crowd. With Britney Spears, Bobby Brown, and Johnny Cash on the jukebox, you'll be happy to wait in line to order a plate of perfect greasy hash browns or an omelet as big as your face. Watching the line cook make your food is almost as entertaining as the guaranteed late-night freaks and post-prom high school students. Thank goodness for that security guard. *RM*

Voodoo Doughnut

22 SW 3rd Ave

241.4704

www.voodoodoughnut.com

Daily 24 hours

After Voodoo Doughnut works its magic, donuts become a thing of beauty, of cultural importance, and of romantic commitment. Yes, romantic commitment. For a mere $200, Voodoo employees (who are ordained ministers) will provide a legal tying of the knot, as well as donuts and coffee for 10 witnesses. But the best reason to come to Voodoo is to satisfy a late-night craving for some unconventional donuts. Try the ever-popular Bacon Maple Bar, a sugar crystal–covered donut with two strips of bacon set in the syrupy glaze. You might gorge on the Memphis Mafia Fritter, stuffed with bananas and drizzled with melted chocolate and peanut butter, or some equally divine vegan donuts. Come in the first Friday of the month at midnight to take the ultimate challenge: How many fried rings you can gobble down? For those more into the speed-eating thing, take the Tex-ASS donut challenge—the current champ downed one of these plate-sized glazed giants in under 90 seconds. *SB*

Voodoo Doughnut

$ La Casita

607 SE Morrison St

234.8894

Mon–Wed 11a–11p, Thurs–Sat 11a–6a, Sun 11a–12a

La Casita's hours fluctuate between late and very late, so anytime is the right time to gobble down one of the $1.50 tacos and free chips and salsa. Nothing goes better with a cool midnight horchata and some Spanish-language MTV. *SB*

$ The Hawthorne Theatre

3862 SE Hawthorne Blvd

233.7100

www.hawthornetheatre.com

Showtimes vary, most start at 8p

For a real all-nighter of dancing, head to the Hawthorne Theatre. Electronica, DJs from all corners, and the more hard-core sounds take the stage every night of the week. Party your heart out with fellow Portland music lovers and boogie addicts. Tickets usually won't run you more than $10, and if you're lucky there will be a free show on the night you decide to invite yourself to the party. *SB*

Pambiche

2811 NE Glisan St

233.0511, ext 3

www.pambiche.com

Sun–Thurs 7a–10p, Fri–Sat 7a–12a

Cuban food fans, rejoice! Pambiche has brought the best of edible Cuba to Glisan Street. It is, perhaps, one of the most vibrantly colorful restaurants in Portland, and happily the food matches the decor in terms of vivid flavor and visual appeal. The main dining room is a cozy space that the management augments during the warmer half of the year with a string of outdoor tables (they are under cover and propane heaters ward off the chill). There is often a line around the block, as Pambiche does not accept reservations. The Ensalada de Remolacha (beet salad) is not to be overlooked, the fried yucca is melt-in-your-mouth good, and the waitstaff are chatty and full of suggestions. It's hard to go wrong with a menu so packed with winners, but

I'm quite fond of the Ropa Vieja. No need to dress up here, but you won't get sideways stares if you do fancy up before stopping in. *MM*

Dots Cafe

 2521 SE Clinton St
235.0203
Daily 12p–2a

While Portland does occasionally sleep, if you know where to look, there's a veritable bounty of late-night eats available. One local favorite is Dots Cafe. If you've got a post-show hankering for a plate of hand-cut cheese fries or a big, happy sandwich, Dots is the place. It's the sort of spot where the folks at the next table will end up joining your conversation and offer you the last of their chips and salsa as they leave. On a good night, the music will be spot-on and the service will be friendly. The dimly lit room, gold-flecked wallpaper, and velvet paintings just add to the atmosphere. Dots has been around for more than 15 years now and has long been a gathering place for people who like an alternative flair to go along with their late-night eats. Order Spiked Rikkis or strong well drinks and toast your neighbor in style. *MM*

$ The Roxy

 121 SW Stark St
 223.9160
Tues–Sun 8a–3a

Owned by a famous Portland drag queen, The Roxy is a boisterous place where you can eat all day and all night. Order the Britney Spears blueberry pancakes (I hear that they are her very own recipe), and sit in a booth covered with autographed memorabilia. *SB*

$$ Doug Fir Lounge

 830 E Burnside St
231.9663
www.dougfirlounge.com
Daily 7a–2:30a

Connected to Jupiter Hotel, one of Portland's most ideal lodging situations, Doug Fir Lounge is the site of many a great night out. Just imagine as you walk down the southeastern Portland streets that almost everyone you pass on the sidewalk has a memory or a tale of a night well spent at Doug Fir.

Order festive food, froofy drinks, microbrews, and a heaping helping of vintage lounge appeal. *SB*

$$ Vault Martini

 226 NW 12th Ave

224.4909

www.vault-martini.com

Mon–Wed 4a–1a, Thurs–Sat 4p–2a, Sun 1–10p

Sit at a bar that looks as if it were carved from ice and pore over the "book" of drinks, including 44 unique takes on the classic martini, shaken or stirred. The Hot and Dirty is made with hot pepper–infused vodka and olive juice; the Geisha is ginger-soaked vodka and sake. Flatbreads, toasty paninis, and heaping salads are made with the same care as the drinks. Vault Martini caters to the Ruski in all of us, treating vodka like the czar. *SB*

$$ Le Happy

 1011 NW 16th Ave

226.1258

www.lehappy.com

Mon–Thurs 5p–1a, Fri 5p–2:30a, Sat 6p–2:30a

At two in the morning, few things outdo the Le Trash Blanc, the bacon and cheddar crepe from Le Happy, served in combination with a cold can of Pabst Blue Ribbon. This cafe is *très mignon*, but it also serves a serious steak, in addition to great coffee drinks and my favorite curry crepe. Whether you are wanting sweet or savory, these crepes are better than your average French roll-ups. *SB*

Someday Lounge

 125 NW 5th Ave

248.1030

www.somedaylounge.com

For a night of messy, musical fun, Someday Lounge is waiting around the bend. This lounge is loaded with new music—local DJs and touring acts in various popular genres fill out the schedule and help make the Someday Lounge a busy place for people looking to dance into the night. Whether you like industrial beats, or retro dance tunes, just skim over the upcoming events on the web site and find your ideal night to rock out. *SB*

Pamper

Shelters from all the hustle and bustle, simple enjoyments, and all things feel-good

Part of the whole pampering process is good, hot comfort food. The classic is chicken soup, but I look for the spots that avoid adding too much salt as a substitute for slow-cooked flavor. Overdoing the salt is bad news for the body—instead of pampering you get dehydration! So in this chapter, I've paid special attention to not only the in-the-moment effects, but also the aftereffects. Here is a selection of feel-good foods, restful spaces, and, of course, spas and salons to refresh, revitalize, and restart your engine.

Tour de Crêpes

 2921 NE Alberta St

473.8657

www.tourdecrepes.blogspot.com

Wed–Thurs 9a–9p, Fri–Sat 9a–10p, Sun 9a–6p, happy hour 9–10a & 3–7p

On a blustery day, few things satisfy better than a steamy bowl of French onion soup. Sadly, this favorite is often misunderstood in West Coast versions, but luckily Tour de Crêpes has maintained a delicate slow-cooked flavor in its offering. Served with a crunchy baguette and some stinky Gruyère, the soup at Tour de Crêpes does justice to my answer to rainy-day fever. But that's not all—this homey spot dollops goat cheese and kalamata olives, or fig onion chutney and prosciutto, onto perfectly thin crepes to suit whatever mood change you are in need of. If sweets are your thing, be sure to have them make yours with chocolate crepe batter before piling on toasted coconut, smearing Nutella, drizzling Grand Marnier, and squeezing lime juice. For an extra smile, slurp on a cayenne hot cocoa and look out at the less lucky passersby on Alberta Street. *SB*

The Parlour St. Johns

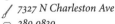 *7327 N Charleston Ave*

 289.0830

www.theparlourstjohns.com

There's no way you can walk out of the cool and cruelty-free Parlour and not look like a million bucks. Keen fashionista eyes and clever clipping skills come together for even picky hotheads. If you aren't in the mood for a cut or color, there are plenty of other lavish ways to get pampered, or you can just hang out and check the local art on the walls. This is a vegan salon, which in this case means the hair and pampering products used have not undergone animal testing and are not animal based. *SB*

Tea Chai Té

734 NW 23rd Ave
228.0900
www.teachaite.com
Daily 10a–10p

Besides having notably good tapioca bubble tea, home-brewed healthful kombucha, and authentic Japanese matcha, this second-floor nook in the Pearl District guides the ailing toward ebullient health through lessons in tea. Even amid the chic shops along the neighborhood's posh main drag, solace and silence can be found at this relaxing abode. Did you know adding some hibiscus to your black tea can instantly help with constipation or the annoying symptoms of a bladder infection? How about that cloves can reduce nausea, even for hangovers, and relieve toothaches? Licorice root aids in combating depression and fatigue, and those "I didn't get enough sleep last night" sore throats. Browse a wall full of loose-leaf teas in every variety, and mix your own according to your day's desires, then find a cozy spot among the serious writers and studious types that hover here. *SB*

Root Whole Body

2526 NE 15th Ave
288.8972
www.rootwholebody.com
Mon–Fri 6a–9p, Sat–Sun 9a–6p

Even with all of our time-saving gadgets, it seems our collective stress levels have skyrocketed lately. Preventing stress can be our biggest lifesaver, as more and more studies come out linking stress to disease. If you have a few extra bucks to spend in the name of relaxation and health, you'll find many ways to regain spiritual and physical balance at Roots Whole Body. Meditative yoga classes, expert massage and acupuncture treatments, and a visit to the sauna are all offered here, together with a hot cup of antioxidant-rich tea. *SB*

The Meadow

3731 N Mississippi Ave
288.4633
www.atthemeadow.com
Sun–Tues 11a–6p, Wed–Sat 11a–7p

Wanna pamper me? Send me to The Meadow with some money. OK, the same could be said for many of the great spots on these pages, but at this particular oasis in the flurry of Mississippi Avenue businesses, an inner, not just outer, beauty is brought out of many shoppers. Somehow those who enter this shop of fine finishing salts, special flowers, rare wines, and bold chocolates have a lightness about their faces when they exit, with or without a purchase. When you witness beauty honored in such a multifaceted way—through delicate flavors, subtle colors, and unique scents—it's hard not to feel pampered through and through. *SB*

$$ Wax On

734 E Burnside St
595-4974
www.waxon.com
Daily 10a–7p

Girlie-girls beware! It's easy to spend hours and dollars here. Wax On is the best place for princess pampering around, with the highest quality hot wax and talented divas to do whatever job necessary. For a modest price, you can prepare for a special night in romance land or just feel a little fresher with a long-lasting eyebrow wax. You can even purchase locally made punky-cute underwear. Whatever your choice, you're certain to feel secretly prettier after a trip to Wax On. *SB*

The Barefoot Sage

1844 SE Hawthorne Blvd
239.7116
www.thebarefootsage.com
Mon–Thurs 10a–8p, Fri–Sat 10a–9p, Sun 12–6p

As far as I am concerned, there should be a big sack of foot massage coupons from the Barefoot Sage at every intersection in Portland—but you'd only realize a sack was nearby when you really needed a moment of true peace and relaxation. Then you'd find a coupon and take yourself to heaven. This incredible place is well suited for those ready for a complete spa overhaul, with river rock treatments, salt baths, and reflexology, but you can also keep it simple and give yourself a well-deserved pamper by just dropping in for a cup of warm tea and a nice long foot rub. *SB*

$$ The Tao of Tea

2112 NW Hoyt St, 223.3563
3430 SE Belmont Ave, 736.0198
www.taooftea.com
Wed–Sun 11a–11p, Leaf Room closes at 10:15p

Walking into The Tao of Tea is like stepping into a monastery where tea is the deity. The atmosphere is always quiet and reverent thanks to a few small water features and a knowledgeable staff who seem to always be in a state of meditation. The tables are rustic and unique, hidden under bamboo tents and surrounded by tall ikebana arrangements. But, oh, the tea! This is by far the best tea in Portland, with an unimaginably large selection of the best quality leaves you can find stateside. You can even buy in bulk at the store, on the Web, or at a grocer like New Seasons Market (see page 197). *RM*

Bishops Barbershop

2132 NE Alberta St (and other locations)
546.4171
www.bishopsbs.com
Mon–Sat 9a–9p, Sun 11a–7p

Going to the salon should never be likened to a trip to the dentist. All the fuss, all the fear, and all the questions about your new look fade away at Bishops Barbershop, where you are welcomed with a complimentary beer and stacks of cool mags. The salon operates on a drop-in-only basis and caters to a huge audience ranging from tattooed teenagers to hip soccer moms. Cuts are mostly under $20, and color starts at $40, so take yourself for a true treat at this unique Portland barbershop. Fundraisers for school arts programs

The Tao of Tea

and other initiatives are a regular happening, so don't be surprised if your next haircut comes complete with a jaw-dropping fashion show. *SB*

Noble Rot

2724 SE Ankeny St
233.1999
www.noblerotpdx.com
Mon–Sat 5p–12a

I get in moods when the energy is sapped from my body, a sniffle is in full effect, and I need a comforting, hot meal. The trouble is, when I get into that state, I never want to go out of the house. Noble Rot would draw me out of the finest hotel room or off a high mountaintop—discovering this steamy enclave is an experience I can never turn down. Perfectly roasted Brussels sprouts, warm frisée salad, a healthful butternut squash soup, poached fish . . . I am deeply involved with each course of this sublimely good meal. I chose a wine flight of three matched vintages and finished with hot tea and a quart of white root and black truffle soup for tomorrow. *SB*

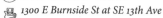 Old Wives' Tales

1300 E Burnside St at SE 13th Ave
238.0470
www.oldwivestalesrestaurant.com
Sun–Thurs 8a–8p, Fri–Sat 8a–9p

Rumor has it that a well-to-do lawyer with a heart of gold opened the original spot as a soup kitchen for the hungry and strapped for cash. With humanitarian acts still a part of this restaurant's philosophy, everyday customers can relax with classical music and booths in the back, and a friendly play area and high chairs in the front. All this and one of my favorite menus in Stumptown, where European foods, vegan delights, ethnic cuisine, and an extensive dessert list are all included. In all my travels, I haven't yet found a restaurant so successful at serving such a vast crowd of picky eaters at once. Whatever your food allergy, if you keep kosher, if you have choosy kids, if you have diabetes, or if you have any other possible reason to think twice before chowing down, you'll be able to do so here and enjoy every minute. Line-caught salmon prepared with ginger and tamari glaze is perfection together with the inexpensive soup and salad bar. Don't miss the Hungarian Mushroom Chowder, an Old Wives' Tales specialty. Each menu item lists all ingredients, even those in the unbelievably good dressings at the salad bar. Whether you're allergic to kids or have 10 of them, eat red meat or only steamed veggies, your needs will be met in the warmest, most relaxed way at this true Portland treasure. *SB*

Löyly

2713 SE 21st Ave
236.6850
www.loyly.net

This Scandinavian-style bathhouse, steam house, sauna, and massage paradise is a great place to recoup in complete, holistic fashion. Let out all your worries and troubles through the pores of your skin, or have them kneaded out by professionals. Prices are affordable for the high skill level and the unique and blissful atmosphere. *SB*

Sweet Tooth

All things sweet converge here—these are the best places to discover your soft spot for sugary treats

Even the healthiest of us crave a sugar rush every so often, and satisfying that craving is a task Portland's bakers, chocolatiers, pastry chefs, and dairy gods and goddesses have heartily taken up. Pack your toothbrush and brush in between licking ice cream cones, munching handmade candies, and seducing your senses with a triple-chocolate cupcake. I figure as long as I keep walking, swimming, riding, and doing whatever else I drum up in the "Get Active" chapter, also heeding my dentist's advice, I can enjoy all the wonders herein.

Bleuet

1019 NW 23rd Ave
295.5981
www.bleuet-yogurt.com

Tart and cooling, zingy and refreshing—all words that come to mind when I reminisce about my new frozen yogurt discovery: Bleuet. Family owned and run, and serving a more sophisticated version of the Americanized frozen treat, Bleuet hits the spot, especially after a cross-city pedal. *SB*

Sweetpea Baking Company

1205 SE Stark St
477.5916
www.sweetpeabaking.com
Mon–Fri 7a–8p, Sat–Sun 9a–5p

Pix Patisserie

Imagine a carefully orchestrated pile o' cupcakes decorated with rustic vertical chocolate hearts and lusciously lumpy icing. Or a wedding cake designed mod with fondant dots and pecking birds. All your imaginings become delicious reality at Sweetpea Baking Company, my favorite place to eat sugar in PDX. *SB*

Pix Patisserie

3901 N Williams Ave (and other locations)
282.6539
www.pixpatisserie.com
Mon–Thurs 7a–12a, Fri 7a–2a, Sat 8a–2a, Sun 9a–12a

Enter Pix Patisserie (a Top Pick, see page 14), a place where any Francophile, Europhile, or other phile can be him- or herself, indulge in quite possibly the best macaroons this side of the pond, and sip mind-numbing Belgian brews while reminiscing about other lands. Beyond the ever-present macaroons are the stunning desserts, all dressed up and ready for the ball. The Amélie, a suave indulgence of orange crème brûlée, chocolate mousse, and toasty hazelnut praline, garnered the chocolate award in the Patisfrance Competition. Other mousse favorites include the Aphrodite with passionate cherries; another chocolate incarnation, the Royale with Cheese, comes with fine French brie à la Tarantino. There's a smattering of fruitier deserts, French classics, meringues, and even dolled-up cheesecake, but for me the choice is between my perennial aforementioned favorite and the pure chocolate decadence of Shazam! and Queen of Sheba Truffle Cake, two rather extreme versions of 75 percent dark chocolate, the first with caramel marvel, the second just pure molten goodness. Don't miss the handmade truffles, of which there are a spectrum of flavors and shapes, or the holiday party and seasonal specialties. Shake off your sugar buzz with some fine cheese, a single malt, or some Chimay, one of many other elegant beverages to sip on. If you go to one place in Portland, you'll have a really tough choice between Powell's and Pix—it is that good. *SB*

Helen Bernhard Bakery

1717 NE Broadway
287.1251
www.helenbernhardbakery.com
Mon–Sat 6a–6p, Sun 8a–3p

Helen started baking up mouthwatering cookies and hearty breads in the 1920s, and this neighborhood bakery carries on the same friendly family legacy to this day. Known for its "M&M" cookies, both *Ms* for "mouthwatering," the cozy shop is piled high with many varieties, such as pfeffernüsse, Mexican wedding cookies, chocolate nut, and more. Inventive loaves like English muffin cornmeal and cobblestone bread are a close second to the outstanding challah, baked fresh every day of the week. Holiday cookies, candies, and cakes help reel in the celebrations and traditions of each season. Service is warm and samples are plentiful. Come early on Sunday morning, when day-olds are half price. *SB*

Piece of Cake

8306 SE 17th St
234.9445
www.pieceofcakebakery.net
Mon–Thurs 9a–8p, Fri 9a–10:30p, Sat 10a–10:30p

With the message that all shall be happy and indulge, Piece of Cake has something surprisingly moist and delicious for everyone: vegan, wheat-allergic, and all. I'm no vegan, but I am careful about the sources of the foods I eat. Honestly, I make fun of my vegan friends on the regular, but I've been fooled more than once by the tasty treats here; I've tasted two versions of carrot cake and couldn't tell which was vegan. Some magic takes place at this spot, voted best cake and best bakery in Portland by local papers a number of times. The vegan Black Forest Cake with chocolate fudge frosting and marinated cherries tastes about as un-vegan as one can imagine. The less sweet Irish Oatmeal Cake and Pumpkin Bread are best-sellers—try the latter under scrambled eggs for a delicious breakfast twist. Cakes and pies with sugar and wheat are in one case, and those without any so-called essential ingredients are in the other—test your own skills and see if you can differentiate. Under the vintage cookie tins, cake stands, aprons, and scattered decor, there's no question this place takes the cake! *SB*

Cupcake Jones

302 NW 10th Ave
222.4404
www.cupcakejones.net
Mon–Sat 10a–8p, Sun 12–6p

Much to my dismay, there is actually a good reason for so many cutesy cupcake shops to open their doors each morning in this rosy city. Whether you are new to the trend or tired of it, there's no mistaking the unique takes these sugary places offer. Cupcake Jones stands out to me, a consummate lover of all flowers, because of the candied rose petals, violets, and other sugar-dappled blooms topping the treats. Wednesday's special white chocolate marionberry rendition is the happiest mid-week indulgence, but whatever your tastes, a trip to Cupcake Jones will require a smile, even if it is just for the attention to detail the community-centric bakers pay to the tops of their little cakes. Think mini gingerbread men, little maple leaf cookies and, of course, lots of flowers. *SB*

Bakery Bar
2935 NE Glisan St
546.8110
www.bakerybar.com
Mon–Sat 7a–3p, Sun 8a–3p

One word, well, two: coconut scone. That is, if you can eat just one. After I sit down with my Stumptown coffee and my perennial Bakery Bar favorite, I have a hard time staying in my seat after finishing the last crumb—I need another, just one more! After a few repeat trips for this sensational pastry, I was told by the barista that it is vegan. I was surprised to disbelief, needless to say. It was then that I decided to venture out and try other sweet treats from that dangerously tempting display. I make biscuits and jam at my house, but I still order Bakery Bar's version when I am in town. Tastes like home! *SB*

Dovetail Bakery
www.dovetailbakery.blogspot.com

The sweet appeal of Dovetail Bakery's treats can be found all over town—my favorite wheat-free marble cake is the subject of my Portland snack-time scavenger hunt. Here's how I play: I take the streetcar and get off at a random stop. I walk until I see the signs of a New Seasons Market, Three Friends, Red and Black Cafe, Proper Eats, or some other fine establishment that stocks the stuff. Other highlights of owner Morgan Grundstein-Helvey's baking repertoire include lemon ginger cookies, sage and caramelized onion corn muffins, chocolate cherry cookies, and Earl Grey tea cake with chocolate ganache. *SB*

Vegan Chewy Ginger Molasses Cookies with Orange Zest
(Recipe courtesy of Morgan Grundstein-Helvey, Dovetail Bakery)

Makes about 2½ dozen 3-inch cookies

3 cups all-purpose flour
2¼ teaspoons baking soda
2 tablespoons ground ginger
½ teaspoon ground allspice
⅔ cup chopped crystallized ginger

1 cup Earth Balance Original Buttery Spread (79 percent vegetable oil)

1½ cups sugar (divided)

zest of 2 oranges

⅔ cup blackstrap molasses (Aunt Patty's or Bob's Red Mill brand is preferred)

1½ teaspoons Ener-G Egg Replacer

Heat oven to 350° and line two baking sheets with parchment paper. In a medium bowl, sift together the flour, baking soda, ground ginger, allspice, and crystallized ginger; set aside. In a mixing bowl, beat the Earth Balance spread, 1 cup sugar, orange zest, and molasses until well incorporated, 30–45 seconds at medium speed if you're using an electric mixer. Add the egg replacer and mix to incorporate, scraping down the sides of the mixing bowl. Add the flour mixture and mix until well incorporated.

Pour the remaining ½ cup sugar into a small bowl. Shape 2-tablespoon-sized portions of dough into balls and place in the bowl with the sugar. Roll the dough balls around until they're completely coated. Place on baking sheets about 3 inches apart. Bake for 10–12 minutes or until they have all puffed up and are starting to look crackly. Cool for 10 minutes on the baking sheet, then transfer to a cooling rack and cool completely.

These cookies are great for potlucks, thank-you gifts, and last-minute guests. The dough freezes well, so it's a great thing to keep on hand during the holiday season. The easiest way to keep this dough is to scoop it out into 2-tablespoon-sized balls, freeze on a baking sheet, then wrap thoroughly in plastic and keep frozen. You can bake these directly from the freezer without defrosting—simply toss them in sugar and bake for 15–20 minutes, or until puffed and crackly.

Stay In

The best takeout and take-home activities in town

Sometimes I try to pack too much into a day. By evening, all systems are not go. But taking in the town can be done inside, too. Many great restaurants specialize in to-go food and even deliver it, while others are more suited to take out, so you can choose one of those low-energy nights to enjoy an in-home or in-hotel dinner. While you're at it, why not rent a flick and make a cozy night of it?

Video Vérité

3956 N Mississippi Ave
445.9902
Daily 12–11p

Situated along the main Mississippi drag, Video Vérité is the pillar of cinematic culture in this hood. Come here for quality flicks in all varieties. Take home a DVD or catch a free screening in the Video Vérité basement. *SB*

$ Cha Cha Cha

3433 SE Hawthorne Blvd (and other locations)
236.1100
www.chaportland.com/taqueria.html
Daily 10a–10p

This local chain, with four Stumptown locations, boasts reasonably priced and delicious Mexican food. Cha Cha Cha offers homemade horchata and a chiles rellenos–stuffed burrito that will leave you full and with leftovers. You can get any burrito smothered in red or green chili sauce, or try it Christmas style and do both. My favorite location on Hawthorne Boulevard makes a great pit stop between perusing the shops. *SB*

$ HOTLIPS Pizza

2211 SE Hawthorne Blvd, 234.9999
721 NW 9th Ave, 595.2342
5440 NE 33rd Ave., 445.1020
www.hotlipspizza.com
Sun–Thurs 11a–10p, Fri–Sat 11a–11p

This family-owned, community-oriented pizzeria encompasses almost all of the GrassRoutes criteria while delivering the best slices right to your door. Your pizza comes decorated cheerfully, with frills of locally grown spinach, free-range organic chicken, and cheese that's free of bovine growth hormones or anything else funky. HOTLIPS even bottles its own soda. No doubt this is authentic Portland without leaving the sofa. *SB*

Clinton Street Video

2501 SE Clinton St

236.9030

Mon–Thurs 12–10p, Fri–Sat 12–11p

To the first-timer it may appear as a tiny indie video shack where it is impossible to find a flick in English with a beginning, middle, end, and explosion. But you're fooled! This small space houses a rather complete collection of DVDs from the '80s, '90s, and '00s (or aughts, as they're sometimes called). Don't fear that just because the place has a primitive air that you'll be stuck watching a Japanese-made silent documentary about Gaudí . . . for three hours. *SB*

Movie Madness Video

4320 SE Belmont St

234.4363

www.moviemadnessvideo.com

Sun–Thurs 10a–11p, Fri–Sat 10–12a

Movie Madness Video is a maze of movies. Organized how people actually think—"Hmm, I feel like a Scorsese film tonight"—this video store arranges by director, actor, and genre. Film fanatics will be able to select from a wide array of international features, and TV aficionados can schedule weekend-long marathons of every season of *Arrested Development* or the like from the extensive TV series collection. Smattered throughout the store is a museum of movie costumes and props, and you might even get to enjoy a Lionel Richie music video screening as you check out. *DL*

$ Monsoon Thai

4236 N Mississippi Ave

280.7087

Mon–Fri 11a–3p & 4:30–10p; Sat–Sun 11:30a–10p

This Monsoon Thai location is attached to a laundromat, but don't be deceived by the modest veneer; this place has pumpkin curry to die for, noodles that explode with flavor, and fresh vegetable dishes to go. The Mississippi locale is near artsy Alberta Street, the First Thursday art walk destination, in the Mister Rogers-esque Mississippi Avenue area. If you are staying at the John Palmer House across the street, another jewel in the North Portland crown, Monsoon might end up being a part of your daily explorations. Reasonable prices and a parade of classic Thai dishes are always crowd-pleasers, especially when those dishes are served with a few video rentals. Call in your order ahead of time for fast service. *RM*

Dove Vivi

2727 NE Glisan St

239.4444

www.dovevivipizza.com

Tues–Thurs 4–10p, Fri–Sun 11:30a–10p

Yummy, comfy, cozy, belly-hugging, deep-dish pizza. This is my panacea for whatever ails me, or whatever doesn't ail me. It's simply a solution to order a pizza from Dove Vivi—think Chicago and California meeting up and making beautiful children, then moving to Portland. Hooray! *SB*

It's a Beautiful Pizza

3342 SE Belmont St

233.5444

www.beautifulpizza.com

Daily 11a–10p

Partial to loud music and loud pizza? Then this is your pizza place. Order delivery for easy nights of noshing. Each pie is named for a different stellar rock star, and of course the ingredients are local and mostly organic. *SB*

Van Hanh Vegetarian Restaurant

8446 SE Division St
788.0825
http://vanhanhrestaurant.com/
Wed–Mon 10a–9p

The big yellow sign, shaped like an old hut, is the beacon for great vegetarian Vietnamese food. The soup broth at the base of many of the dishes is simply sublime. Lemongrass is used inventively with ginger as a glaze for tofu sticks and other delectable appetizers. Feast on assorted veggie and fake meat dishes, it is all incredibly good and affordable, but the restaurant itself is not particularly fabulous in terms of atmosphere, so send a friend to pick up your order and you'll be in store for one great dinner. *SB*

International Grocery

A world of cuisine in your own backyard

Often the taste of a new place is what makes me fall in love: mochi when I lived in Japan, lavender and goat cheese–stuffed anchovies in Croatia, white asparagus in Switzerland. In Portland, with its incredible number of authentic eateries and international grocery stores, the flavors bring a new excitement and enable your taste buds to travel within the city limits.

People's Food Co-op

3029 SE 21st Ave
674.2642
www.peoples.coop
Daily 8a–10p

One of the first co-ops to gain popularity and influence the foodways of Portland is People's, a place that is all about living wisely, lightly, and joyfully on the planet. With or without membership, you can shop here for organic, fair-trade produce and groceries, but members get exclusive benefits and it is easy to join if you are here for an extended stay. *SB*

People's Food Co-op

 Otto's Sausage Kitchen and Meat Market

 4138 SE Woodstock Blvd

771–6714

www.ottossausagekitchen.com

Mon–Sat 9:30a–6p, Sun 11a–5p

This sausage shop, meat market, and sandwich counter features local, grass-fed, and free-range meats, and the tastiest homemade sausage around. Buy in bulk and invite everyone around to a barbecue in the park, or just hop in for a Weiner Boutique lunch of sausage sandwich. *SB*

Fubonn Shopping Center

2850 SE 82nd Ave

517.8877

www.fubonn.com

Daily 9a–8p

Oregon's largest Asian super-mall is a complete afternoon of tasty exploration. Here you'll find lots of types of produce, pantry items, live and dead meat and seafood, and a lovely selection of drinks and frozen treats. Go for the unexpected, rather than your usual peanut butter and jelly or pasta and marinara. *SB*

Steve's Cheese

2321 NW Thurman St, located inside Square Deal Wine Shop
222.6014
www.stevescheese.biz
Tues–Sat 11a–7p, Sun–Mon 12a–6p

Steve saw his grandfather's Iowa farm taken over by corporate American agribusiness, so his love for all things small business and artisan is deep-seated. This incredible cheese case inside one of Portland's best wine stores takes even the fanciest small-batch cheeses off the pedestal and into your mouth. Try the enormous flavors of northern Italian cheeses Robiola and Brescianella, or sample some divine peasant cheeses from Estrella Family Creamery, or Rogue Creamery (see page 202). Even Portland's top chefs get their cheese from Steve—he's the cheese guru, after all. *SB*

New Seasons Market

1214 SE Tacoma St, 230.4949
1954 SE Division St, 445.2888
5320 NE 33rd Ave, 288.3838
www.newseasonsmarket.com
Daily 8a–10p (most locations)

This local chain of grocery stores will leave even the most food-oblivious person enraptured. And for the active foodie, it's like a trip to the Holy Land. Local and organic produce is arranged with an artistic eye, the health and beauty section is a chemical-free oasis, the bulk section spans multiple aisles, and there is a dedicated, knowledgeable staffer stationed in the wine and beer row. Oh, and did I mention that the store offers an array of trinkets, books, and must-have knickknacks, which makes it possible for you to complete your holiday gift shopping while also buying groceries?

New Seasons Market came to be when a national chain absorbed a local Portland natural foods store. Three former employees of that organization were determined to build another market that would make it a point to stay local and focus on creating a sustainable and engaged business. The city has embraced New Seasons and it's expanded to seven stores around town. *MM*

🏬 Food Front Cooperative Grocery

2375 NW Thurman St
222.5658
www.foodfront.coop
Daily 8a–9p

One of Portland's original cooperative grocery stores, Food Front has been charming shoppers for more than 35 years by stocking local items. The bulk section offers a deep and quirky assortment of grains, pastas, dried fruits, nuts, cookies, and pretzels, making it the perfect place to pick up the building blocks of a meal or just a quick snack. I particularly love the fact that you can buy real maple syrup and honey in bulk here, as not too many places offer that option (and if you're staying with friends or family, a reusable bottle of local honey makes an amazing hostess gift). Toward the back of the store, you'll find the deli, where you can get soups, salads (many of them vegetarian and vegan), and made-to-order sandwiches. There are a couple of picnic tables in front of the store, where, at least on dry days, you can sit down and take a few minutes to enjoy your meal. Food Front also stocks a thoughtfully curated selection of beer and wine that spotlights the locally produced and organic. *MM*

Detour

My favorite side trips

I've always been a daydreamer, and despite criticism of my meandering ways, I see the beauty in distractions. En route I find myself frequently taking unplanned side trips. A new addition to GrassRoutes guides is this "Detour" chapter, which focuses on an area nearby, but not next door. Portland is served by the adjacent fertile farming valleys, the Willamette Valley being the most famous, but the lesser-explored Applegate and Rogue River Valleys charm me to no end. Any trip to Oregon must now involve a side trip here. Discover more about this region and other detour trips at *www.grassroutestravel. com/detours.*

Summer Jo's

1315 Upper River Rd Loop, Grants Pass

541.476.6882

www.summerjos.com

Fri–Sun 9:30a–2p & 5–8:30p

The unsuspecting traveler will be inspired to write a stack of postcards after dining at this magical eatery. Summer Jo's is the perfect discovery—its lush organic gardens feed the kitchen and provide lots of hideaways for stealing kisses or learning the medicinal benefits of yarrow. Pass through the wine cellar and sit in the glass-enclosed porch for a meal to remember. House-cured corned beef and fabulous seasonal salads are highlights, as are the exquisite pastas and sumptuous desserts. To say the owners are dynamic and interesting is an understatement, but how else could a place like this come into being? *SB*

Treehouse Treesort

300 Page Creek Rd, Cave Junction

541.592.2208

www.treehouses.com

Go a little outside of the of the Grants Pass area to Cave Junction and a very unique, albeit kitschy, type of lodging: a tree house. But these tree houses are seriously nice, and the intersecting zip lines, ladders, and tree-to-tree bridges will make you want your own tree house to live in. The owner will build you one, too, if you want it that badly! *SB*

Hellgate Jetboat Excursions Canyon Boats

966 SW 6th St

541.479.7204

www.hellgate.com

Making it possible for anyone and everyone to get out on the Rogue River and enjoy the incredible wildlife and scenery, Hellgate Canyon boat tours include a big, club-style barbecue feast in the middle of an epic canyon tour with views of diving ospreys and bald eagles. *SB*

The Lodge at Riverside

955 SE 7th St

541.955.0600

www.thelodgeatriverside.com

For a comfortable and not-too-showy riverside stay, ask for a room with a view of the pool and river from the second floor. Free happy hours include local wine sips and organic apples within view of the river and its bridges. *SB*

Punch Buggies and Mopar in Southern Oregon

When I realized how doable it was to convert my 1989 Camaro to use a new and hopefully more efficient form of ethylene (with an edible byproduct for livestock to feed on), I got on the project. Cars are a soft spot for both me and my car-crazy hubby, who hides his favorite rides in drawings. But there's a way to enjoy them sustainably, and refitting older cars with sustainable systems is getting easier as the days go by. Also, it doesn't hurt to look. Grants Pass has a notable collection of punch buggies and mopar muscle—if you like cars you can't help but ogle something every few blocks. Even if these are guzzlers, they do represent a community element in all-American Grants Pass, and there are lots of ways for visitors to get involved in the scene. The following are just a few annual car events in southern Oregon. *SB*

February
Southern Oregon Rod and Custom Show, Central Point

June
Truck and Motorcycle Festival, Grants Pass
Lions Club Classic and Antique Car Show, Cave Junction
Rooster Crow Weekend, Rogue River

July
Back to the 50s Summer Celebration, Grants Pass
Corvette Weekend, Grants Pass

August
Cars of Summer, Ashland

September
Old-fashioned Car Show Contest, Grants Pass
Caveman Vintage Car Club Show and Swap Meet, Grants Pass

Taprock Northwest Grill

 971 SE 6th St, Grants Pass
541.955.5998
www.taprock.com
Sun–Thur 8a–10p, Fri–Sat 8a–10p

A big American eatery envisioned by local bank owner Brady Adams, Taprock Northwest Grill has something beautiful to look at in every corner. Local artists came together to weld, paint, sculpt, and even scrape the walls, elevators, decks, and doors into beautiful additions. Order crab and artichoke dip and a local beer, grab a seat on the patio, and bask in the riverside scene. While reconstructing and strengthening the riverbank during construction, a Native American burial site was uncovered, and every respect and honor was given to the tribes to protect their traditions and wishes. Rarely have I seen such mutual understanding around a business venture—look for the statue that commemorates their findings in the meandering gardens just to the side of Taprock. *SB*

Weasku Inn

5560 Rogue River Hwy, Grants Pass

541.471.8000

www.weasku.com

An old hangout of past presidents and Hollywood hotties, the Weasku Inn has all the rustic allure of southern Oregon combined with a good measure of comfort and historic charm. Stay by the river in new cabins with fireplaces, porches, and very comfortable beds, and lounge on hot summer afternoons in comfy plank chairs under rosy rhododendron bushes on the beautiful property. Right in the center of the valley's attractions, but out of the way of the Grants Pass main drag, Weasku is more than memorable. *SB*

Wild River Brewing

595 Northeast F St

541.471.7487

www.wildriverbrewing.com

I was so excited to be drinking a beer with a label on it depicting an R4 rapid I had run earlier that day. And to top it off, it was a great beer! Wild River Brewing is a Grants Pass local watering hole provider, sudsing things up with classy microbrews and hearty ales. Take a second look at the label and call up Rogue River Journeys (see page 203) to experience the Blossom Bar rapids yourself. Visit the brewing facilities or the Grants Pass pub location (533 NE F St, Grants Pass)—there are also a few other southern Oregon locations on your way north to PDX. *SB*

Pennington Farms

🐾 Rogue Creamery
 311 N Front St (Hwy 99), Central Point
541.665.1155, ext 3
www.roguecreamery.com
Mon–Sat 9a–5p, Sun 12–5p

Cheese, glorious cheese. Portland is highly influenced by the stuff, despite all the veganism. Tillamook County is the home of a lot of famous cheddar, and so is its southern cousin Rogue Valley. Rogue Creamery artisan cheese is easy to find in the international section of the many grocery stores, but you can get a closer look at the farm itself. Buy cheese while in sight of the cows, or come on a Saturday for wine tastings to go with. *SB*

🐾 Pennington Farms
 *1115 Williams Hwy, Grants Pass*
 541.846.0550
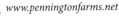 *www.penningtonfarms.net*

Ever get caught in those nasty blackberry brambles by the side of the road? Turns out they might be tasty heirloom Cascade blackberries or invasive Himalayan blackberries. After a visit to Pennington Farms I know the difference. In fact, I've tasted my way through lots of heirloom berries, including rare tayberries, a cross between the black raspberry and the blackberry. Jam, scones, pies, and sweet agave lemonade are made fresh in the renovated red barn, and you can stay with your family for very reasonable rates in the agri-chic farmhouse. Wake up to strawberry pie and choose to work alongside the big family in the kitchen or along the trellised rows. *SB*

 ## Rogue River Journeys

866.213.7754

www.roguerivertrips.com

Ask for Springer (especially if you like to fish—just know you're lucky if you get him!), Scott, or Brent, and you'll be in the best hands on the Rogue River for optimum adventure. Learn about the rocks, the water, the history, the historic lodges, or just how to enjoy the silence while on these steady rafts. Choose to hike or raft, or mix it up with both, and stay either right by the river in a tent or in one of several incredible riverside lodges. Expect to see the wild side of America, kept pristine in this protected river region. The area has committed locals working to protect an ever-wider swath of land out from the river. Watch carefully and you'll see brilliant yellow wild irises, ospreys, incredible swim-walking ouzel (also known as American Dipper birds), and some incredible rapids, like my favorite, Blossom Bar. This is one trip for the young and the old, the experienced and the novice—work with the knowledgeable folks at this premier rafting outfit and you'll be setting out on one life-changing trip. *SB*

Wine Roundup

The winegrowing regions of the Rogue River and Applegate Valleys are harvesting and pressing some great vintages. Each year there are more since the 1850s when vines were first planted here for commercial use. These are some of my favorites, but there is an ever-growing number of unique places to sip, so follow your nose along this rather undiscovered wine trail. Find out about all the local wineries at the Wines Northwest web site: *www.winesnw.com/ rogue.html*. *SB*

Del Rio Vineyards and Winery

52 N River Rd, Gold Hill
541.855.2062
www.delriovineyards.com

Winemaker Jean-Michel is a joy. He draws inspiration from his classical French winemaking upbringing and sprinkles in his own fresh style. Del Rio is the oldest winery in the area. *SB*

Troon Vineyard

1475 Kubli Rd, Grants Pass
541.846.9900
www.troonvineyard.com

Another established name in the valley, Troon Vineyard has an incredible array of varietals, a mean malbec I could drink barrels of, and a great wine-pairing setup. *SB*

Wooldridge Creek Winery

818 Slagle Creek Rd, Grants Pass
541.846.6364
www.wcwinery.com

The winemaking couple behind these fabulous vintages are talented community members and do a great job keeping alive the vision of this old Oregon winery. The sparkling rosé and the other unbelievable bubbly wines are highlights, but even the reasonably priced red table wine is textured and complex. (I was lucky enough to taste the first fermentation cuvée juice—a delightful foreshadowing of vintages to come!) *SB*

Plaisance Ranch

16955 Water Gap Rd, Williams
541.846.7175
www.plaisanceranch.com

Once a huge dairy farm, Plaisance Ranch has been reinvented by the original owners, a sweet couple with both sheepdogs and poodles, chickens, horses, and cattle. Grass-fed beef is shipped to the best restaurants in Oregon from this beautiful ranch, where you can visit and enjoy the taste of its stellar wines (very new!) and locally made baked goods. *SB*

Lodge
Every place to rest your noggin

Portland is a wonderful place to live and a fabulous and unique vacation spot. I much prefer to experience this city over a week or two at minimum, either by calling ahead to B&Bs and hotels and asking for extended stay discounts or going on Craigslist and finding short-term rentals. There are tons, I mean tons, of great things to see and do in this city, and I don't want to be too biased, but Portland is really exceptional when it comes to the density of conscientious, interesting, and community-centric businesses and activities in each and every neighborhood. All of these spots are environmentally and socially smart in one way or another. I recommend you reserve a spot in advance. Sweet dreams!

Bed-and-Breakfast Inns

The Blue Plum Inn
2026 NE 15th Ave
288.3848
www.bluepluminn.com

Staying in a historic Irvington home is the ideal way to experience the softer side of Portland. You'll feel like a local locking up your bike and walking up the wood-shingled porch at The Blue Plum Inn after a morning bike ride. The owners are not only friendly and extremely handy in the kitchen (especially when it comes to handmade brioche!), but they genuinely care about their effect on the neighborhood and the surrounding environment. Rooms are usually under $100, and never more than $200, even for a two-bed suite. *SB*

The Fulton House
7006 SW Virginia Ave
892.5781
www.thefultonhouse.com

Just a few short blocks away from the riverside Willamette Park and boating area, The Fulton House is a cozy home away from home in the central southwest Portland area. Convenient to downtown, and to transit for points east, the gardens, shaded porches, and epic wine cellar at the house can tempt you to stick around before venturing out. Comfortable beds, robes to use during your stay, and all the amenities you'd look for to connect with the outside world (like wireless Internet), are included in the room price. *SB*

The Georgian House

1828 NE Siskiyou St

281.2250

www.thegeorgianhouse.com

A standout in the long list of quaint Portland B&Bs, The Georgian House is just what it sounds like—in fact it is one of only three Georgian–Colonial style homes within the city limits. The classic brick front opens up to three floors of sunny rooms with large leaded windows, leading out to a living collage of color—the backyard. Several gazebos, a vegetable patch, and a wild mesh of berry vines are set off by seasonal shades of blooms and hanging plants, making this one of the best backyards to hang out in. Between Portland discoveries, it is easy to call The Georgian House home. *SB*

Terwilliger Vista Bed and Breakfast

515 SW Westwood Dr

244.0602

www.terwilligervista.com

With just five bedrooms, this B&B feels all grown up, and much more on the luxurious side than the homey side. Sit by the crackling fireplace after a day of adventures, and head back to your room to put your feet up and enjoy the views of the Willamette River, Mt. Hood, and beyond. English-style crepes and eggs Benedicts are among the tasty morning fare options, and soda and water are always available. The refined atmosphere lends itself to a Portland vacation full of romance, good food, and fine art. *SB*

Heron Haus Bed & Breakfast Inn

2545 NW Westover Rd

274.1846

www.heronhaus.com

Heron House is just like a road that used to appear regularly in my dreams. It was just like this highly recommended Portland stay, covered with ivy, full of craftsman details, and equipped with a large, well-lit parquet sunroom, perfect for sketching or writing postcards in between excursions. Sweeping city views and exceptional service make this one of the most gracious stays in the Rose City. Breakfast is served early and finishes at 9:30am, but there are always fresh-baked cookies in the afternoon for an extra sweet treat. *SB*

Portland's White House

1914 NE 22nd Ave

287.7131

www.portlandswhitehouse.com

This West Coast White House looks a lot like a miniature version of the one in DC, and the fine wall murals, garish furniture, Colonial accents, and sophisticated atmosphere are unlike any other B&B in the entire Northwest. The palatial scale to everything here make it ideal for a classical wedding or a secret vacation designed to wow your partner. Canopy and Rose Suites both have footed tubs in their private bathrooms, but the small Blarney Room is just as comfortable and fine. Breakfasts are a tasty affair, but don't resist the urge to sleep in and enjoy the sumptuous and romantic decor until late unto the morning; you can always send your honey down to bring you something in bed. *SB*

Top-End Hotels

The Benson Hotel

309 SW Broadway

228.2000

www.bensonhotel.com

This classy hotel has the Old World looks of dark woods, leaded glass window panels, studded leather and luxurious textiles on the fine furnishings, and five-star service that make you feel like a guest in some Scottish estate rather than a popular wedding hotel in downtown Portland. One of the few privately owned hotels in the Top End category, it isn't prohibitively expensive to stay here, but it might be impossible to leave once you get accustomed to the location, luxury, and service that set the Benson apart. *SB*

The Westin Portland

750 SW Alder St

294.9000

www.starwoodhotels.com (search "Westin Portland")

The Westin is a world-class chain of hotels, and their downtown location exemplifies the fine style for which they'd like to be known. In addition to high ceilings and extra-plush bedding in the rooms, the lobby areas and full fitness center are worth taking advantage of. Book online for special deals and to ensure your room is complete with a soaking tub. *SB*

Boutique Hotels

 Kennedy School

 5736 NE 33rd Ave
 249.3983
www.kennedyschool.com

While other hotels are sought out once a destination is chosen, Kennedy School is the inspiration behind many a vacation to Portland—it is really that unique a place to stay. Picture staying in an old schoolhouse, complete with modern comforts and old schoolhouse charm, then add a microbrewery and an art-house movie theater. There's a complete restaurant menu downstairs that features one of the best burgers in Portland, and you can take it—plus a fine aged whiskey—with you to detention! Erase memories of your school days and replace them with good times had at Kennedy School. *SB*

Jupiter Hotel

800 E Burnside St
230.9200
www.jupiterhotel.com

The coolest place to stay in Portland has got to be the Jupiter Hotel, connected to the lumberjack-chic Doug Fir Lounge (see page 178). The decor in the rooms is fresh and modern—oversized bamboo wallpaper on a feature wall, flatscreen wall-mount TVs, edgy bedding, and luxurious amenities are all part of it. The outdoor lounge, complete with bamboo hedges and glowing-white armchairs, comes alive with late-night concerts, garden parties, or impromtu meetups at all hours, and the soundproofing still affords restful sleep for those early-to-bed types. Stay in luxury, right near the Burnside Bridge but surrounded by the exciting Eastside arts scene, with a full eating and drinking hole right at your fingertips. *SB*

 Hotel Modera

 515 SW Clay St
 484.1084
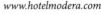 *www.hotelmodera.com*

Run by the same classy hoteliers at Seattle's Andra (see *GrassRoutes Seattle*), Hotel Modera is a fab new addition to the lodge menu in PDX. Each and every square inch of the property is steeped in fine design—from the living walls of ferns in the courtyard and the bold-patterned throw pillows on the guestroom beds to the linear hardwood fences and the specific use of modern art and live flowers. You can host a barbecue in the spacious courtyard, get good work done in the chic lobby (I pretend it's my very own corner office when I'm staying here), or stay in bed and order food from Nel Centro (of the same chef as Vindalho, page 113, and Lauro Mediterranean Kitchen, page 171) like handmade pansotti pasta with walnut sauce, which goes great with a classic British gangster film like *Mona Lisa*, at least in my opinion. Thankfully Modera is near some great local movie rental spots, and outfitted with flatscreen TVs with DVD players. Staying in at least one night seems a must if this is where you're hanging your hat in Stumptown. *SB*

$$$ Hotel Fifty

50 SW Morrison St

221.0711

www.hotelfifty.com

With an eye for upscale business-chic design, the atmosphere at Hotel Fifty is perfect for a dream vacation. Bring your discerning travel partners here and pick between a river view or one of the city center. There are a good number of queen and king singles, but availability for double-double rooms is usually flexible. Also, you don't have to leave your room to start your journey into the fabulous food scene in Portland—H5O Bistro and Bar is right downstairs. My personal recommendation is to live the lux life by sleeping in and ordering Grand Marnier custard–soaked brioche French toast, and house-made quiche with Mexican chorizo and fresh spinach to eat in bed. Now that's the start of a great day! *SB*

$$ Hotel deLuxe

729 SW 15th Ave

219.2094

www.hoteldeluxeportland.com

Roll back the clocks, keep them rolling. Back to the '40s and '50s in Hollywood, where so many American icons were nourished. Each and every detail is steeped in this romantic theme, with a lobby full of gold shades and sultry wall sconces where there aren't large-sized prints of favorite silver-screen moments. Specials make it cheaper to stay during weekdays, plus you can get a third night free if you book two nights at the standard rate. These rooms are sure to spark romance, so book this hotel for a hot date or to rekindle the flames! When you are in Seattle, reading *GrassRoutes Seattle*, of course, check out Hotel de Luxe's sister hotel, Hotel Max. It's another fab, and surprisingly affordable night's rest. *SB*

White Eagle Saloon & Hotel
836 N Russell St
282.6810
www.mcmenamins.com

This pub hotel dates back to 1905 and is a main stop on the Beyond Bizarre tour since it's known to host ghosts from the Shanghai Tunnel era. Now it's a veritable rock 'n' roll pub with great live music every night, sumptuous McMenamin's brews, and comfortable amenities upstairs. Private queen rooms are just $60 a night on weekends (and sometimes even cheaper). As long as you're here to jam into the night—and not for an early bedtime— you'll love the value and charm of this historic place. *SB*

Ace Hotel
1022 SW Stark St
228.2277
www.acehotel.com

The artsy charm of Ace Hotel is slowly spreading across America with new locations in Palm Springs and New York, and I certainly hope the idea catches on in more great cities. Ace inspires its guests with extensive use of recycled and reused materials, local art displayed everywhere from the lobby to the cheapest rooms, and free bicycles for guests to use around town. The amenities are worth writing home about, and while you do have to be willing to share a bathroom with one or two other rooms, you'll enjoy being in the heart of the Pearl District, just a couple blocks from Powell's Books (see page 35) for under $100. Dogs are always welcome, and WiFi is free in every room. *SB*

Avalon Hotel and Spa

455 SE Hamilton Ct

802.5800

www.avalonhotelandspa.com

The riverside Avalon Hotel is the best place to stay is you want a comfy king bed (there's one in absolutely every room) and an incredible view of the Willamette River. Rooms and suites—even the smallest—hover around 350 square feet, making it all too easy to kick back, especially if you've chosen a deluxe riverside suite with the wraparound balcony for entertaining. You can't help feel a bit coy and romantic at this lush, centrally located spot. Make a trip to the spa for a luxurious massage or the popular Equavie Eco-Escape Facial and you'll have your cherry on top. *SB*

Hotel Lucia

400 SW Broadway

225.1717

www.hotellucia.com

The spotless, spacious rooms at Hotel Lucia are home to my favorite beds in the city. A pillowy top-layer makes a great mattress even greater, and the fine linens don't hurt either. There's even a pillow menu! Lucia is the more traditional stay when it comes to boutique hotels in Portland, but that doesn't mean this place is straight edge. Suave Asian-influenced design—and attentive service—create an unforgettable atmosphere, plus there's interesting art by David Hume Ketterly displayed throughout the hotel. My only complaint would be the funky showerheads. Whatever the issue, the staff are there in minutes to fix it. If I were a bride again, it would be hard *not* to pick a Lucia suite for my bridal shower. Lucia is in the same family with the local Provenance Group, which also includes the Hotel DeLuxe and Hotel Max in Seattle. *SB*

Inn at Northrup Station

2025 NW Northrup St

224.0543

www.northrupstation.com

When all the other hotels seem to be another shade of beige, Inn at Northrup Station is a splash of color. Each room (including the rainbow-hued lobby), is dripping with brilliant purples, greens, and magentas. Each room has a small kitchen area, and most rooms also have a balcony. The rooftop here is one of the best places to chill in the city, so the minute the sun comes out, I recommend rushing up there. Cafe tables and beautiful plants add to the city view from the upper deck, and public transit and city attractions are just a few steps from the lobby. If you plan on eating out a lot, you can easily stash leftovers, and if you're a farmer's market junkie, you can cook your own simple meals from your hotel room. I took my yummy eats upstairs to the rooftop to enjoy, obviously. *SB*

Airport Hotels

Clarion Hotel
11518 NE Glen Widing Dr
252.2222
www.stayclarion.com (search "Portland, OR")
Coffee is always brewing in the Clarion lobby, and there are snacks to grab for breakfast. Forget the bells and whistles, and stay at this comfortable, user-friendly hotel near the airport. The bus and MAX lines are nearby, the rooms are clean and quiet, the WiFi works reliably in the rooms and the lobby, and the price is right. You might not get a sense that you're in Portland while you're inside the hotel, but for some vacations, a basic room is just what's called for so you can focus on exciting adventures in the city. *SB*

Embassy Suites
319 SW Pine St
279.9000
http://embassysuites1.hilton.com (search "Embassy Suites Portland, Downtown")
While this might be the more generic of Portland stays, the Embassy Suites sure does rack up points for the lux indoor pool, the plentiful exercise equipment, and the high standard of cleanliness that caters to even allergy-ridden guests (what other hotel do you know of that makes regular practice of dusting the pillows with a special sani-vacuum?) These features—plus flat screen TVs and convenient MAX access (see page 12)—create a comfortable stay for your family. *SB*

Fairfield Inn

11929 NE Airport Wy
253.1400
www.marriott.com

A little more relaxed than the main Marriot brand hotels, Fairfield Inn still offers the business-ready amenities, and some of the pampering ones, that you'd look for, and for less moolah. There are zero smoking rooms, so no second-hand fumes, and there's always a hot breakfast served in the morning for hotel guests. It might be standard, but this place is a great plain canvas from which to jump off and explore this crazy city. *SB*

Comfort Suites

12010 NE Airport Wy
261.9000
www.choicehotels.com

On the northern outskirts of town, just outside of the main airport circle, Comfort Suites is ready to help you get your rest. With new fleece bed coverings, more floor-to-ceiling windows and a full fitness center, complete with indoor pool and whirlpool, this place is an even bigger deal than a few years ago. Take the free shuttle from the airport to the hotel, then look for convenient buses or green rental cars (see page 229) to get you and yours to the main drag. *SB*

Monarch Hotel and Conference Center

12566 SE 93rd Ave
652.1515
www.monarchhotel.cc

Pillowtop beds, relaxing surroundings, plush service and a slew of green practices, it's no wonder this convention complex and hotel are always buzzing with activity. Monarch is a popular place for conferences and business meetings, but it is also good for family get-togethers or couples' vacations. You'll find energy efficiency being taken into account without feeling like you are losing warmth, sacrificing water pressure, or spending too much time sorting recyclables. It is comfortable and clean here, but not so fancy that you can't let your hair down and feel homey. *SB*

Hyatt Place
9750 NE Cascades Pkwy

288.2808

www.hyattplaceportlandairport.com

This chain hotel is relatively new to Portland, and when it was built, the design included little upgrades that go a long way—rainfall showerheads, flat screen TVs, granite countertops, and a spacious lobby that caters to the large groups this hotel accommodates. The hotel is near the airport and a block from the Mt. Hood MAX station (see page 12), so you can easily get from A to B without paying the steep downtown hotel prices. The staff are used to catering to groups, family reunions, babies, and other guests who value affordable comfort over boutique hotel style. Bulk discounts, special multi-night rates, and packages can be purchased directly from Hyatt *SB*

Traditional Hotels

$$ The Mark Spencer Hotel
409 SW 11th Ave

224.3293

www.markspencer.com

You can often tell a lot about a hotel from the lobby carpet pattern. This busy, yet classic weaving of auburn tones leads to a pretty dead-on idea of The Mark Spencer. The haughty brown tones continue throughout, and the impeccable service and traditional furniture, the live orchids and the European flair all come together to create a hotel experience that can only be designated as classic. The pet-friendly rooms are as clean and well cared for as those ready for guests with allergies, and the free parking, green considerations, and surprising reasonable rates don't hurt either. Plus, you are right in the middle of downtown, easy walking distance to many great attractions and restaurants. *SB*

Best Western—Inn at the Meadows
1215 N Hayden Meadows Dr, 286.9600

9901 NE Sandy Blvd, 256.1504

www.bestwestern.com

Both of these Best Western locations have the great service for which this affordable chain is known. Work with the concierge here to get specific directions all around the maze that is the Expo Center, and enjoy free Internet access in between meetings or outings, whatever you are in town to do. All guest rooms have microwaves and mini fridges, so when you are finished taking in the tastes of the town you can reheat them for a savory breakfast, unless you'd rather explore the "Up Early" chapter instead (see page 16), much more civilized, I'm sure. *SB*

Hotel Monaco Portland

506 SW Washington St

222.0001

www.monaco-portland.com

Even though this chain hotel can be found in most major cities, its presence in Portland does make a unique impact. There's no lobby quite like the one here—decked out in bright red and maroon textiles, the original 1912 structure, with its ornate features, is one fine place to sit with a cocktail to people watch. Check out the local Portland artists on the hallway walls, too. *SB*

Hotel Vintage Plaza

422 SW Broadway

228.1212

www.vintageplaza.com

The snazzy design of each and every detail at Vintage Plaza—from the metallic studs in the modernized wingback chairs to the bold bands of color in the blown-glass lighting fixtures—makes it easily one of the most comfortable boutique hotels in town. And I'm not the only one who thinks so—this Kimpton property has achieved "Gold List" status with its brand new renovation on the Condé Nast Top Hotels in the World. If you are craving a party for your girlfriends this would be my first pick, but it is also ideal for quick romantic getaways . . . *SB*

RiverPlace Hotel

1510 SW Harbor Wy

228.3233

www.riverplacehotel.com

Perched right at the river's edge at the tip of Portland's waterfront, River-Place is a chic stay with all the modern comforts. Romance on the River packages include a deluxe guest room, champagne, locally made Moon-struck truffles, free parking, breakfast, and plenty of roses and rose petals—a bargain considering the sweet service you'll receive. Try the spa and the restaurants here before you head on your way home—they are true pillars of pampering. *SB*

Crowne Plaza—Downtown Convention Center

 1441 NE 2nd Ave

233.2401

 www.crowneplaza.com (search by city)

Recently renovated and conveniently located, the Portland Crowne Plaza is another energy efficient hotel that's worth checking out. Using recycled cooking oil to make biofuel for hotel vans is just one of the eco-savvy steps this chain has taken to be green. Try their special packages, many of which come with welcoming lavender spray for the linens, and a funky sleep CD to help you meditate your way to sweet dreams. *SB*

Cheaper Stays

Hawthorne Hostel

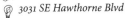 *3031 SE Hawthorne Blvd*

236.3380

www.portlandhostel.org

The hostel in Portland's indie shopping hood of Hawthorne is one of the best hostels in the country. It isn't the fanciest stay in PDX by any means, but with a slogan "your eco-home away from home," and crazy-cool sustainable features like a rainwater harvesting system and a full event calendar for visitors—it's hard to top when it comes to eco-conscious and memorable. You can volunteer while you are there to further interact with the cool staff people and groovy guests that abound. Take part in a group hike with your new friends to nearby Mount St. Helens, or grab the microphone for an après-feast open mic session. *SB*

 $ Northwest Portland International Hostel and Guesthouse

 425 NW 18th Ave

241.2783

 www.nwportlandhostel.com

Part of the Hosteling International organization, Portland's Victorian home-cum-youth hostel is more than meets the eye. There are loads of freebies and friendly new faces to share them with—grab free bread in the lobby, get a free city map and travel info, free parking and Internet use, and perhaps best of all, the convenient location is inside the free transit zone, so taking public transit from here is also, you guessed it, free! The shared rooms are clean and cozy, plus the rooms are always open, unlike most European hostels. *SB*

$$ Silver Cloud Inn

2426 NW Vaughn St

800.205.6936

www.scinns.com

Local Seattle-based lodge group Silver Cloud's first, and so far only, location in Portland is a great addition to the lodge offerings here. These well-run, beautiful hotels are known around the Pacific Northwest for being both classy and affordable, albeit more pricey than some of the other options in this section. Full workout equipment, plus a few fireplace rooms add to this comfortable home away from home. *SB*

Holiday Inn Express—Portland NW Downtown

2333 NW Vaughn St

484.1100

www.hiexpress.com (search by city and choose NW Downtown location)

This business-savvy location is great for writers like me—there are outlets everywhere, and barely any Internet issues. The northwest Nob Hill area of Portland is now dotted with corporations and hospitals, so it's no surprise that there are a good number of suites as well as many hipster haircuts floating around the lobby. Rooms are comfortable and more scaled up than other cheaper stays. *SB*

Thriftlodge—Portland Central

949 E Burnside St

234.8411

www.travelodge.com (search by city)

Right on Burnside Street, the city of Portland is easily accessible from this low-key lodge. Don't expect fancy frills, but do expect free coffee, free wireless Internet, and one of the best cheap lodging locations around. Walking from here means discovering some of the best this city has to offer. *SB*

Downtown Value Inn

415 SW Montgomery St

226.4751

www.downtownvalueinn.com

The Downtown Value Inn is actually more hooked up than you'd think—each room I've seen has extra lounge chairs, and at least one that's primed and ready for a nice reading session. TVs with sliding, angling trays make it easy to watch from anywhere in the room, and small desks make it easy to get work done, even if the proximity to the city's top attractions distracts you. The convenient location of this motel makes it even more of a bargain, considering PSU and OMSI are just minutes away. *SB*

The Palms Motel

3801 N Interstate Ave

287.5788

www.palmsmotel.com

Other than the fantastic vintage motel sign, this place isn't that fancy or particularly pretty, but it does a great job of housing your tired, traveling bones for less money than most. Queen beds with polyester bedcovers aren't exactly the most luxurious, so I remove the cover as soon as I arrive. There's free wireless Internet, surprisingly accommodating service at the front desk, and a small bill at the end of the stay. No bells and whistles, but I'm not complaining. *SB*

America's Best Value

4911 NE 82nd Ave

255.9771

www.americasbestvalueinn.com

In the midst of a hot Portland summer day, the outdoor pool at this affordable hotel hits the spot. Also, all the rooms are suites, and most are dog friendly for a low fee of $15, plus they come with a handy kitchenette and beds with extra fluffy pillows. If you call ahead and request allergy-sensitive cleaning, they'll do an extra good job cleaning your room with nontoxic, nonchemical cleaners. *SB*

Best Western—Pony Soldier Inn

9901 NE Sandy Blvd

256.1504

www.bestwestern.com

There's a free shuttle to and from the Portland International Airport, and a free continental breakfast every morning. I grab extra danishes before heading out of Portland to Mt. Hood to hit the slopes, and when we all get back from the mountain, the indoor heated pool and steam room and free HBO are great for wind downs. Plus there are plenty of locally-owned restaurants that deliver to this convenient location. *SB*

Briarwood Suites

7740 SE Powell Blvd

788.9394

www.briarwoodsuites.com

This comfortable roadside motel is great for groups or for travelers who want to explore PDX on the cheap. There are mini fridges in most rooms—great for all those leftovers—and there's friendly service at the front counter. Instant coffee is served in the morning, but who wants that when there's Stumptown? *SB*

Camping

Columbia River RV Park

10649 NE 13th Ave, Vancouver, WA

360.285.1515

www.columbiariverfrontrvpark.com

Champoeg State Park

8239 Champoeg Rd NE, St. Paul, off US 99, 7 miles east of Newberg

633.8170

www.oregonstateparks.org/park_113.php

Milo McIver State Park

24101 S Entrance Rd, off Springwater Rd and Hwy 224, 4 miles west of Estacada (45 minutes from Portland)

1800.452.5687

www.oregonstateparks.org/park_142.php

Fir Grove RV Park
5541 NE 72nd Ave
252.9993
www.traveloregon.com (search "Fir Grove")

Jantzen Beach RV Park
1503 N Hayden Island Dr
289.7626
www.jantzenbeachrv.com

Oxbow State Park
3010 SE Oxbow Pkwy, Gresham
663.4708
www.metro-region.org (search "Oxbow State Park")

Calendar

Annual cultural events and festivities are part of what makes Portland come to life. Check out what will be going on when you'll be in town, and take the opportunity to get involved in a Stumptown celebration. There's something for everyone!

January

RiverCity Music Festival
Oregon Convention Center, 777 NE Martin Luther King Jr Blvd
224.8499
www.rivercitybluegrass.com

O-Shogatsu New Year's Celebration
Portland Japanese Garden, 611 SW Kingston Ave
223.1321
www.japanesegarden.com

Portland Seafood and Wine Festival
Oregon Convention Center, 777 NE Martin Luther King Jr Blvd
360.210.5275
www.metroproductions.net/seafoodandwine

ChocolateFest
World Forestry Center, 4033 SW Canyon Rd
228.1367
www.worldforestry.org

February

Hollywood Lux
Hollywood Theatre, 4122 NE Sandy Blvd
281.4215
www.filmaction.org

Portland Jazz Festival
Various locations
228.5299
www.pdxjazz.com

Portland International Film Festival
Various locations
221.1156
www.nwfilm.org

Oscar Night America
Hollywood Theater, 4122 NE Sandy Blvd
281.4215
www.hollywoodtheater.org

March

St. Patrick's Day Festivities
Holy Rosary Church, 376 NE Clackamas Rd
691.2078
www.holyrosarypdx.org

Oregon Arbor Week
World Forestry Center, 4033 SW Canyon Rd
228.1367
www.worldforestry.org

Festival of Quilts
Portland Expo Center, 2060 N Marine Dr
222.1991
www.northwestquilters.org

April

Party for the Planet
Oregon Zoo, 4001 SW Canyon Rd
226.1561
www.oregonzoo.org

Wordstock
Oregon Convention Center, 777 NE Martin Luther King Jr Blvd
546.1012
www.wordstockfestival.com

Spring Plant Sales
Berry Botanic Garden, 11505 SW Summerville Ave
636.4112
www.berrybot.org

Portland Japanese Garden, 611 SW Kingston Ave
223.1321
www.japanesegarden.com

Astronomy Day and Vernal Equinox Star Parties
Rooster Rock State Park (22 miles east of Portland)
www.omsi.edu/visit/planetarium/starparties

VegFest
Various locations
224.7380
www.nwveg.org

Spring Beer and Wine Fest
Oregon Convention Center, 777 NE Martin Luther King Jr Blvd
222.4644
www.springbeerfest.com

Taste of the Nation
Oregon Convention Center, 777 NE Martin Luther King Jr Blvd
222.4644
http://strength.org/portland/

May

Doggie Dash
Waterfront Park
285.7722
www.oregonhumane.org/doggiedash

Pug Crawl
MacTarnahan's Tap Room, 2730 NW 31st Ave
285.7722
www.oregonhumane.org/pugcrawl

UFO Festival
McMenamins Hotel Oregon, McMinnville
www.ufofest.com

Memorial Weekend in Wine Country
Yamhill County, various locations
646.2985
www.yamhillwine.com

Cinco de Mayo Fiesta
Tom McCall Waterfront Park, SW Naito Pkwy at Columbus St
232.7550
www.cincodemayo.org

Portland Indie Wine Festival
Urban Wine Works, 407 NW 16th Ave
595.0891
www.indiewinefestival.com

Annual Shell Show
OMSI, 1945 SE Water Ave
797.4000
www.omsi.edu

Alberta Art Hop
Alberta Street
www.artonalberta.org

Living Green Expo
OMSI, 1945 SE Water Ave
797.6674
www.omsi.edu

Zompire: The Undead Film Festival
Various locations
800.494.8497
www.zompire.com

Mother's Day Plant Sale
Crystal Springs Rhododendron Garden, SE 28th Ave at Woodstock Blvd
771.8386

June

Waterfront Village
Tom McCall Waterfront Park, SW Naito Pkwy and Columbia St
www.rosefestival.org/events/waterfrontvillage

Portland Rose Festival
Various locations
227.2681
www.rosefestival.org

Portland Queer Documentary Festival
Clinton Street Theater, 2522 SE Clinton St
www.queerdocfest.org

Chamber Music Northwest, Portland
Reed College campus, various locations
233.3202
www.cmnw.org

PedalPalooza
Various locations
www.shift2bikes.org

Lake Oswego Festival for the Arts
368 S State St, Lake Oswego
636.1060
www.lakewood-center.org

North American Organic Brewers Festival
Various locations
www.naobf.org

July

Oregon Lavender Festival
Various locations in and near Portland
662.4488
www.oregonlavenderfestival.org

Wednesday Zoo Tunes
Oregon Zoo, 4001 SW Canyon Rd
www.oregonzoo.org

Portland Highland Games
Various locations
www.phga.org

Oregon Brewers Festival
Tom McCall Waterfront Park, SW Naito Pkwy
778.5917
www.oregonbrewfest.com

PDX Pop Now!
Various locations
616.4433
www.pdxpopnow.com

Waterfront Blues Festival
Tom McCall Waterfront Park
973.3378
www.waterfrontbluesfest.com

Molalla Buckeroo Rodeo
Molalla, just outside Portland
829.6941
www.molallabuckeroo.com

August

Mt. Hood Jazz Festival
200 NE Hood Ave, Gresham
661.2700
www.mthoodjazz.org

Homowo African Storytelling

Washington Park

288.3025

www.homowo.org

Bridge Pedal

Various Willamette River locations

www.providence.org/BridgePedal/

Festa Italiana

Various locations

www.festa-italiana.org

Soapbox Derby

Mount Tabor

493.9465

www.soapboxracer.com

September

Time-Based Art (TBA) Festival

Various locations

242.1419

www.pica.org/tba

Muddy Boot Organic Festival

St. Philip Neri Church, 2408 SE 16th Ave

www.muddyboot.org

Polish Festival

3900 N Interstate Ave

287.4077

www.portlandpolonia.org/festival

Annual Reptile Show

OMSI (see page 73)

797.4537

www.omsi.org

Wintering-In Harvest Festival on Sauvie Island

Bybee House, Sauvie Island

222.1741

www.ohs.org

October

Portland Marathon
226.1111
www.portlandmarathon.org

Greek Festival
Holy Trinity Greek Orthodox Cathedral, 3131 NE Glisan St
www.goholytrinity.org

Apple Tasting
Portland Nursery, 9000 Division St
788.9000
www.portlandnursery.com

November

Wine Country Thanksgiving
Various Willamette Valley locations
www.willamettewines.com/thanksgiving.shtml

Northwest Food and Wine Festival
Memorial Coliseum in the Rose Quarter Complex
800.422.0251
www.nwfoodandwinefestival.com

Portland Opera Season
Keller Auditorium, SW 3rd and Clay Sts
www.portlandopera.org

Sustainable Forestry Tours
Hopkins Demonstration Forest, 16750 S Brockway Rd, Oregon City
632.2150

The Northwest Knockdown (Roller Derby Championships)
Expo Center, 2060 N Marine Dr
224.0368

December

Holiday Artisan Market
Pioneer Courthouse Square
222.6073
www.pioneercourthousesquare.com

Holiday Ale Festival
Pioneer Courthouse Square
252.9899
http://holidayale.com/

Holiday Cheer and Authors Party
Oregon Historical Society
306.5221
www.ohs.org

Community-Supporting Banks

Here are a few of the community-supporting financial institutions around town

Albina Community Bank
8040 N Lombard St, 285.9966
2002 NE Martin Luther King Jr Blvd, 287.7537
430 NW 10th Ave, 445.2150 (and other locations)
www.albinabank.com

Advantis Credit Union
3717 SE 17th Ave
785.2528
www.advantiscu.org

The Bank of Oswego
310 N State St, #218 (and other locations)
635.1699
www.bankofoswego.com

Northwest Priority Credit Union
715 NW Hoyt St, #4, 223.1669
12630 SE Division St, 760.5304 (and other locations)
www.nwprioritycu.org

Consolidated Federal Credit Union
2021 NE Sandy Blvd, 232.8070
2055 NW Savier St, 226.4991
www.consolidatedfcu.com

Urban Eco Resources

Companies and small businesses in Portland, and statewide throughout Oregon, are exploring the use of wind, solar, geothermal, hydropower, and bioenergy in a serious way. According to *Portland Oregon Magazine*, the state is taking on the green energy revolution speedily, creating one of the fastest-growing industries in Oregon. That also means there are plenty of ways to travel more sustainably. If you aren't walking or utilizing the great public transit in Portland (see the "Getting Around" chapter, page 10), then here are some resources to help you green up your next adventure.

Renting and Buying Greener Vehicles

The Portland airport features a standard array of car rental places. A few, like Enterprise Rent-a-Car, offer carbon offsets for purchase from reputable companies, donate money to green auto research, and offer many fuel-efficient vehicles. Others, like Hertz, have many diesel, hybrid, and sometimes even fuel-cell cars for rent. Also, National has joined with EuropeCar in Portland to offer an expanded range of eco-vehicles. For more information, check the Portland International Airport web site *(www.portofportland.com/PDX)* and also the RezHub site *(http://www.rezhub.com/CarRentals/Portland CarRental/tabid/402/Default.aspx)*.

Autoblog Green
http://www.green.autoblog.com/tag/portland/
Get the latest green auto news at this blog.

Tonkin Green
877.223.4753
www.tonkingreen.com
Buy an affordable used or new hybrid or diesel vehicle here.

Portland Green Streets
www.portlandgreenstreets.org
This is another great blog that offers info on the latest green ways to get around.

Biodiesel

With a market expected to grow rapidly in 2010, biodiesel is becoming easier to find, and there are also more vehicles that can use it. Where it used to be something found only in rural areas, biodiesel is now more readily available in America—especially in eco-friendly cities like Portland. Here are some resources to get you going:

Jay's Garage
734 SE 7th Ave
239.5167
www.jaysgarageportland.com
Mon–Wed, Sat–Sun 9a–5p, Thurs–Fri 8a–6p

GoBiodiesel Cooperative
www.gobiodiesel.org
This veggie-oil collective has annual membership dues that ensure low eco-fuel prices, but it's only really viable for residents of Portland.

SeQuential Biofuels
620 SW 5th Ave, 978.3210
10111 NE 6th Dr, 978.3210
www.sqbiofuels.com

Lovecraft Biofuels
1216 Division St
888.834.4645
www.lovecraftbiofuels.com

NearBio
www.nearbio.com
Use this site to send the location of the nearest biodiesel station to your cell phone.

Columbia-Willamette Clean Cities Coalition
www.cwcleancities.org
If you are looking for a spot to fill up on alternative fuel, you want the latest prices on biodiesel, or you'd like to find a green transit event happening in the near future, this coalition web site is the best place to start.

Don Thomas Petroleum

2727 NW St. Helens Rd, 277.0145
www.donthomaspetroleum.com

At the northeast location B20 is available available, and at the northwest location B5, B20, and B99 are all sold. Note that all locations are closed on weekends.

JL Mini Mart

6021 NE Portland Hwy
289.5558

This spot sells B99 biodiesel. Note that it's closed on Sundays.

Mr. Car Wash

510 SE Grand
235.9740

This spot sells B20 biodiesel. Note that it's closed on weekends.

BlueskyFuel

SE Portland, call for directions
544.3558
www.blueskyfuel.com

BlueskyFuel is co-op for B99 biodiesel. A one-time orientation gets you directions to this centrally located yet tucked-away fueling spot, which is then available to you for 24-7 self-service.

Star Oilco

4504 SE 17th Ave, 800.532.9620
8445 N Kerby Ave, 283.1256
www.staroilco.net

Star Oilco is open 24-7 to members; it's easy and acceptable for travelers to apply. B20 fuel only.

Leathers Fuels

18145 SE Division St
666.8198
www.leathersfuels.com

B99 fuel is offered here every day until 10pm.

Olson Brothers Tire Factory

14115 SE McLoughlin Blvd, Milwaukie
659.5141
www.olsonbroserv.com

Olson Brothers offers B5 and also E85 fuels. Note that it's closed on Sunday.

Natural Gas

Used in both the compressed natural gas (CNG) and liquefied natural gas (LNG) forms (only for larger vehicles like industrial trucks and school buses), natural gas is touted as the cleanest burning fuel. Unfortunately, as of yet it can be tricky to get your hands on a CNG vehicle, and it's a bit of a waiting game to fuel up, as there aren't tons of stations with CNG pumps, and it can take a while to refuel due to the high pressure it takes to store the stuff.

In Portland, surprisingly, natural gas is more difficult to obtain, and I am not sure why. Other cities like San Francisco and Seattle are much better equipped with CNG. In fact, California by far has the widest array of public CNG access.

Even with all this trouble, the Civic GX is near the top of my wish list (along with that fancy gadget that turns sludge into drinking water). In order to buy this car, you'll have to go to California anyway, because as far as I have researched they aren't yet for sale in Oregon. For more info, check out *www.fueleconomy.gov/feg /bifueltech.shtml* and *www.ngvc.org/*.

There are a slew of private-access CNG stations in Portland, including one at the airport, but unless you are especially good at haggling or are on a government mission, they won't let you fuel up. Bummer.

Pacific Pride Bretthauer Oil Company

21180 NW Amberwood Dr, Hillsboro (not far to the west of Portland)

615.3370

Daily 24 hours

There are two public CNG stations in Medford, but this town is hours south of Portland. (See the "Detours" chapter for more southern Oregon adventures, page 198.) If you are driving to Portland from the south on I-5, Pacific Pride is convenient on your way into town.

Rogue Valley Transportation District

3200 Crater Lake Ave, Medford

541.779.5821

Mon–Fri 5a–8p

This cash-only spot has great service and always has domestic natural gas at your beck and call—just remember to stop at an ATM first.

Jackson County Motorpool

808 W Main St, Medford

541.774.6960, call ahead for availability

Electric

In this city, there are many forward-thinking businesses that aren't signing on to a petroleum-fueled future; rather, they are aiming to create an EV (Electric Vehicles) culture where people can easily and affordably get from A to B. Visit *www.evworld.com* and *www.dont beapassenger.com* for more information on the latest news and ways to get involved in transitioning our great nation towards a brighter and cleaner future. While you're in Portland, there are some great resources for getting started:

Oregon Electric Vehicle Association

www.oeva.org

Porteon Electric Vehicles

625 NW 17th Ave

595.7676

www.porteon.net

Oregon Electric Car Co.
18203 SE McLoughlin Blvd, Milwaukie
799.6141

Electric Wheels Inc.
1555 12th St SE, Salem (about 30–40 minutes south of Portland)
485.0588

MC Electric Vehicles
6311 NE St. Johns Rd, Ste B, Vancouver, WA (about 10–15 minutes north of Portland)
www.mcev.biz

Index

V

Valentine's, 65–66
Van Hanh Vegetarian
  Restaurant, 195
Vault Martini, 152, 179
Vega Dance+Lab, 43
Vegan Chewy Ginger
  Molasses Cookies with
  Orange Zest (recipe),
  190–91
Vegan Mall, 101
Veloce Bicycles, 69
Vendetta, 15, 67
Vera Katz Eastbank
  Esplanade, 112–13
Veritable Quandary, 120
Video rentals, 192, 193
Video Vérité, 192
Vindalho, 113
Vita Cafe, 63–64
VOAR, 144
Voicebox Karaoke Lounge,
  163
Volunteer, 70, 83, 141–44
Volunteer.gov, 144
VolunteerMatch, 144
Voodoo Doughnut, 175, *176*

W

Walking and jogging, 14, 19,
  23, 39–40, 41, 42, 78, 112–13,
  114, 122
Walking clubs, 41
Walking tours, 78–79
Washington Park, 79–82
Wax On, 182
Wealth Underground Farm,
  57
Weasku Inn, 201
Weather, 7–8
Weekend, 111–20
Westin Portland, The, 207–8
Westmoreland, map of, xxviii
"Wet and Rusting"
  (Menomena), 155
White Eagle Saloon & Hotel,
  210
Whole Bowl, The, 60
Widmer Brothers Brewery
  Tour, 77
Wild Abandon Restaurant,
  170
Wild River Brewing, 201
William Temple House
  Thrift, 108
Wilshire Park, 42–43
Wine festivals, 220, 222,
  223, 227
Wine information resources,
  84, 147, 203
Wine stores, 182, 197
Wineries and wine tastings,
  84, 147, 202, 203–4, 223
Wonders of Walking Club
  (Hosted by REI), 41
Wong's King Seafood, 118
Woodstock Park, 32
Wooldridge Creek Winery,
  204
Working Artists, 87–88
World Cavalcade, 135–36
World Forestry Center, 80
Writing workshops, 83

Y

Ya Hala Lebanese Cuisine, 46
Yarn Garden, 95
Yarn shops, 85, 95
Yoga, 24–25, 44, 181–82
Yoga Bhoga, 25
Yoga Space, The, 24–25

Z

Zach's Shack, 174
Zell's, 17
Zines, 37, 38, 88
Zipcar, 13
Zoo, 80–81, 225
Zoobomb, 71